CHEQUES AND BALANCES

MEMOIRS OF A BANKER

CHEQUES AND BALANCES

MEMOIRS OF A BANKER

BOB WHITE
CECELIA CLARKE

VIKING

Viking
Penguin Books Australia Ltd
487 Maroondah Highway, PO Box 257
Ringwood, Victoria 3134, Australia
Penguin Books Ltd
Harmondsworth, Middlesex, England
Viking Penguin, A Division of Penguin Books USA Inc.
375 Hudson Street, New York, New York 10014, USA
Penguin Books Canada Limited
10 Alcorn Avenue, Toronto, Ontario, Canada M4V 3B2
Penguin Books (N.Z.) Ltd
182-190 Wairau Road, Auckland 10, New Zealand

First published by Penguin Books Australia, 1995
10 9 8 7 6 5 4 3 2 1

Typeset in 11/14 Palatino by Midland Typesetters, Maryborough Vic. 3465
Made and printed in Australia by Australian Print Group

National Library of Australia
Cataloguing-in-Publication data:

White, Robert J. (Robert James), 1923– .
Cheques and balances.

Includes index.
ISBN 0 670 85734 3.

1. White, Robert J. (Robert James), 1923– . 2. Westpac Banking Corporation. 3. Bankers–Australia–Biography. 4. Banks and banking–Australia–History. I. Clarke, Cecelia. II. Title.

332.10992

To the memory of my dearly beloved late wife, Molly,
whose loyalty and support contributed so much to the story of this book.

R.J.W.

ACKNOWLEDGEMENTS

I would like to give special thanks to the thousands of Bank staff who served with me, for their loyalty and support; to my secretary, Jan Milne, who has served me faithfully for over twenty years and who provided so much of the impetus for this book; to my co-author, Cecelia Clarke, whose professionalism and dedication has added so much to the quality of the final manuscript; to Lorrie Graham for her assistance with photographs.

Many thanks also to: Geoffrey Allen, Prof Heinz Arndt, The Rt Hon Sir Garfield Barwick, Dianne Beer, Sir John Bunting, Esmond Cawsey, Dr William Clarke, Margaret Connolly, Jamie Grant, Sir Harold Knight, Alan May, Dorothy Simons, Christine Bacher Smith, John Valder.

And my former colleagues at the Westpac Banking Corporation: Carolyn Beveridge, Dr Keith Carpenter, June Chapman, Peter Davidson, Peter Douglas, the late Douglas Farquharson, Douglas Ferdinands, Barbara Filipowski, The Hon A H Jago, Bob Leonard, Ian Matheson, Lyn Milton, Sir Robert Norman, Ross O'Brien, Jan O'Dea, Ron Owen, William Paget, Keith Phillips, Louise Reid, Murray Stewart, Eric Tait, Geoffrey Thompson, John Twycross, the late Frank Ward, Geoffrey Ward, Geoffrey White.

R.J.W.

CONTENTS

PROLOGUE

My banking career spanned fifty years; it was hatched in the simple surroundings of a small Riverina farming village, and was to take me to the top executive suite in Australia's first bank. It ended when I was confronted by the agonising decision of resigning from the Board to express my lack of confidence in the direction then being followed.

It all began in 1940 when I joined the Bank of New South Wales at Echuca, Victoria in the aftermath of the depression of the 1930s and shortly after the commencement of the Second World War. My return in 1947 after war service coincided with the announcement by Prime Minister Chifley of the government's intention to nationalise the banks. The drama which followed set the pattern for the next forty years of my career, a career which was marked by achievements, disappointments and frustrations, by travel and new experiences, by successes and failures and finally by turmoil and change.

It is sometimes difficult to recognise the face of modern banking. It was so simple in 1940 when there were only cheque accounts, fixed deposits and overdrafts. Banking products now come in many shapes and sizes, but the fundamental precepts of banking remain the same. Banking is about providing a safe haven for our savings; facilitating the exchange of money for goods and services; buying and selling money as our savings are marshalled to finance development and production. It is also about returning a satisfactory profit to the proprietors of our banks since it is they who bear the primary risks. Banking should be about serving the customer – in an industry so heavily people-oriented, it cannot be otherwise. Banking should be about reliability; it should be about helping school children and others to learn the value of thrift. Banking should be about following the time honoured principles of credit. The checks and balances of a market-oriented financial system mean these fundamental precepts will continue to drive financial markets. Some old bankers say 'beware when the marketers take over from the bankers'.

Fifty years on Westpac was not alone in its difficulties – Royal Commissions had been appointed to investigate events at the State Bank of Victoria and the State Bank of South Australia.' The financial crisis which followed Australia's bicentenary in 1988 was arguably the worst in Australia since the one which followed the centenary in 1888. The investigations into the two state banks, both with roots stretching back to the last century, had been conducted in the full glare of the public spotlight whereas the crisis in Westpac, a publicly listed company incorporated under its own Act of the New South Wales Parliament, was to some extent concealed behind the traditional veil of corporate secrecy.

In relating this story, there are conflicts between one's duties to the institution, to confidentiality, to history, and to the public interest. It is difficult to describe the circumstances concerning these events without confronting these conflicts. In doing that I have endeavoured carefully to balance what I perceive to be my duty to the public interest against the other conflicting duties so as not to damage the institution which I served for fifty years and not to harm any individuals, be they customers or servants of the Bank. I have endeavoured to achieve my aim by concentrating on the importance of the facts rather than personalities.

A bank is not a public utility. But does the privilege of a banking licence impose a wider duty to the public? Crises in large financial institutions affect more people than the individuals directly involved. With its huge branch network, carefully built up over time, Westpac touches the hearts and minds of a large percentage of the population. In the aftermath of any crisis in banking, some people are pardoned; many more people are punished. I believe that all bankers have a duty of care to ensure that the lessons learnt from the financial crises of the 1980s are not repeated. As an active observer of the banking industry, my task is to relate some of those lessons.

MY EARLY YEARS

1

It was 1935. I was about to leave the one-teacher primary school at Conargo which had been my sole source of education for the previous five or six years. Conargo, a tiny village in the south-west Riverina, is about 400 kilometres from Melbourne and more than twice as far from Sydney. The mail car came three times a week, bringing two daily papers at a time from Melbourne: the newspapers for Saturday and Monday arrived on Tuesday. Although Conargo is in NSW, Sydney seemed so far away that nobody was prepared to wait yet another day just to read the *Sydney Morning Herald*. My father used to say the only time they think of us in Sydney is when we pay our taxes.

Life was simple, happy, free and uncomplicated, for the most part, save for the hazards of floods, bushfires and drought. I learnt to drive our T-Model Ford utility truck when I was about eight so that my father could dole out hay from the back of it to the starving sheep. Our principal amusement was the Saturday night dance on the store verandah to the music of an old-time dance band broadcast by the ABC through our new wireless, in a handsome walnut cabinet powered by four batteries each the size of a house brick.

My knowledge of banking was limited to the school savings account in which I had been depositing one shilling per week. The first passbook was brown with a hard cover, and it had been replaced a couple of years later by a smaller book with a blue cover from the Commonwealth Savings Bank. I have a vivid recollection of seeing my parents around that time with worried looks on their faces, contemplating what seemed to me to be a bundle of cash and a brown passbook. Without knowing it, I was witnessing the demise of the Government Savings Bank of NSW, with its takeover by the Commonwealth Savings Bank. Were my parents a part of the run on the Government Savings Bank of NSW which led it to close its doors in 1932, an unprecedented event for a government-owned savings bank?

I was to leave home for the neighbouring town of Deniliquin to enter the intermediate high school. Here I watched in fascination the construction of four new, two-storey buildings in the main thoroughfare, Cressy Street: first there was the Commonwealth Bank; next door was the Bank of New South Wales; and over a side street the Bank of Australasia next door to the Rural Bank of New South Wales.

From my backblocks childhood, two-storey buildings were something of a novelty, so I was greatly impressed with the strength and stability presented by these four banks being built almost next door to each other in a small pastoral town with a population of about 3000 people. Five years later I was to walk through the portals of one of those buildings to apply for a job.

My three years at the Deniliquin High School were relatively uneventful. I made my first public speech from the stage of the Deniliquin Town Hall before I became a teenager. It was the occasion of the Jubilee of the reign of King George V, and in the atmosphere of the current republic debate, it is interesting that my schoolboy recollections of the death of George V, the abdication of Edward VIII, and the coronation of George VI, remain clear almost sixty years later. Empire Day, or Queen Victoria's birthday, was still celebrated with a half-day holiday. Memories of school in Deniliquin are overwhelmed by my mother's illness and her death before I was fourteen. In the aftermath of that sad event, which left a gaping hole in my life, I moved in 1938 to begin my final two years of high school at the War Memorial High School in Hay, 150 kilometres away – four hours by dirt road in the mail car with stops at Wanganella and Booroorban to deliver and pick up mail.

The move was a big event in my life, not only because none of my companions followed the same path and I was now living in the school hostel, but also because life with sheep, dust, flies and drought held little attraction for me. It had long been planned that I should not follow in my father's footsteps and further education was seen to be the key to unlock that plan.

Life in the larger school was more sophisticated, more enjoyable and more satisfying. My principal interest outside the classroom was debating, and I felt privileged to lead the school debating team against a team from the Albury High School on the subject 'That the colonies taken from Germany by the Treaty of Versailles be returned'. This was in 1939, and war clouds were beginning to gather. We were debating the negative case and we won.

The clouds erupted into a storm in September that year when Great Britain declared war on Germany, and the Australian Prime Minister, Robert Menzies, announced that Australia also was at war. That dramatic event took place during the school holidays, and I well recall that on the first day back at school those of us in the Leaving Certificate class were summoned to the 'Boss's' office. The 'Boss', or, to give him his proper title, the Principal, no doubt drawing on his experience as an ex-serviceman from the First World War, gave us sombre advice – we should not follow his example but seek a secure position of employment before enlisting in the services. It was taken as a matter of course that we would ultimately enlist. But since I was not yet sixteen it all seemed so far away.

However, I took his advice and within the next few days submitted my application for a job to the local branch of the Bank of New South Wales. It seemed that only a few days elapsed before approval came through. When I mentioned that I would not be able to commence work until after Christmas and the Leaving Certificate examination, back came the terse reply, 'When Master White is ready, he should submit another application which will be considered in the light of the circumstances existing.' That was the end of my first attempt to get a job with the Bank of New South Wales.

I duly sat for the Leaving Certificate, and with a favourable result in hand, I applied to the Deniliquin branch of the Bank in January 1940. Once again the application was approved, this time 'as a special matter', whatever that may have meant; but there was also a condition that I should commence work at a branch away from Deniliquin, where my family had lived for many years, and where they were well known to many of the Bank's valuable customers.

At that time, all applicants for a job in the Bank were required to lodge two bonds from suitable guarantors, each for £500, accepting responsibility for any loss the Bank might suffer as a result of employing the new applicant. Fortunately my father had two friends of sufficient means and with sufficient trust in me to sign the required guarantee.

Early on the morning of 26 February 1940, my father and I set out from Conargo to catch the train from Deniliquin to Echuca where I had been directed to commence work as a probationer. Echuca, on the Murray River, had been an inland port and the Bank's branch was close to the wharf where the river boats used to load and unload their cargoes, mainly wool.

The manager, Mr Allen, met me at the railway station in his brand new Chevrolet. Motor cars held a strong fascination for me and I knew all the makes and models, dreaming of the day when I might own one. I felt a stir of excitement when I saw this sparkling, navy-blue 1939 model Chevrolet, a symbol of the new career I was about to commence. A car was something to strive for.

Mr Allen had arranged for me to board with a widow and her two daughters who quickly accepted me almost like an adopted son. The Echuca branch was an attractive late-19th century building, with the manager's residence on the upper floor, exhibiting all the strength and stability of Australia's first bank. I was to be an addition to the staff and would be known as a staff probationer. My three colleagues were the manager, the second officer and the ledgerkeeper who was shortly to leave to join the army.

Of my duties, those I remember the most clearly were in the banking chamber where I was responsible for seeing that the writing pads and blotting paper were clean; the inkwells filled and clean; the nibs in the pens were clean and not worn out; and most important of all, that the date blocks showed the correct date. I suppose this was good training in customer service but few of us were sorry to see the departure of such symbols as the pewter inkstand with its china inkwell insert and the pens which had to be regularly refitted with new nibs. I became reasonably expert in making ink by mixing water with ink powder, but I could never master the art of filling those narrow-necked china ink wells without spilling as much as I used with disastrous results. It's hardly a sign of success when you have to spend the rest of the day with one or both hands stained with blue ink.

After six months, my probation expired and I was relieved when the Inspector, the big boss in Melbourne, approved my admission to the permanent staff. With that approval, I was told to advise my guarantors that their bond was released for future events but would be retained to cover any misdemeanours which may yet come to light from the period of probation.

I was now to be known as the Junior. There were six banks in Echuca in 1940, and the Juniors of those banks met each morning in a room at the Town Hall to exchange cheques, theirs in exchange for ours, keeping a running record of the amounts owing between us for settlement at the end of each week in Melbourne.

Before the next six months had expired, I was transferred, this time with the exalted title of Ledgerkeeper at Benalla where there were five banks; ours was similar in size to Echuca. Service in these small branches, where the only machinery was a typewriter, provided invaluable experience in the basics of banking and in the banker-customer relationship.

To the interested and inquiring young bank officer, hand posting of the ledgers provided a unique insight into the financial or cash flows of a whole range of businesses: the local retailer, the local branch of the chain retailer, the garage/service station, the farmer, the co-operative butter factory, the dentist and the doctor. With the war in its second year, an elementary flying school was established in Benalla and the Wales was chosen to look after the school's banking requirements.

Despite the good experience, I discovered that my pay was becoming less adequate as I grew older. My commencing salary at Echuca was £90 per annum plus an away-from-home allowance of £55 per annum, paid on the fifteenth and last day of each month – £6 and 10 pence each time. Weekly board was £1, 7 shillings and sixpence – $2.75 in today's terms.

With twenty-four pay days per annum and twenty-six fortnightly payments for board and lodging, my financial planning expertise was often seriously tested, particularly when I broke my tennis racquet, with the cost of a new one equal to half a month's pay. Another near financial catastrophe occurred when I agreed, as was almost a duty for young bankers, to partner a debutante in the Younger Set Debutante Ball. The Ball was the social event of the year in Benalla demanding nothing less than black tie and dinner jacket. I was saved when I was able to negotiate the purchase of a second-hand dinner jacket from one of my fellow boarders who was about to join the Air Force. Life might have been more prosperous if my first annual increase of £15 had not been applied by the Bank to reduce my away-from-home allowance by £15. To avoid paying these allowances to adults, the Bank was quick to phase them out as teenage officers grew older.

Having reached the age of eighteen by 1942, my immediate problem was to answer the call to join the army. My boss at Benalla, a traditional banker, threatened to resign if they sent him a woman to replace me. The manager's attitude was typical of the times. Prior to the war few women had been employed by the Bank and then only in jobs such as typists. When something of the order of 70 per cent of the Bank's male staff enlisted in the services, it was only the widespread entry of women that enabled the Bank to carry on its business. However, it was not until some time after the war that women were accepted in wider roles in the Bank and then only after disputes over differentials in pay rates and job security.

On 14 February 1942, a little less than two years after joining the Bank, and just five days before the first air attack on Darwin, I was on the train on my way to Melbourne with a number of others to join the army. From the transit camp at Royal Park, I was drafted to a transport company to enjoy the contrast of sleeping six to a tent in the damp, industrial atmosphere of Fishermens Bend. With the deterioration in the war position, this transport unit was being reactivated for an active service role. When our motley mob arrived from Royal Park, wearing ill-fitting uniforms characteristic of rookies, I heard the Staff Sergeant bark at me, 'And where did you come from, son?' After I had replied, 'From a bank', he said, 'Good, you can take charge of the oil store.'

I soon found myself telling drivers that Hypoid 90 was the right oil for the differential and that SAE 60 should only be used in the gear box. As the newly formed 118 Australian General Transport Company, we moved to St Kilda to prepare for bigger things.

I was glad that I had that exalted position in the oil store, part of the workshop platoon, because we moved to Allerdices Junction Garage at St Kilda with sleeping accommodation in the loft, while the transport platoons were accommodated in the grandstand in the nearby St Kilda Cricket Ground.

A few months later we joined a troop train bound for the showground in Adelaide, and on to Terowie, Alice Springs and our final destination: Darwin. The final stage of three days was by truck convoy over a badly worn dirt road. As a measure of our defence capability in 1943, that track was the only supply line from Adelaide to Darwin, then already under attack by the Japanese.

On the eve of our departure from Melbourne the workshop platoon of the 118 Australian General Transport Company organised a valedictory dinner at the Australia Hotel. I was prevailed upon to say a few words. We had already developed a team spirit and relationships which seemed destined to last and I launched into an appeal to make a vow to continue our association after the war. We did, and I became one of the first secretaries of the 118 Australian General Transport Association in 1947, and I am proud to say that the Association continues fifty years later, thanks to the dedication of a special bloke, Albert Hart. During my term as the Secretary, the Association experienced a minor setback when the Treasurer unsuccessfully attempted to double our wealth by investing it at the races, but we survived.

It was feared that the air raids, which had commenced in February 1942, would be followed by the arrival of land-based forces from Japan who would attempt to isolate the Top End cutting off the supply route from the south. At the beginning of 1943, it was said there were over 60 000 troops in the Top End including a large contingent of Americans and some Dutch. Regular raids from Darwin were carried out by American Liberator and Dutch Mitchell bombers against neighbouring Japanese bases and they were supported by Royal Australian Air Force squadrons equipped with the famous Spitfire fighter aircraft from Britain. When I first saw one, I was aghast at its speed, but the Concorde, some thirty years later, was to fly at over four times that speed.

With its fleet of trucks, our 118 Australian General

Transport Company had detailed orders of the role we were to play in the event of an invasion, but the general impression was that the Japanese had over-stretched their lines of communication particularly as the air raids were declining in their frequency and severity.

Each time there was an air-raid red alert, our major concern was the security of the above-ground pipeline which carried the only supply of fresh water from the dams about 80 kilometres to the south of Darwin. As a result, we had to detail a motorcyclist each time to patrol the pipeline in our adjacent area until the all-clear was sounded. Invariably this was a lonely late-night patrol over about 20 kilometres of pipeline.

On my first visit to the township of Darwin not long after my arrival, I was anxious to see the branch of the Bank, a substantial brick building which had been completely gutted by an incendiary bomb, leaving the four walls standing almost without a blemish. After the war, the Bank re-opened its branch in Darwin and reconstructed the old building within its existing four walls. It is ironic that in December 1974, a little over thirty years after the air-raid damage, the Board voted a sum of $2 million or so to rebuild the Darwin branch in order to cope with the rapidly expanding business opportunities. Within two weeks of that fateful decision, Darwin was struck and almost destroyed by Cyclone Tracy but that wonderful old bank building again survived, this time almost unscathed, and it still survives to this day.

At the end of 1944, I was transferred to Headquarters Norforce located in the Larrakeyah Barracks which had been constructed just before the Second World War for the permanent army. These relatively new buildings remained almost totally undamaged throughout the war and the accepted explanation was that Larrakeyah would be the Japanese headquarters after the invasion. While we may have treated the prospect of an invasion with some scepticism, the Japanese authorities had already printed invasion currency, and I have seen samples, the last in a currency museum in Osaka.

My new job at Norforce was an administrative posting in the Office of the Director of Supplies and Transport, a job I found interesting and satisfying as well as useful in my future bank career.

My promotions in the army were anything but meteoric as I moved slowly to Lance Corporal with its proverbial one stripe to Acting Corporal, Corporal, Lance Sergeant, Staff Sergeant and finally to Warrant Officer Class II when my responsibilities in the Supplies and Transport Directorate expanded as many of my seniors moved south for discharge following the cessation of hostilities.

My job in 1945 involved me in the arrangements to ensure that the first contingent of returning prisoners of war from Singapore were made welcome and comfortable during their short stopover in Darwin. It was late morning on 21 September 1945, a typical 'dry season' Darwin day: cloudless blue sky, calm blue waters of the Arafura Sea and the stark contrast of the lone white hospital ship SS *Oranje* as she steamed slowly towards Darwin Harbour. She tied up to the music of the Norforce Military Band and then the passengers disembarked, some walking but few without help, others being carried – all emaciated with the visible signs of the privations of the last three and a half years, but home – home as if they never doubted that they would come home. There was not a dry eye on the wharf in Darwin that morning.

With the war over, civilians returned to Darwin including bankers to re-open the branches of the banks and the Allied Works Council, later to become the Department of Works and Housing charged with reconstruction of the city. With the latter group was one Molly McKinnon of Hepburn Springs, Victoria who was to become my wife five years later and who was to remain my faithful supporter until her death.

The army had a system of establishing priorities for discharge using points related to age on enlistment supplemented by additional points for a wife and children. Since I was 18 on enlistment, and with no wife or children, my points hardly registered on the scale, and so it was not until early 1947, or almost two years after the war had finished that I was free to return to Royal Park, for my final discharge and return to civilian life. My five years in the army and the friendships I forged left me with a footprint, the focus of which has remained clear and sharp over the intervening years.

Following my discharge from the army, I reported back to the chief office of the Bank in Melbourne and was assigned to South Yarra branch as the ledgerkeeper, this time in a five-handed branch.

A PEN, A NOTEBOOK AND A MOTIVE

2

On the afternoon of Saturday, 16 August 1947, I was walking down Swanston Street in Melbourne when, in shocked disbelief, I heard a newspaper boy yell out: 'H-E-R-A-L-D – EXTRA – BANKS TO BE NATIONALISED'. I immediately purchased the paper and there it was, blazoned right across the front page: MOVE TO NATIONALISE BANKS, SENSATIONAL DECISION BY FEDERAL CABINET.

The paper went on to say that the Prime Minister, J.B. (Ben) Chifley, had been authorised by Cabinet, with the Attorney-General, Dr Evatt, to prepare legislation for submission to the Federal Parliamentary Labor Party for the nationalisation of banking other than state banks. Not long returned from World War II, I could, like the great majority of bank officers at that time, be described as politically neutral, but the Chifley announcement suddenly put an end to that. The paramount consideration in those days was not only the availability of a job but also the security of the job and the continuing guarantee of that security into the post-war period. The Bank had offered me all of these benefits in 1940, but now it seemed to me and to many others on the staff that those benefits were being threatened by Chifley's announcement which would undoubtedly bring with it rationalisation of the individual bank branch network. My political neutrality gave way to political activism.

I, like most other people, was stunned by Chifley's decision, but for the participants and close observers of the political processes, all the signs had been there for some time. Banking had been well to the fore in the policies of the Labor Party since the Party's 1921 Conference at Brisbane affirmed 'the nationalisation of banking and all principal industries' as a plank in the platform. No doubt reflecting the tensions in the government/bank relationships of the great depression of the 1930s, nationalisation of banks featured as a major issue in the Labor Party's election campaign of

1934. But it was the government of the United Australia Party, the precursor to the Liberal Party, under Prime Minister Lyons which announced the appointment of a Royal Commission on the Monetary and Banking System in 1935.

The Labor Party's nominee to the Commission was Chifley, a minister in the former Scullin Government, and the man who was to become Prime Minister a decade later. In broad terms the Commission's final report in 1937 endorsed a system which included private banks with a strong publicly-owned central bank exercising control over their activities. However, Chifley dissented through a minority statement which said:

> With this opinion, I am unable to agree. Evidence given before the Commission, personal observation and experience led me to believe that there is no possibility of the objectives being reached, or of any well ordered progress being made in the community under a system in which there are privately owned trading banks which have been established for the purposes of making profits.[1]

There was a longstanding and bitter debate on the requirement that the trading banks hold on deposit with the Commonwealth Bank a declared proportion of their own deposits. This requirement was substantially endorsed in the Commission's call for a strong central bank control. The strength of the trading banks' opposition, and the approach of the 1939-45 war, delayed legislation which would have given effect to the Commission's findings. A.C. Davidson (later Sir Alfred), the General Manager (the term then used for the chief executive officer) of the Bank of New South Wales during the depression, argued strongly against any compulsion on the banks to lodge Special Deposits with the Commonwealth Bank, which then also carried out central banking functions. So great was the standing of the Bank of New South Wales and its chief executive officer in those days that when a meeting called to discuss the lodgement of Special Deposits was boycotted by Davidson, it was described by L.F. Giblin in his book, *The Growth of a Central Bank*, as being 'like a production of *Hamlet* with Hamlet left out'.[2]

A legend from those days recorded that the Commonwealth Bank was mimicking the Bank of England's tradition by answering the phone with the word 'Bank'. Davidson's response was to instruct the Wales switchboard to answer 'The Bank' to all incoming calls.

The pressures of a wartime economy ultimately led to a voluntary scheme of Special Deposits with the Commonwealth Bank. The subsequent defeat of the Menzies Government in 1941 saw Chifley re-emerge, this time as Treasurer in a new Labor Government under Prime Minister Curtin. The private trading banks did not have hard facts, but they were concerned that the government would continue to limit bank profits or, in the worst case, to nationalise the banks. Their common concerns prompted L.J. McConnan (later Sir Leslie) of the National Bank of Australasia, who was also Chairman of the Associated Banks (Victoria) (the precursor to the Australian Bankers' Association), to attempt to galvanise the private trading banks into public opposition.

The banks shared a common objective. They had accepted to a degree that there was a need for some control of credit in order to minimise the effects of the business cycle. On the other hand, they wanted to resume with a post-war banking system free from profit controls and other wartime restrictions, operating free from political interference and in an essentially 'free market' environment. However, the banks disagreed on a strategy to change the government's bank policies. The disagreement was delineated along state lines and the state differences which emerged in 1944 continued to influence the strategy of the whole anti-nationalisation campaign.

McConnan of the Melbourne-based National Bank of Australasia wanted the banks to express their opposition immediately by circularising their customers. The Commercial Bank of Australia and the English Scottish and Australian Bank, both Melbourne based, and the Bank of Adelaide, lined up behind McConnan. In contrast, Sir Alfred Davidson from the Wales was concerned that if the banks acted without real knowledge of the government's intentions, the government could cut the ground from under the banks.

As the war drew to a close, legislation followed to formalise the wartime regulations, but that legislation stopped short of implementing the Labor Party's policy of nationalisation of banking. The legislation, introduced in March 1945, comprised two bills, the Commonwealth Bank Bill and the Banking Bill. Special Accounts, advances (lending) policy, and interest rate controls were the key elements. The Commonwealth Bank Bill extended the wartime regulations and formalised the requirement that the banks lodge special deposits (Special Accounts) with the Commonwealth Bank, and required the Commonwealth Bank to develop and expand its general banking business. Founded in 1912, the Commonwealth Bank had predominantly remained a savings bank supported by the Post Office Agency network. Its trading bank business and branch representation were relatively small, but this was now to change. The government-inspired boost to its growth could only be achieved at the expense of the private banks.

The companion Banking Bill which later became the Banking Act, 1945, retained the qualitative and quantitative lending controls established during the war. For example, the Special Account provisions covered under s18-22 required that each private bank deposit a certain proportion of its deposits with the Commonwealth Bank. The Special Accounts, as these deposits were called, remained a contentious issue for years to come. They were a restriction on money available for lending by private banks and by tying up bank assets in low interest-bearing deposit accounts, profits were to some extent controlled. Although there was a requirement that the Special Accounts be separated from the Commonwealth Trading Bank, the private trading banks remained convinced that the Commonwealth Trading Bank would have access to their funds and could therefore enjoy an unfair competitive advantage.

As a portent of things to come, s48 in the Miscellaneous section of the Banking Act 1945 prohibited private trading banks from accepting accounts of the states or their agencies. This meant that state governments, state authorities, city and municipal councils would be required to bank with the Commonwealth Bank. In order for the Commonwealth Bank to absorb this new business and to expand its general banking business, it was necessary for it to build up its branch network. Hence s48 was applied progressively to enable that build-up to be achieved.

Notwithstanding wide opposition and strong protests, the

legislation was passed and survived, to many people's surprise, without challenge for two years. The other surprise was that the challenge ultimately came not from a bank, but from the Melbourne City Council, a customer at that time of the National Bank of Australasia.

An added complexity was the fact that the trading banks continued to lobby the Commonwealth Bank for some concessions on aggregate profit limits, achieving some small successes. When the government announced that it would invoke s48 of the 1945 Banking Act, and when the Melbourne City Council announced it would challenge the legality of s48 in the High Court, T.B. Heffer, General Manager of the Bank of New South Wales, was anxious not to jeopardise the delicate negotiations over these concessions.

In February 1947, at a meeting with the trading banks, the Governor of the Commonwealth Bank foreshadowed that, 'under pressure from the Prime Minister', the Commonwealth Bank would be taking over the accounts of the New South Wales and Victorian governments. Initially, it would take over the Main Revenue and Trust Accounts, leaving the trading banks with the Departmental Accounts. This announcement prompted a concerned comment from the Wales that the Commonwealth Bank would be 'taking the cream and leaving us with an unprofitable residue'.[3] The business of the Government of New South Wales had been substantially with the Bank of New South Wales since its foundation in 1817 and was, of course, extremely valuable to the Bank.

At the same meeting the Governor foreshadowed that the Commonwealth Bank would also take over municipal accounts. In April 1947 Chifley announced that s48 of the 1945 Banking Act would be invoked, and that local councils banking with the trading banks would be required to transfer their accounts to the Commonwealth Bank by 1 August 1947.

In the interval following the signalling of the government's intentions to the trading banks and its official announcement regarding s48, Garfield (later Sir Garfield) Barwick, KC, opined that s48 of the Banking Act was invalid. Again an important dispute arose between the Wales and the Associated Banks (Victoria), led by McConnan.

The Wales wanted to send a joint letter from all the trading banks to the Commonwealth Bank saying that they had been advised on s48 and would 'reserve all legal rights'.[4] With the ongoing negotiations regarding trading bank profits, the Wales wanted to adopt a more circumspect approach to the added difficulties with s48.

'I am anxious not to start an open campaign by this bank as I feel that we would stir up the resentment of the Government and the Commonwealth Bank and probably invite discrimination', wrote T.B. Heffer on 15 April 1947 to A.H.B. Jones, Inspector, Victoria, of the Wales, also Heffer's representative on the governing body of the Associated Banks (Victoria). 'That does not mean that we have been idle here; we have been at work through others in the Press and in political circles and you could do the same down there as long as you keep under cover.'[5] One can almost see the hair rising on the back of Heffer's neck as he penned that communication.

In late May 1947, Heffer's anxieties about possible government retaliation were further increased when the Melbourne City Council advised that it would also challenge s18-22 of the 1945 Act. In June 1947, in an exchange of correspondence between himself and McConnan he continued to urge McConnan to 'use every endeavour to dissuade the Melbourne City Council from raising the question of the validity of sections 18-22'.[6]

Initially McConnan refused to do this. He was annoyed when the Melbourne City Council decided to challenge s18-22 because he, too, was concerned that the government might retaliate. However, he was equally angry that the banks seemed to be retracting an earlier agreement to fight the government's enforcement of s48.

Heffer's perceptions that Chifley considered s18-22 to be the cornerstone of his banking legislation were correct. Sections 18-22 of the 1945 Act were the key credit sections of the Act. If these provisions were found to be invalid, the foundation of Chifley's monetary policy could be jeopardised. Although the Melbourne City Council at the last moment abandoned its claim on s18-22, it pressed on with its challenge to s48.

On 13 August 1947 the High Court found s48 to be invalid, and the following day senior Commonwealth Bank officers attended a meeting with the Prime Minister and were asked to prepare a two-page memorandum on the technical and other aspects of nationalisation.[7] On Saturday, 16 August, only three days after the High Court's decision, Chifley announced that the Cabinet had authorised the preparation of legislation for the nationalisation of banking.

It was a first order donnybrook. On one level an intense legal challenge with some of the best legal resources was mounted. At another level one of the most sophisticated propaganda campaigns was conceived and executed. This campaign, in which I played an active role, was one of the most impassioned since conscription. The objective in NSW was not only to destroy the legislation through the courts and to oppose the legislation publicly, but also to ensure that the government would not be re-elected in 1949. The NSW banks were convinced that a legal decision as such would not provide sufficient protection for the future. It was a very powerful motive. It would be better to remove the government and thus prevent a recurrence of attempts to nationalise the banks.

The Sydney approach was to go through the courts and do everything possible as far as nationalisation was concerned. To that end a strategy document, the 'Preliminary Plan for Borderline Electorates and Recommendations' (hereafter called the Plan) was prepared for the Wales. Although archival materials do not categorically state whether the Plan was endorsed and used, there is little doubt in my mind that the Plan was the basic strategy document for the anti-nationalisation campaign. Initially the objective of the Plan was:

> . . . to affect the Government so that it will drop its proposal to take over the trading banks.
>
> It must be realised that this does not envisage a campaign to win the mass of the people over to our side
>
> Rather it means that we must impress the politicians in such a way that they come to believe that the public supports our cause.

> Our job is to *inspire and arrange evidence to this end*, to make vocal these groups who do support us and to as far as possible render impotent those who are against us.[8]

The determination of the propaganda plan is reflected in T.B. Heffer's correspondence with the Wales branch staff. 'Our immediate objective', said Heffer, 'is to inform and arouse the public so that the electors, by letters, telegrams, public resolutions and the signing of protests and petitions might force the Labour (sic) government either to reject the bank nationalization proposal or to submit it to a referendum.'[9] As the covering letter of the Plan recommended, 'I think it would be very helpful to our cause to have key members of Parliament aware of the inauguration and prosecution of a high-powered campaign deliberately aimed at undermining them at the most vulnerable part of their anatomy, which is their seats.'[10]

Throughout the campaign a series of letters to Inspectors, branch managers and staff reflects the determination of the Bank to win the battle, and the importance that Heffer placed on inspiring staff morale and support.

Perhaps because I was stationed in Melbourne from 1947 to 1955, I have always been conscious of the banking and political view that L.J. McConnan was the undisputed leader of the anti-nationalisation campaign. Of all the banking leaders, he was the most able performer in public and provided good leadership. Few, if any, in the banking fraternity would diminish his contribution. In recent times, and with a lifetime of banking experience behind me, I have come to a better understanding of Tom Heffer's perceptive assessment of the politics of banking and his strategic capabilities.

Sydney felt that the Melbourne approach savoured of a 'banking public relations campaign' rather than a positive effort to unseat the government. It was self-criticism to describe it as a 'banking' public relations campaign, implying that it was one which lacked professionalism. Though the need to resolve the differences as to the form of the campaign might have been recognised, those differences were never really resolved. McConnan criticised the Sydney banks for their decision to use the socialism issue rather than the specific nationalisation issue. 'I have been long enough in the political game to know that you do not get very far preaching against some abstract quality',[11] fumed McConnan.

Staff in each state organised their own protest committee. The committees liaised with each other, but they largely determined the format and the execution of their campaigns independently.

State differences which featured throughout the lead-up to 16 August continued to affect the strategy, structure and execution of the banks' campaign. I was not conscious of the state differences, because at my level the objective was always to get the government out of power. The legal processes did divert attention, but there was nothing one could do until the government lost office.

I found it easier to talk to the public about the 'evils of socialism' than the niceties of banking legislation. It was easy to relate the socialist objective to the government's desire to impound people's savings. This threat would possibly be more real if the banking system were totally owned by the government. During the 1983 election campaign Malcolm Fraser resurrected the threat of the Labor Party confiscating private savings when he commented that money would be safer under the bed. But Bob Hawke, being the skilful politician, joked that the Reds were there already. In the modern context the threat was meaningless – but in 1949 it was perceived as real.

Melbourne carried on with its program, and Sydney carried on with its own ideas, apparently agreeing to disagree. Little has changed since then.

Though unaware of it, I guessed some organisational plan existed. Now, I am fascinated by the strategy documents which reveal the thought and planning that went into the propaganda side of the campaign. They expressed organisational detail in military language: 'The problem is thus seen to be one in which a military type of organisation will be most effective.' The proposed organisational structure consisted of a War Council, and a Chairman of a Working Committee was to be a 'dictator' or 'Supreme Commander'. The bank officers were 'shock troops'. The military references are not all that surprising, since many of those involved in the planning and execution of the campaign had only recently returned from serving in one or another of the armed forces.

The campaign used the available media techniques, such as advertising, films, radio programs, opinion polls, articles and editorials in the press and, of course, was structured in such a way that it reflected the views of the banks. For example, little or no mention is made in the press that the French had nationalised their banks in 1946, albeit with a different structure than the one proposed for Australia.[12]

The Bank of New South Wales had substantial fire power. The *Bulletin* was helpful, as were the professional advertising agencies. The connections between the officers of the Wales were wide and often linked with military service. Harry Jago, a relatively junior officer of the Wales and ex-serviceman, assumed leadership of the NSW campaign because he was an office bearer of the Bank's sub-branch of the Returned Servicemen's League, where he had the opportunity to speak about freedom of choice to rally support. Harry's chance meeting with a former military colleague who was then with the advertising agency J. Walter Thompson led to its involvement in the campaign.

The banks were nevertheless nervous about appearing to be too aggressive. They were happy to support and to provide material for other organisations to do the real fighting. In keeping with its policy not to have its campaign viewed as a mere public relations exercise, the Wales decided not to occupy more advertising space than was usual and not to increase the frequency of advertising. Advertising would also be confined to institutional matters such as the merits of individual banks and/or the merits of the banking system. These advertisements made no specific reference to bank nationalisation. They were concerned to adopt what would have been considered a 'proper' stand on nationalisation.

The propaganda campaign loosely extended the definition of socialism to include both communism and national socialism. There was a genuine fear about what had happened in Europe. Professor Hayek's book, *The Road to Serfdom*, was freely circulated and widely quoted. There was probably a measure of self-interest on the part of the bank officers in going beyond the narrower issue of nationalisation of banking which, by itself was not considered a very persuasive argument.

The nationalisation issue had remained on the union

agendas even during the war. The unions which represented the staffs of the private trading banks were the Melbourne based Australian Bank Officials' Association (ABOA), the Sydney based United Bank Officers' Association (UBOA), and the Associations based in other states. They were divided along state lines with the chief differences also between Victoria and NSW, a division which originated in the early days of the creation of the respective unions.

As early as 1934, L.P. Harrison of the Melbourne based BOA, the precursor to the ABOA, had warned members that nationalisation would lead to the replacement of competent bank officers with political appointees, and thus to unemployment for some bank officers.[13] The major point of disagreement continued to be, if nationalisation should occur, whether the Associations should oppose it outright or endeavour to win the best conditions for their members regardless of who owned or controlled the banks. The Victorian Association favoured the latter course of action. In 1944 J.H.O. Patterson, President of the ABOA, may have been influenced by his contacts in Federal Cabinet. His conclusion was 'even if the union made it clear that they were not attacking the government but only the proposed legislation, it would nevertheless be viewed as an attack on the government, and they would not forget.'[14]

These important differences of opinion divided the Associations during the lead up to the nationalisation announcement and throughout the campaign which followed. Chifley, who was then the Treasurer, added to this perturbing situation. The union delegation which met him in January 1945 received few assurances from him about future job security.

The unions were largely unable to resolve their differences during the campaign which followed Chifley's announcement. The UBOA, led by the General Secretary, S.E. Card, announced on 19 August 1947 its intention to take the side of the banks, and informed the chief executives of the various banks that members of the UBOA would side with them in the fight. Their Victorian counterparts demurred. The ABOA did not wish to come out in open protest against the proposed nationalisation legislation because it felt that any open conflict would prejudice any hope of influencing the legislation to contain clauses to protect the interests of bank officers. While declining to take an active part, the ABOA was prepared to allow its members freedom of action.[15]

In those pre-television days public rallies encouraged direct participation with sometimes startling results. Murray Stewart, long-serving Wales staffer and active ABOA member, remembers being pushed away from the microphone at a large Prahran ABOA rally to avoid any impression there was opposition to the ABOA line. In contrast, a photograph of a large UBOA anti-nationalisation rally in the Sydney Domain was prominently featured in the press giving the impression of solidarity. And, as the late Fred Daly recounts in his book, *From Curtin to Kerr*, bank officers also took the opportunity to interrupt Labor-organised meetings.[16]

An active, relatively independent and supportive bank staff was essential, because the cornerstone of the political campaign was in the marginal electorates where sitting Labor members would communicate their fears to Caucus. The work on marginal electorates was to be done directly between the Bank Employees' Protest Committees and the branches, while Liberal headquarters were not to be approached on account of their 'proven political incompetence'.[17]

The campaign was vehement. Certainly some of the cartoons depicting Chifley as Field Marshall Goering were nasty. In retrospect I believe that Chifley was a modest individual, and probably didn't realise that what he was doing was so much against the public's wishes. If Chifley considered himself to be a 'moderate', the public at that time, myself included, did not find him so to be.

As a young man I found the anti-nationalisation propaganda material totally convincing. I was still at school when the war started, and spent five years in the army. In that time away from 'civvy street' I was bitter about the impact of the war on my life. I disliked the constraints of army life and longed for the freedom and security of life back at the Bank. Now that my job security was threatened by nationalisation, I, like many young people, had no problem with the argument that it was a socialist plot. I think I was typical of the majority of young ex-servicemen in holding this point of view.

Job security was important to me because I had grown up during the depression and had direct experience of the hard times. The idea of a secure career in the Bank had been very attractive and the guarantee of a job on our return from the war was important. Insecurity intensified when the Minister for Postwar Reconstruction, The Hon. J.J. Dedman, announced in 1947 that some 5000 fewer bank officers would be required after the absorption of the private trading banks. Despite the damage control that followed Dedman's statement, and assurances that our conditions and benefits would be protected, we were not convinced.

The anti-nationalisation campaign was very much a young bank officers' campaign. The older bank officers were supportive and would ask people to sign the petition being circulated. Nevertheless, it appears that the Bank did have difficulty in persuading some of the 'older men' that this was a serious business, and that we were really under challenge. To some extent the reaction was understandable from that conservative group whose long careers had been moulded in those non-threatening days when the Bank appeared unchallengeable. The age group that had actually seen service in the war was much more active in its response to the seriousness of the problem.

In this well devised and orchestrated campaign, the bank officers learned about political involvement and organisation. They developed public speaking skills and could lead discussions on the subject. We learned a lot about people and what influenced their thinking. For some bank officers, such as Harry Jago, who went on to become Mayor of Ku-ring-gai on Sydney's north shore and later a minister in the state government, the experience opened new horizons and career opportunities. Another of my fellow campaigners in Melbourne became a member of the Victorian State Parliament. I think most of us were richer for the experience.

Patricia Drummond, my beloved English and History teacher at Hay, where I led the school debating team, had urged me to contemplate a political career. A decade later, the nationalisation campaign provided a flirtation with politics from which I could not suddenly disengage. However, I quickly came to the conclusion that there was infinitely more entertainment for the audience in the farce which would continue on the political stage than there was for the cast.

Nationalisation changed my political reticence. No federal election was due until 1949, but I participated in the dramatic

Victorian state election in 1947. The election was called because the Legislative Council had rejected the Supply Bill and forced an election on the provisions in the 1945 Act relating to government bank accounts; the Cain Government was defeated. It is one of history's ironies that Premier John Cain Snr was defeated on a banking issue and his son, Premier John Cain Jnr, was also forced out by what was substantially a banking issue following the State Bank's problems. I was boarding in Albert Park in Melbourne when the Nationalisation Bill was introduced. The Manager of the local English Scottish and Australian (ES&A) Bank held a meeting in his home for all the bank officers of the district, and I went to it.

The Bank Employees' Protest Committee distributed to us brown-covered handbooks about 25cm long, held together with circular metal rings. The handbooks were invaluable because they contained possible questions which we were likely to encounter when canvassing voters or leading discussions. Sample answers were also provided.

An example of a sample question and sample answer indicates the detail in our briefs:

Question. Is it true that Professor Hytten speaking for the Banks advocated 6–8% unemployment as a 'steady national policy'?

Answer. Definitely no. The facts are:-

(a) Professor Hytten was, at the time, Economic Adviser to the Bank of New South Wales. He attended the Science Congress at Hobart in his personal capacity as a Professor of Economics as he was perfectly free to do and indeed over the years has attended similar Congresses in many parts of the world as an individual. He was not even representing the Bank of New South Wales let alone any other Bank.

(b) He did not use the words 'steady national policy'. He quoted the figures 6–8% as the rate of unemployment existing in the best years of the 'twenties' and said that 'it should not be impossible to attain the conditions which prevailed in those years as a fairly stable level of employment'. That this was a more satisfactory level than the figures suggest was demonstrated by the capacity of the country to absorb large numbers of migrants.

It is a wicked twisting and misquoting of words to give an entirely erroneous meaning.[18]

Other information at our fingertips included a list of social services which were initiated by non-Labor governments such as the introduction of the old age pension by Deakin in 1908 and the first anti-cancer program introduced by the Bruce-Page Government in 1926.

The sample questions and answers aided the tuition of bank officers to prepare them for public debate. Some of the material was not related to nationalisation but it added to the arguments against the Labor Government, and showed the growing capacity of bank officers to cope with the wider political debate.

The way in which the officers and their relatives worked on the campaign indicated their value as publicity agents. The strategists seemed to know what they were doing. Banks collectively had a widespread branch network. Their staff were respected members of the community, and it was traditional for bank officers and bank managers to be leaders in most districts. Indeed, they were encouraged to be so for business reasons. Bank officers in the Bank of New South Wales were instructed in the Bank's *Book of Rules* not to frequent hotels or billiard halls or gamble. They could not hold a second job. They had to get permission to marry if they earned less than £250 per annum. Although banks were viewed by some people as having added to the suffering in the 1930s, I believe that it is fair to say that the community's perception of the bank officer was that of an upright citizen with no vices. In some country towns people who worked in banks were regarded as just slightly below the doctor. When I joined the Wales, the bank manager's residence on the top of the 19th-century branch building was equipped with an intricate bell system to summon the maid to the various rooms in the residence, a demonstration of the standing of the bank manager in earlier years.

Over the years and in several quarters the banks have been

accused of coercing young bank officers to participate in the anti-nationalisation campaign. In referring to literature distributed by the banks to their employees, Chifley commented that, 'It almost directed their employees what they were to do, irrespective of their personal views regarding the Government proposals.'[19] If this form of intimidation did occur in other banks, I was not aware of it. If the bank officers employed by the Wales were coerced, I saw no evidence of it. Although some individuals may have acted incorrectly, the archival material cautions against exerting too much overt influence. The Wales' circulars on campaign tactics were more guides than directives to the kinds of activities in which officers could be involved. The language of the General Manager's circulars suggested, 'ways in which you could help the good cause' rather than 'must'.[20] As the election of 1949 loomed, Heffer advised that no officer must feel any obligation to take part in the forthcoming election campaign and that the Bank respected officers' personal views.[21] As Murray Stewart explained, 'I never felt in conflict with the Bank's line because I personally believed in it . . . I did not like to be pushed around . . . I don't think we ever felt as if we were being coerced.'

By today's standards, the Bank's strict code of conduct in the 1940s, as set out in its lengthy *Book of Rules*, seems to intrude on the public and private lives of bank officers, but in those days the Wales was regarded as the leading employer and, as Murray Stewart reminded me, 'It was a street ahead as far as attitude was concerned.'[22] So we were loyal to the Bank because we knew the Wales offered more benefits and looked after its staff better than other banks.

For example, the superannuation scheme of the Bank of New South Wales, established in 1862, was believed to be Australia's oldest. At one stage the Bank had its own award. Respondents to the award were described as 'Bank of New South Wales' and 'Bank of Australasia and the others'. All of that came to convince bank officers they were better off staying with the boss and taking part in the campaign.

I don't recall any hostility between the Commonwealth Bank officers and the private bank officers. I had the impression that they were on our side. I suppose they didn't see themselves as benefiting greatly because they would be swamped by the private bank officers.

The campaign was not easy. I remember talking to the chief of the Victorian Division of the Bank in a get-together in the aftermath of the Victorian State election, before we were to embark on the next phase. I was saying how distasteful I found this activity and was surprised by his reaction. He seemed concerned and asked me why I was doing it, and I remember saying, 'It is now or never.' His immediate sense of relief was obvious.

During this time I had to go into a repatriation hospital for an operation to correct a problem arising from war service. Throughout the couple of hours of my surgery, in which I was conscious, the sole topic of conversation between the surgeon and his support team was the nationalisation of medicine. I was too sick with all the blood and gore to join the debate, but I was tempted to tell them where I stood.

In the lead up to the federal election personal contact with members of the public was seen as the best policy, and the bank employees themselves were considered the best people to handle this contact. Every assistance possible was given to bank officers to take up the challenge. Men from all states were released to take up full-time duty on committees. Attention was given to filling in the gaps in political party organisations. As for myself, I went to work full time on the campaign in Ballarat with two locals from the Union Bank and the ES&A Bank. Ballarat was a marginal seat held by the Labor Party. We took over the distribution of material and undertook an extensive canvass of the city and surrounding district. The Liberal Party could not believe its luck. Approximately 60 000 homes were visited in the state of Victoria. As canvassers we got a mixed reception. People who were dedicated to the nationalisation cause were hostile. Frequently they made comments such as 'What are you doing here?' and 'Who is paying you?'

I got a particularly hostile reception from one fellow who asked me if I were a qualified accountant. When I said I was not, he replied with a very authoritative voice, 'Well, I am and when you are you can come back and talk to me', and he slammed the door. When I went next door, I had a sympathetic reception. I asked who their neighbour was and related my story, and they said laughing, 'He's a shearer.'

From the outset, the campaign created a volume of work for Parliamentary staff. On 16 September 1947, it was reported that the volume of telegrams was such that the telegraphists protested to the Prime Minister about the amount of work. It is evident from the archival material that the banks worried about maintaining the momentum. On 20 September 1949, Heffer warned his staff that the Privy Council verdict in favour of the banks on the government's appeal against the High Court decision was 'not necessarily the end of the story. The only real answer is for the electors to decide in the forthcoming election to get rid of the government.'[23]

We used to meet after our canvassing sessions and compare notes trying to assess what the outcome was going to be. It was interesting how the results varied in different parts of the City of Ballarat. There was a speakers' group, substantially a Liberal Party initiative, but the Bank Employees' Protest Committee was very much involved in finding appropriate speakers and people trained to be members of the speakers' group. In addition to canvassing marginal electorates, we also organised a petition containing a demand that the question of bank nationalisation be submitted to a referendum. Each state organised its own petition. In NSW alone some half million signatures were obtained out of the total population of 3.2 million (men, women and children) for the state.

Now, so long after these events, I find it difficult to understand how the broadly based rejection of the nationalisation policy and the resounding defeat of the Cain Government in Victoria did not convince Chifley to withdraw his legislation. History tells us that Chifley was totally convinced that he was correct and I doubt that anyone would question his sincerity in wanting the best for his country. However, I believe that it was an act of folly to pursue a course of action which was strongly perceived by the constituency to be against their interests. The opinion polls showed the depth of public antipathy. The Ashby Research public opinion poll called a straw vote on 19 September 1947. It disclosed that 64.5 per cent were opposed to bank nationalisation and 24.5 per cent in favour, with the rest having no opinion. The Gallup polls showed a shift in preference from Labor to the Liberal-Country Party, between

July 1947 (prior to the decision to nationalise) and November 1947 from 51 per cent to 46 per cent, a dramatic drop of 5 per cent. In persisting with nationalisation the Labor Party created a great deal of public hostility and in the end became its victim. The loss of government in 1949 was a blow from which the Labor Party did not recover for 23 years until the election of the Whitlam Government.

Bank officers celebrated when the legal milestones were achieved in 1948 and 1949, but always with the knowledge that legal victories alone were probably not enough and that we must press on with our political campaign. In the December election, four ministers lost their seats, as did seven other Labor members of the House of Representatives, with the Liberal-Country Party coalition winning 74 seats to Labor's 47. In the Senate, Labor held 34 out of 60 seats having retained a majority of 12 from the previous election.

Ultimately we achieved our objective with the fall of the Chifley Government in December 1949 and the reaffirmation of the right of private trading banks to exist. The banks were not nationalised. However, the dispute between the banks and successive governments over the level of profits, and over special deposits in various guises such as Statutory Reserve Deposits, continued until the era of so called 'deregulation' in the 1980s. The principles of central bank control over monetary policy established during the war were grudgingly accepted by the trading banks and remained in place.

Is it not ironic that a political campaign to nationalise the banks in the late 1940s has come half circle in the 1990s with the partial privatisation of the Commonwealth Bank and moves to privatise the state banks? The Commonwealth Bank, established in 1912, long regarded as the people's bank and designated less than fifty years ago as the instrument of bank nationalisation, joined the private sector in the 1990s with its shares listed on the Stock Exchange.

Is it not also ironic that a political campaign to save bank officers' jobs has also come half circle? Now the private banks are 'shedding' their own staff, and not by government directive. What has happened to the implicit contract which was so highly valued by the banks and their staff – a contract which motivated bank officers to take uncharacteristic political action in 1947? Would today's bank officers have the same motivation to defend their employers, the banks, from a similar hostile takeover? I think not.

3 A WIG, A GOWN AND A COURT

While I was out drumming up public support against nationalisation the management was organising the anticipated legal wrangle. Douglas Farquharson of the Wales was the epitome of a traditional career banker, a recognised authority in his time on banking practice and procedures, the author of many text books on banking, and the obvious choice to lead and co-ordinate the campaign to win the battle for the banks in the courts in 1947. There is no doubt that the Bank of New South Wales immediately assumed the leadership role in the legal battle. Following the startling announcement by the Prime Minister on Saturday, 16 August 1947, Farquharson had already met early on the following Monday morning with lawyers representing the two Sydney banks. The banks were taking steps to brief senior counsel (KCs in those days) and communicating with the banks in Melbourne urging them to follow suit.

Before the day was out, seven counsel and seven juniors were retained and arrangements were set in train to retain estate agents in every capital city in Australia to argue compensation. By Wednesday, Garfield Barwick, KC (later Chief Justice of the High Court) emerged as leader to the legal team when three of his seniors agreed to stand aside because the strenuous and exacting nature of the long task which lay ahead required a younger man.

While the general managers and the bank staff were planning to marshall all of their energies to defeat the government at the polls, Farquharson identified the danger of early legislation, framed within the powers of the Constitution, giving the government the power to achieve its objectives before the election, not due until December 1949, a little over two years later.

He faced a monumental task in preparing a case and briefing legal counsel without any knowledge of what form the legislation would take or its timing. By Friday, or day six, plans had been developed to co-ordinate the activities of the Sydney and Melbourne legal advisers. Barwick was outlining the research work to be undertaken. At that stage he thought that the government appeared to have the constitutional power to do what it proposed to do, but, as nearly always in these matters, it was when they attempted to put their intentions on paper in the form of a bill that they ran into difficulties. He believed that s92 of the Constitution would be the banks' strong point and cited several cases which should be researched. All Australians interested in the preservation of our Federal system should be familiar with s92 which reads:

> . . . trade, commerce and intercourse among the States, whether by means of internal carriage or ocean navigation, shall be absolutely free.

In a lighter moment, Farquharson once told me that he had directed one of the Bank's officers seconded to him for the campaign, who happened to carry high academic qualifications particularly by 1947 standards, to prepare a paper discussing all possible interpretations of the word 'intercourse' as this word appeared in s92. He was not amused when he found the first nine pages of the resulting paper were devoted to the sexual connotations of the word. While I often wondered what the founding fathers had in mind, there could be no doubt about their intentions. As Barwick observed to me almost fifty years later, 'Not free, but absolutely free.'

As the discussions continued, steps were taken to retain counsel in London in anticipation of proceedings before the Privy Council. But with no proposed legislation available, speculation continued about what it might contain. One of the first concerns to arise was the future of the Fidelity Guarantee and Provident Fund which had been established by the Bank in 1862, and which was, in simple terms, the superannuation fund. The trustees were, ex officio, the three most senior directors of the Bank and the three most senior officers. If the Bank were compulsorily acquired and new directors and officers were appointed, it would follow that this old fund would be caught up in the acquisition. The pensions from the old fund were based on salary averaged throughout the whole of the officers' service and, since the Bank had long seen that amount as inadequate, there was a standing arrangement for the Bank to supplement pensions to 60 per cent of the average salary over the last five years of service and to pay a retiring gratuity as well.

Of course, the bank was under no legal obligation to continue these supplements and, not surprisingly, the question flashed up – what would happen in the event of nationalisation? Urgently, the rules of the fund were amended by the trustees to provide for their appointments as individuals and not as the holders of particular positions. The rules were further amended to provide that no future alterations could be made without the unanimous written consent of the *individuals* who were now the trustees.

With the 'superannuation fund' thus protected the Bank then entered into a Deed of Guarantee with the trustees, as representatives of the staff, which effectively converted the gratuitous supplementary retirement payments to legal obligations of the Bank.

There was also another fear that the government would attempt, in the Bill, to restrict the directors' powers and prevent the Bank dealing with its own funds. This could have had the effect of preventing the Bank from briefing counsel or incurring other expenses to oppose the legislation. To counter this, a separate company was formed by the Sydney based banks and it was funded so that, if necessary, it could independently carry on the challenge to the legislation.

The Bill to nationalise the banks was introduced on 16 October 1947 and provided that after the takeover of the banks the only payments to retired officers to be authorised would be those to which they were legally entitled and, had Farquharson's changes to the pensions not been made, retired officers would have been seriously disadvantaged. Also, the Bill attempted to give the government the power to dismiss, at a moment's notice, the directors of the banks and replace them with nominees of the Commonwealth Bank. Likewise, had the changes to the appointment of trustees for the superannuation funds not been made, the new nominees could also take over control of the funds.

Obviously the government was not pussyfooting and Farquharson's warning about early legislation was vindicated. A nerve centre was established on the fourth floor of the Head Office of the Bank of New South Wales at 341 George Street, Sydney where legal advisers from all states assembled four days after the Bill was tabled. They conferred daily for the next two weeks. One can only guess at the level of tension that pervaded the atmosphere – and at the cost. Nine KCs, eight juniors and six solicitors battled away with Farquharson's help to develop the fabric of the banks' challenge. Early on the first day F.W. Kitto, KC (later Sir Frank and a judge of the High Court) interrupted the discussion to highlight the 'dangerous provisions' in the Bill which enabled the directors to be dismissed 'at a moment's notice' and to paint the scenario if some protection were not obtained against this provision. The banks could, for all practical purposes, be taken overnight. With the directors gone, the briefs to counsel could be withdrawn, the banks' funds controlled and the position would become desperate.

Kitto argued strongly for steps to obtain an injunction from the High Court, before the Bill received Royal Assent, to prevent the government implementing it until the Court had decided its validity. He said such a move was vital and urgent, but he met with opposition, almost ridicule, especially from the Victorian counsel. The argument continued throughout the day until the group finally appointed a committee (called the Injunction Committee) to investigate the detail and report back by 11.00 a.m. the following morning. The final decision was that two applications should be made to the Court, one by the Australian banks and one by the English banks since the English banks were not affected by the Bill in the same way as their Australian counterparts. In 1947, three of Australia's major banks were incorporated in England, controlled by London boards of directors and substantially owned by British shareholders. They were the Bank of Australasia, Union Bank of Australia and ES&A Bank.

While the two Injunction Committees continued work on preparing the applications, the wider conference, after several days of discussion, concluded that there was a good chance of success and sought authority to proceed which was granted. Six subgroups of the conference were formed to concentrate on state governments and staff provisions of the Bill, and five particular sections of the Constitution. The Bank of New South Wales was to lead for the Australian banks and the Bank of Australasia for the English banks.

Largely at Barwick's suggestion, the application for the injunction was to be supported by an affidavit from Heffer, the General Manager of the Bank of New South Wales, giving reasons why the injunction should be granted. Since this was to serve as a basis for the legal actions to follow, a mass of detailed information and figures was called for from every bank.

It is fascinating to look at the method by which this huge task was approached. For example, to prove to the Court that it would be disastrous to the banks to have their directors dismissed out of hand, the affidavit would canvass the details of each director and his experience, what powers they had, when and where they met, what business they transacted at their board meetings, what decisions they were called on to make and what were their relationships with their executive officers.

A raft of information was to be brought forward to demonstrate to the Court at an early stage the complex network of the banks' interstate transactions and to provide a platform for the possibility that the Bill would be found invalid under s92 of the Constitution. Similar details were to be brought forward to explain the interstate ramifications of lending with loans granted in one state financing activities in another state. All of this had to be supported by factual data. And so it went on to cover the network of branches, agencies, shares and share transfers, people and people transfers across state boundaries. In addition, there was the possibility of interference with the business relationship of the banks with state governments.

Time was short and in the final run there were problems in producing a draft which satisfied the requirements of the high-powered legal team and which at the same time was capable of being sworn by the General Manager of the Bank. The poor old General Manager had to be word perfect both in presentation and cross-examination. Farquharson said in his report, 'As all the world knows, legal people and laymen do not always speak the same language.' It was also necessary to obtain the approval of each of the other banks to what was said about them in the document, and that was no simple task.

A director from each bank was joined in the application because the possibility existed, in the absence of an injunction, that the director could be dismissed and his shares seized, thus disqualifying him from any further action as a director. It was also decided to join in the application a London shareholder whose shares could not be seized because they were held outside Australia on the London register.

The whole of the preparatory work had to be carried out in absolute secrecy to avoid any hint to the government of what was happening. This added to the strain because of the need to limit the numbers of people in the know, but also because of extended and exasperating criticism that the banks had gone to sleep and were letting the matter go by default. Still, no one cracked and all was ready to go by 15 November, just thirty days after the Bill was introduced. The question was when? If the move was too early or if the government amended the Bill on the way, the result could have been disastrous.

It was decided to wait until the debate in Parliament was nearing its end, and, so as not to be caught unawares, two members of the Bank's staff were sent to Canberra with instructions that one of them must always be in the chamber day and night, to follow proceedings and report hourly to Farquharson. Communications in 1947 were primitive by today's standards – no fax, no STD – and so hourly trunk telephone calls were booked ahead each day – 9.00 a.m. to 6.00 p.m. to the Bank and 7.00 p.m. to 8.00 a.m. to Farquharson's home. One of the officers sent to Canberra was Charles Ord, who later left the Bank to set up the stockbroking firm which carries his name to this day. The other was Alan Richardson who subsequently became Secretary of the Bank.

To illustrate the plan which he had devised with meticulous care, or perhaps to highlight the drama which was being played out, Farquharson, in his report, expressed his fear that the Bill would be passed and receive the Governor-General's assent in the early hours of the morning, with the directors dismissed and replaced before the Bank could get to the Court for protection.

> Had Messrs Richardson and Ord advised us say at 2.00 a.m. that the debate had concluded and that the Bill was being submitted to the

> Governor-General for Assent, we would have approached the Chief Justice (Sir John Latham) in his bed at the Australian Club and obtained an Injunction from him, there sitting, as Mr Heffer put it, in Chambers. However, it never came to that.

Some wag has desecrated the Bank's archival record by altering the penultimate sentence to read, '. . . and obtained an injunction from him, there sitting, as Mr Heffer put it, in, *or on*, Chambers . . .'

Eventually on Friday, 14 November, it was decided to lodge the Application for Injunction and the affidavits with the High Court at 10.00 a.m. on Monday, 17 November. Frantic activity continued over the weekend to perfect the affidavits and the various other documents, and to produce the required number of copies. There were no photocopiers, no word processors, no computers, and the old roneo machine had to be inked up for the job. This was left to Monday morning for security purposes, and, as is usual in such tight situations, the roneo machine broke down. This mishap must have impressed itself on Farquharson's mind because his full report, written over two years later, describes the incident and its consequences in some detail, even to the inclusion of the words, 'The Bank's machine was not being used.' What a relief, but I still wonder why the Bank's machine was not used.

That mishap left them with only twenty minutes to reach the High Court at Darlinghurst and it was raining heavily. Although this was deadly serious business about saving Australia's first Bank, I could not resist a smile as I read Farquharson's account of what followed. They set off to travel via Hunter Street – it was blocked off – they tried Barrack Street/Martin Place, and were caught in a traffic jam. Almost fifty years later, with a *few* more cars on the streets, and both of these latter thoroughfares now pedestrian plazas, is it any wonder Sydney has traffic jams! Finally, via York Street and Park Street, they reached the Court with four minutes to spare.

But there were even more problems. The Registrar insisted that the matter could not come before the Court until each of the six justices was provided with a separate copy of every document. No doubt with thoughts of the roneo machine fresh in their minds, they were relieved when the Chief Justice agreed to detach Mr

Justice Dixon to deal with the application. Following adjournments and conferences, the government ultimately agreed to refrain from implementing the Bill for forty-eight hours following the Governor-General's assent to enable the banks to approach the Court.

During the interval provided, the General Manager, Heffer, began the laborious task of familiarising himself with all aspects of the substantial documentation to be submitted, in preparation for the grilling trial cross-examination by a Victorian counsel. Assent to the Bill was given on 27 November, and following further proceedings, the matter was adjourned by the Court to 15 December. The whole undertaking was then dealt a heavy blow when Heffer became seriously ill and could take no further part in the proceedings. His affidavit had to be replaced by someone who would be available for cross-examination and time was short. Barwick was strongly of the opinion that the Court was entitled to have before it the most senior officer available and so it was that the Acting General Manager, S.J. Gandon, with only ten days to go, faced the task of familiarising himself totally with his own lengthy and complex affidavit, and all of the other documents to be submitted to the Court. Given the normal tension between Melbourne and Sydney and the not unnatural disdain which characterised the relationship between the Bank of New South Wales, Australia's biggest bank, and McConnan's National Bank, the second biggest, it would have been easy to predict the reaction of the extrovert McConnan, to the hurried substitution of the introvert, Gandon.

McConnan expressed his concern at the position in which Gandon was placed and impressed on him the great responsibility he carried. In a separate note, Gandon said that McConnan dwelt on what he described as the serious and dangerous position that had arisen and highlighted the danger to all the trading banks if anything went wrong with the affidavits or the cross-examination. This was hardly the sort of confidence-building message one would have expected from a colleague stuck in the same legal mire. Farquharson's account of Gandon's response to McConnan was, 'Mr Gandon said that, in view of the last remarks, perhaps Mr McConnan would like to take the matter over, and, if so, Mr Gandon would not be at all offended ... Mr McConnan declined this offer with haste and thanks.'

Gandon's separate account confirmed his response, but it went on to unveil some of his inner feelings when he said that the assumption of the leadership on behalf of the Australian banks had placed a heavy burden of work and responsibility on the Bank of New South Wales and its officers. To illustrate his sense of hurt he went on to say: 'Apart from a letter from the Brisbane Permanent, I have had no hint of any recognition by the other banks of the work done by us, nor have I heard or read anything from the other banks indicating that they were in any measure grateful for what was done by this Bank or its officers.'

All of the anxiety and tension went for nought when the Crown and the banks agreed on Friday, 12 December that they would not cross-examine in the injunction proceedings, so Gandon was released from his task. The injunction was granted on 15 December, but there was criticism of both sides from the Bench on the grounds that their affidavits contained more argument and conjecture than fact. The case ultimately began before the full High Court in Melbourne on Monday, 9 February 1948, and all the books and evidence along with many executives had to be transported to Melbourne.

The case continued for the whole week in temperatures seldom below 38°C and there was considerable sympathy for those who were garbed in wig, gown and stiff collar. While I slaved away at the South Yarra branch, posting the big ledger books, using an inkwell and pen with removable nib, a drama of massive proportions was being played out in the nearby High Court. The Chief Justice, Sir John Latham and five of his fellow judges comprised the Court. The case was unusual in that Dr H.V. Evatt, KC, and Attorney-General for the Commonwealth, appeared for the government.

The Australian banks were represented by six barristers, the English banks by six barristers, the states of Victoria, Western Australia and South Australia each by two barristers, while Dr Evatt led a team of 11 barristers for the Commonwealth. It was hot, tense, grim and almost humourless as no less than thirty-five wigs and gowns grappled with the arguments. The case finally came to an end in Sydney on 15 April, a little over two months after it began, but the decision was not to be handed down for another four months.

On the morning of 11 August, the High Court was crowded to capacity, with hundreds of people unable to gain admission, and the atmosphere was tense as they waited for what seemed like an age for the verdict. Farquharson, surprisingly, was sufficiently relaxed to enjoy some flashes of humour as the Court Orderly struggled to impose his stamp of authority on this historic occasion. With the entrances hopelessly packed, he instructed his two junior orderlies in stentorian tones, 'And don't let no more in.' With the doors closed and order restored, he decided to give those present a lesson in deportment and procedure when the judges took their seats in the Court. His concluding remarks, 'Ladies and gentlemen, if you follow learned Counsel, you can't go wrong,' must have impressed Farquharson because he reported, 'That brought down the house.'

There was not a movement in the High Court as the Chief Justice commenced to announce his decision. As decision after decision in favour of the banks was announced, a sense of relief descended on those present, giving way to audible murmurs of approval. However, there was not much time for rejoicing. Five judgements had to be read and analysed.

When the judgements were analysed, the position of the banks was not as comfortable as first thought. It seemed clear that the findings on s92 of the Constitution offered the main protection against the prohibition from carrying on business, whilst the protection offered in the other judgements could be nullified if the government merely passed an amending act to provide just compensation for the acquisition of shares and assets. So the suspense began again as the banks waited on the next move from the government. They had only two days to wait before the Prime Minister announced that the government would appeal to the Privy Council.

Dr Evatt, by then also President of the United Nations, proceeded to London to argue the case for the government. Four barristers and two solicitors for the banks, with two barristers for the States, journeyed to London to join London-based barristers and solicitors who had also been briefed to appear for the banks. The appeal ran from 14 March 1949 to 1 June 1949 with the Australian team now led by Lord Monckton, KC and Sir Cyril Radcliffe, KC. The Board of the Privy Council comprised seven Law Lords, two of whom died during the case.

The Privy Council's verdict was given on 26 July 1949. At 7.32 p.m., Barwick, Kitto and Cowper, the senior partner of Allen Allen and Hemsley, waited with a number of the Bank's senior officers at head office to receive the cable 'Appeal Dismissed' sent by the London Manager. Bank officers sprang from nowhere and Farquharson described the jubilation as reminiscent of Armistice Night – the Second World War had concluded only four years earlier. But as the sober minds began to reflect, and Farquharson omits to say how sober they were, problems again began to emerge. The Privy Council had given only a bare decision, leaving the reasons to be published after their summer vacation, not expected to end until about 15 October. Would the reasons be satisfactory and would they effectively prevent the government from carrying out its aims? On the positive side, the government faced the same dilemma and day by day the election date drew closer. Thus it was that I, at the ripe old age of twenty-five, was left to pound the pavements in the marginal Labor-held seat of Ballarat with the election scheduled for 10 December.

So determined to preserve Australia's first bank were those senior officers of the day that they used the waiting time to amend the Bank's Deed of Settlement. The Bank was, and still is, no ordinary public company because it was incorporated by its own act of the New South Wales Parliament, which underpinned the Deed of Settlement.

My forebears concluded that, whatever might happen, the government would have difficulty in seizing shares held outside Australia by shareholders (or proprietors as they were rightly called) who were non-residents of Australia. The Bank had for many years conducted a London share register to accommodate non-resident proprietors, who held their shares subject to the provisions of the Deed in the same way as every other proprietor. It was now decided to restrict the voting power of an individual proprietor to 200 votes, irrespective of the size of his or her shareholding. At that time, only individuals were permitted to hold shares in the Bank. Assuming that means were made available for proprietors outside Australia to vote by proxy, and assuming that the government seized all shares on Australian registers, it would only have 200 votes if the Deed could be so amended. It could therefore be out-voted by the non-resident proprietors.

The Privy Council's reasons were published on 26 October 1949, and surprisingly, they dismissed the appeal on the grounds that the government had not obtained the certificate (in effect, leave) of the High Court to appeal. Since it might still have been possible for the government to apply for, and obtain, a certificate from the High Court, their Lordships foresaw that the case might have to be re-argued. Their Lordships also took into account that the government was under a misapprehension as to the meaning of earlier judgements of the Privy Council on the construction of s92 of the Constitution. In stating their views, their Lordships made it clear that the Act to nationalise the banks was a direct infringement of s92 and therefore invalid. Notwithstanding, the youthful Bob White, now turned twenty-six, and his Ballarat banking colleagues carried on to share in the win of the Ballarat marginal seat for the Liberal candidate, Councillor Alan Pittard, the former Mayor of Ballarat, on 10 December.

APPRENTICE BANKER

4

With the election result in the bag, it was back to reality, back to the mundane job of ledgerkeeper/teller at the South Yarra branch in Toorak Road in Melbourne. I felt I had gained a lot from my experience on the hustings and of course I enjoyed the contact with people and the new relationships.

Some of the hostile encounters of the election campaign were in sharp contrast with the cosy customer relationships developed in the relatively prosperous atmosphere of that Toorak Road banking chamber. One customer asked me if I could help her with some mint condition florins for the Christmas pudding and remarked, 'Not like the old days when we used to have sovereigns.' *My* only recollection was of threepences which had been used many times before. I also had a visit at that time from the garbage man asking me if I could change some coins into notes. He emptied a huge pile of coins onto the counter and left with £75 ($150) in notes – another satisfied customer provided with free service. The garbage collector's total Christmas gratuities made my meagre salary seem even more meagre until the florist next door presented me with a big sheaf of flowers for Christmas and the liquor merchant gave me a half bottle of Guinness for looking after his takings outside regular hours. For an ex-serviceman bachelor, boarding away from home, the intrinsic value of a half bottle of stout could not be compared with that of a sheaf of flowers but the thought or recognition in both cases was magic.

Supposedly because I got on well with the customers, though I suspect it was for another reason, I was delegated by the manager to raise with the wife of a prominent stockbroker the delicate, if not embarrassing, subject of the position of her account. It was not surprising that a young woman with upwardly mobile aspirations to match her husband's prosperity would have difficulty in managing her bank account when it came to the temptations of the exclusive Toorak Road boutiques. I carefully planned my approach to her so as not to cause waves with the potential to splash right up to the top and perhaps even to the boardroom of the Bank. After the usual pleasantries about the weather I broached the subject,

'Mrs X, it has occurred to me that it is some time since you have had a look at your passbook.' We had handwritten Trading Bank passbooks in those days, not statements.

'Thank you – do I get it now?'

Having prepared in advance, I produced the passbook and opened it at the appropriate page where I carefully added it up to show in red the debit balance of about £450 ($900).

'Oh thanks, does this mean I have all that money in the Bank?' asked Mrs X.

'No, I'm sorry, it means that you owe that much money to the Bank.'

'Oh goodness, I'll have to talk to Daddy about that.'

I proudly reported to the manager 'Mission accomplished without any tension'.

It is pleasant to recall the simplicity and the bonds between the banker and the customer which characterised banking in the 1950s after the nationalisation furore. It is also fascinating to reflect on the subsequent events which so dramatically changed the banker/customer relationship in the next forty-odd years. However, in 1950, I was already becoming unhappy about the rigidities of a system which precluded us from paying interest on an old lady's cheque account that carried a balance of £10 000 (equivalent to many more dollars in 1990s terms) and which, at the same time, obliged us to charge her an account keeping fee of five shillings (50 cents) per half year. Much and all as I disliked it, I had to say to those small would-be customers who walked in to open an account that their needs were more appropriate to a savings account, because it cost nothing and because it paid a little bit of interest, and that they should, therefore, walk down the street to the State Savings Bank or to the Commonwealth Savings Bank. Is it any wonder that the heat of savings bank competition was later to cause us to enter the savings bank field?

One of the less pleasant aspects of our lives in the immediate post-war period were the shortages of consumer goods. Imports were restricted and there were strict rules about the amount of foreign currency available for overseas travel or for importing goods. Australia had only just begun to produce its first motor car and there was a long wait for delivery. Of the five members of the staff at South Yarra branch, only one, the manager, had a motor car.

Houses were also in short supply either to rent or to buy, and this was of concern to me because I wanted to marry. It was marginally less difficult to find a house to buy, and I finally found one I thought would match my limited resources. It was in suburban Essendon, about twenty years old, offering little more than minimum accommodation with a price tag of £2175. After calculating needs for furniture and other expenses, I applied to the Bank for a loan of £1850. The Bank's valuations were then geared to pre-war prices on the conservative view that there was something inherently unsound about the post-war supply/demand driven inflation in house prices. That policy left me with a valuation of £1450 for security to support my loan of £1850. It is worth mentioning that it was not customary for the wives of bank officers to be in paid employment. Even if this had not been the custom, my wife's earnings would not have been taken into account in the Bank's calculations. Not surprisingly, I was destined not to own a house for the next eight years, when the price I had to pay for a not dissimilar property had jumped to £6150. Such were the ravages of inflation for the purchaser, and such were the advantages for vendors.

Needless to say, the fate of my housing loan threatened the love affair I had developed with the Bank during the nationalisation campaign. It came on top of an earlier disappointment when I was obliged to discontinue the part-time commerce degree course at Melbourne University which I had commenced following my discharge from the army. South Yarra was on the opposite side of the city from the university, involving travel through the city and a change of trams. With late afternoon and early morning lectures and tutorials, inevitable tensions arose about leaving work early or arriving late, particularly on Saturday mornings which were always a bit of a nightmare in a suburban bank. The climax came when I rushed into the Bank one Saturday morning, breathless, about 9.40 a.m., following an 8.00 a.m. tutorial and having missed the connection in the city, to be greeted by the manager, 'Young Fellah, you had better make up your mind whether you want to go to university or work in the Bank.'

That did not seem to be the time to argue, particularly as he had joined the Bank some years before I was born and had advanced to his comfortable niche without higher education, like the great majority of his peers. I opted for the Bank because the alternative would have created so many difficulties. It was a rigorous program of self-education from then on.

My disappointment faded in February 1950, when a phone call came through to inform me that I was transferred to the office of the Inspector for Victoria, the nomenclature then used to describe the chief manager for the state. I interpreted that transfer as a wonderful opportunity to see the bigger picture and to move from the perspective of a single suburban branch to the 100 branches which then comprised the Victorian Division.

I was to remain in the Inspector's Office for five years and here began an invaluable period of basic training in lending procedures and controls as well as in personnel management, because for part of that time I was personnel manager of the Division. The predominant impression left with me at the end of that period was one of tight and centralised control exercised by the Bank over a whole range of its activities. The Inspector had a lending authority of £10 000 delegated to him from Head Office in Sydney, and he was therefore obliged to seek approval from Sydney for loans in excess of that figure. As well, Sydney approval was needed to engage a new entrant or to promote an officer to a classified position, and the Board's approval was required for all managerial appointments. The Board had to meet twice a week to keep abreast of all that activity.

One of the outcomes of a highly restrictive lending environment was that the propositions that did get through were usually of the highest quality. It wasn't until the early 1980s that the Bank developed a special credit assessment and policy unit. Even then, the underlying principles remained unchanged. We knew the people with whom we were dealing, their products and their cash flows.

During the early stages of my banking career, I wanted to learn the art of practical banking and I wanted to become a bank manager. I came quickly to the conclusion that, apart from putting one's hand in the till, the quickest way to get into trouble was to make a bad loan. Branch managers were allowed no formal discretion to make loans but it was accepted that in many cases it would be expedient for the manager to make loans or grant temporary excesses on existing loans, with the expectation that he would seek confirmation in due course. Human nature being what it is, some managers were more adventurous than others or more generous or more aggressive, and those traits were accepted as a means of growing the Bank's business until something went wrong.

The Inspector's control mechanism was a series of returns known as the 8s and 9s, the most hated device in every branch of the Bank. The Number 8 Return comprised the accounts for which there was an approved overdraft limit and the Number 9 Return for accounts for which there was no approved limit. In earlier times, these returns were required weekly but as the Bank grew, their frequency was progressively reduced with the aid of a dastardly device called the 'Surprise Rendition'. All returns were required to show debt at date of rendition, the highest debt since last return, brief details on security, safety and repayment.

None of us likes to admit to a mistake and it is therefore not unnatural for a bank manager to present his lending reports in the best possible light, particularly when the prospects of recovering an outstanding loan are beginning to look grim. The business of the Bank of New South Wales has probably covered every facet of life since its early beginnings in 1817, and it was interesting, amusing and sometimes sad to look over some real life experiences of bankers who lent money. There was the optimism of the manager who made a loan to a garage proprietor against his mother's verbal guarantee and who probably pretended not to see the significance of the comment he was later obliged to add 'Guarantor deceased'.

Then there was the Goulburn Valley manager who made a loan to a tomato grower with clearance to come from crop proceeds, only to find that the grower had used cement instead of fertiliser. This tested the credibility of the Inspector's staff. I remember another manager who sought to gild the lily with the comment that his unsatisfactory borrower was a 'Miss Australia' in the 1920s. It might not be prudent to quote the year even if I could remember it, and of course, the pencilled observation, 'Does he think we should take a stock mortgage?' was sexist in the extreme. (A stock mortgage was the Bank's form of security over livestock, usually sheep.)

When a debt was considered doubtful, the account was transferred to the 'A' List and, of course, to be an 'A' account was the ultimate disgrace. No doubt due to the rigorous lending controls imposed by the authorities and, to some extent, to the internal controls imposed by the Bank itself, lending losses in the aggregate were quite modest, certainly by the standards of the 1990s. The Bank's 1950 *Annual Report* showed that the total assets had almost doubled in the past six years, but made no mention of the amount provided for bad and doubtful debts. That information was to remain undisclosed for many years to come. About one third of the Bank's assets were held in the Special Account with the central bank, while loans to the customers fell as a proportion of total assets, 'to accord with the central bank policy of limiting the volume of Trading Bank credit'; such was the severity of the lending controls in those days.

In spite of my initial period of discomfort there was no doubt in my mind that I had chosen my employer well because I was part of a bank that was 'on top'. On 3 June 1950, with the offer of some basic accommodation over an old city branch of the Bank, I married Molly McKinnon at the Presbyterian Church in Daylesford, Victoria. We were married by the minister who had been at the Echuca church where I joined the Bank ten years earlier. True to her Isle of Skye background, Molly was piped from the church in pouring rain on a typical Daylesford winter's day; but the sun was to shine for most of the next forty years of our career with the Bank as we moved through ten different addresses involving twelve postings in Victoria, New South Wales, London and New Zealand.

5 IN 'THE CITY'

On a day in May 1955, just after 9.00 a.m., I rang Molly to tell her that I was to be posted to London for special training. She was so overcome with emotion she was speechless. For many people of our generation it was a burning ambition to go to London, and here it was provided for us. It was like winning the lottery. I was to discover that London really was the financial capital of the world, its mystique enhanced by the pseudonym 'The City' which was commonly used to describe it.

I was still in Melbourne when the posting to London arrived in the ordinary mail from Sydney like a bolt out of the blue. Bank officers did not bid for jobs in those days, and the whole personnel function was highly secret in that the concept of consultation with a staff member and an agreed career plan as we understand it today did not exist.

It was not usual for assessments to be discussed: this kind of discussion came later. If there were any adverse comments in our reports, these were brought to our attention so problems could be corrected. Every officer was reported on once a year – the fifteenth of August – and the report, called an R20, would consist of no more than three or four lines. They usually started off with a stock phrase 'good appearance and address', followed by something like 'average ability'. Occasionally there would be reference to business-getting ability or ability to meet customers, with these comments tending to be confined to the more senior officers. The reports were bound in a book; one copy was sent to Sydney and the other retained in Melbourne. Every officer was graded. The gradings were A-1, A-Promising, A, B and C. While we knew some of the information contained in the reports, we were kept in the dark about our grades, adding to the mystery of the assessment process. Later, in London, I discovered that the British banks were not all that different. The R20 equivalent in the Midland Bank was known as the 'Elephant' because it never forgot.

I already knew that I was out of the rut because of the 1950 move from South Yarra to join the Inspector's Office, and the London posting was another indication that I was progressing in my career. Apart from my wedding, it was the biggest event in my life and it did leave a lasting impression. London was my first international experience – having been stationed in Darwin during the war – and I was excited to be going to work in the largest financial market in the world.

I had always been interested in international affairs, perhaps because wool and its price played a major part in my early life. One of my memories was of the Ottawa Agreement of 1932, when the old British Empire members got together in Ottawa and came up with an agreement covering commodity trade within the British Empire. Australia gained a preferential position in the British market for primary produce, as did the other members of the Empire. This was a big thing in my father's life. He was a small-time farmer far from Sydney, but I remember him telling me about it when I was nine years old. He could see an advantage for wool at a time when conditions were really tough. This was a time when refugees from the ravages of the depression knocked on our door to beg for food.

At school, history had been predominantly British and European with Australian history only taught in primary schools and confined to the romantic exploits of the early explorers. When I went to London, therefore, I was already familiar with British history and knew the names of all the kings and queens. The first thing I wanted to do was to go to Buckingham Palace. There was also Piccadilly Circus, Westminster Abbey, Big Ben and St Paul's, all of which had been familiar and yet far away. With an upbringing like this, it is no wonder that Molly and I were thrilled to be going there. It was also an opportunity to escape from our drab flat in the markets area of Melbourne.

There was a flurry of activity as Molly and I prepared for our departure – reservations were made on the P&O ship *Himalaya*, passports had to be obtained, inoculations against smallpox, typhoid and tetanus etc. – until we left in mid-July 1955. As we waved goodbye to our friends and relatives and the ship slowly pulled away from the wharf in Port Melbourne, came the realisation we were actually going to the unknown, amongst strangers for an indefinite period. Molly, having lost her voice in the excitement, shed a few tears.

We sailed around the south coast of Australia and across the Indian Ocean to Sri Lanka and Bombay and through the Suez Canal, fulfilling a long-held ambition. We finally landed in Tilbury and were escorted to London. After a few weeks of uncertainty about accommodation we moved into a small semi-basement flat in the mews behind the Bank at Berkeley Square. It mattered little that the standard of the accommodation did not match the lofty heights of the address. We were in London.

I found it exciting to walk down the street and see banks from every country in the world. Right opposite us on Threadneedle Street was the Bank of Montreal. The Bank of England was just down the street, as were Barclays, the Standard Bank of South Africa, Swiss Bank Corporation and a host of others. They were all such big names, and here I was in the middle of it. What an experience it was to visit St Paul's Cathedral for the first time and see the grave of Nelson, and the tomb of Wellington with the cast iron funeral car on which his remains were brought to the Cathedral well over a hundred years earlier.

I had a cultural shock when I first reported for work. By contrast with Melbourne, the office seemed so primitive and overcrowded. My early work was all new as I grappled with the activities of a bank involved in trade and foreign exchange transactions. On the more interesting side I involved myself in research into the European Giro system of payments, staff training practices in UK banks and in developing a system for measuring personnel requirements in London.

The stable relationship between Australia and London during the first hundred years of the Bank's presence in London, reflected in the exchange rate, was remarkable. When the Bank opened its London branch in 1853, pounds (sterling) was the currency of Australia and during my early days as a bank officer, just as some people talked about going 'home' (to the UK), they wrote Australian cheques in pounds sterling even though the parity between the Australian and British pound disappeared in December 1931, when the Australian pound devalued against sterling for the first time during the depression. Even the new rate of £A1.25=£Stg1 remained unchanged until well after the Second World War.

The ANZ was perceived as a major competitor, far more active in international business than we were. We saw the ANZ as having a superior reputation in foreign exchange activities, and that reputation flowed into dollar markets. The other Australian banks were pretty well unknown, but they all had long established offices in London: the Commercial Banking Company of Sydney; the National Bank of Australasia; the Commonwealth Bank; the Commercial Bank of Australia; and the Bank of Adelaide. There was an Association of Australasian Banks and it, in turn, was part of the much larger British and Overseas Commonwealth Banks Association, representing all the banks in the British Commonwealth. It was through that representation that we had a voice in the British Bankers' Association.

In the Bank hierarchy, the London Office belonged to the International Division, which had not long before been called the British and Foreign Department, again reflecting the changes taking place in Australia's identity. The Wales had only three offices: the City office, Berkeley Square and the Kingsway branch. The City office in Threadneedle Street had been in operation since 1853, and when I arrived occupied its second site: in over one hundred years it had only moved once. It had the honour to be the oldest established foreign bank in London, the largest international banking centre in the world. When we protested about the Credit Lyonnais of Paris advertising itself as the oldest foreign bank in London, the response was: but you are not really a foreign bank. I wonder what the response will be in 2000.

Berkeley Square branch, situated on the square where the nightingale sang, was set up in the 1930s as the Travel Branch, and is the source of many tales, both humorous and romantic. The Kingsway branch was opened in 1958. Being close to Australia House, it was designed to provide facilities for employees of Australia House and the States' Agents-General, and also to promote migrant business. We picked up leads on migrants, and even generated leads on migrants, in the hope of securing their banking business. The Migrant Advisory Service was an adjunct to the Savings Bank.

Proud though I was of the name 'Bank of New South Wales', in London the name seemed inappropriate to the spread of its business in Australia, New Zealand and the South Pacific. It gave the impression of a small operation at the other end of the world; in a sense it was parochial. I can still see the ANZ's press advertisements worded along the lines of: 'Thinking of Migrating to Australia or New Zealand? Then consult the ANZ Bank.' It was my early concern about the appropriateness of the name, Bank of New South Wales, in the international market which influenced my thinking about the name change following the merger with the Commercial Bank of Australia in 1982.

The cessation of the Second World War and post-war reconstruction stimulated the production of tradeable goods. Australia's exports consisted largely of foodstuffs and raw materials; between 30-40 per cent of our exports went to the United Kingdom, and we imported about the same percentage of goods from there. In such a stable trading environment, there was little appreciation of the change which was to come a decade or so later.

A wool boom in 1950-51, fuelled by the Korean war, led to an unprecedented 30 per cent increase in the value of wool shipped overseas. The impact of this one commodity on our trade balance was enormous: in 1951-52 wool revenues accounted for two-thirds of total exports. On the other side of the trade balance sheet, the increase in export income, coupled with a relaxation in import restrictions, permitted imports to grow by 37 per cent in 1950-51 and by a further 41 per cent the following year. Much of that increase was for productive purposes – machinery, equipment and fuel.

The surge in imported goods, mainly from the UK, caught the Bank in London totally unprepared. The Export Bills Department was unable to cope, and the resulting chaos spread to the credit lines extended to the London confirming houses. The role of the confirming house was to confirm the order from the Australian importer to the British exporter. It would draw a bill on the Australian importer and present it to the Bank in London for cash. The

Bank, in turn, would present the bill to the Australian importer for reimbursement.

Normally, the system worked well, but when the volume of business forced the Export Bills Department to use window sills for bills and documents awaiting processing, and when a gust of wind scattered a pile of bills and documents into the path of a red double decker bus careering down Threadneedle Street, the system was not as efficient.

Initially, I was surprised at times, by the lack of respect from the senior English staff for their Australian managers although embarassed to discover later that it was sometimes justified. The chaotic bills experience of the early 1950s was one of those times. In the panic of the day, the Head of Export Bills, one Les Pawsey, who was arguably equal to the best in his field, was summoned to the office of one of the expatriate managers, who was probably out of his depth. The manager, with all of the authority he could command, said, 'Pawsey, the Bank has decided that it will not negotiate any more bills.' Somewhat taken aback by the inflexibility of this command, Pawsey sought to discuss the implications, and, not making any progress, and merely as an afterthought, said, 'Of course, Sir, we will continue to negotiate any bills drawn under our Letters of Credit.' He was then dismissed with an all too familiar display of misguided autocracy – 'Pawsey, you heard what I said: NO MORE BILLS.' Pawsey, the professional, retired knowing full well that he would continue to honour any bill drawn under the Bank's Letter of Credit, as he was indeed obliged to do if the Bank was not to hold its head in shame forever more. The crisis was so severe the Bank dispatched a senior executive from Sydney, with prior London experience, to oversee the solution.

I learned a lot about trade and international banking from those old stalwarts in London, and I also learned a lot about the behaviour of Australian managers abroad. No Australian manager in 1955 would address one of his senior staff members by his surname, but they dropped into this behaviour when they worked abroad. Perhaps this was a sign of the cultural cringe from which we suffered, or perhaps it was 'When in Rome, do as the Romans do'. Typical of the cultural cringe, I almost caught the next ship home when I was first addressed by my surname.

In the 1970s this attitude still existed. A senior Australian businessman, who was a personal friend of mine, came to London on business and needed travellers cheques. The young officer in charge of issuing travellers cheques, in complying with the rule that travellers cheques be signed in front of the issuing officer, presented the cheques to our customer for his signature prior to the sale. Our customer replied that he was in a hurry and would sign them later. Even in the face of threats from our customer that he would report her behaviour directly to me, the bank officer stood her ground, and the customer, pride hurt, walked out minus travellers cheques. Her supervisor, the Assistant Accountant, summed up the situation and forewarned me. As the newly arrived Chief Manager, I was so concerned about staff attitude and morale that I went downstairs and commended the young officer. The news of that event went through the office like wildfire, to my surprise, presumably because it signalled a more human approach in contrast to the autocratic style of the past.

Wool bills naturally dominated the activity of the Import Bills Department but I was fascinated to note that come February, for about five weeks each year, we had a flood of bills covering apples and pears, principally from Tasmania, shipped to catch the window of opportunity between seasons in Europe. With the advance of the European community concept that happens no more, and many of us will recall the time when the Tasmanian government was forced to subsidise the destruction of hundreds of fruit trees because of loss of markets.

On early morning visits to the Smithfield meat markets in London to look at beef and lamb imported from Australia and New Zealand, I talked with Borthwicks about our lack of competitiveness. Borthwicks, a big name in the London meat business, was probably one of the Bank's largest single customers in the 1950-70s as we financed their meat purchases in Australia and New Zealand. Today the name no longer exists, principally because of our exclusion from European markets. As a country we have done well in managing the huge shift in our trade which has taken place within one person's career.

In the 1950s and 1960s the Bank was not interested in retail transactions in London other than those imposed on us by our

Australian connections, and I had no quarrel with this policy. But if one took away the travel, export bills, and import bills departments, there wasn't much left. With exchange controls in the UK, Australia and New Zealand, dealing activities in currencies were largely confined to exchange control-approved transactions. There were one or two people on the dealing desk. The Bank also had a responsibility to ensure that currency control regulations were observed. There was no problem with exports, though there was a problem with the disposal of the proceeds, which had to be passed back to Australia. The exporter was not permitted to retain proceeds overseas. But this was all to change.

By the 1970s the Eurodollar market, a market for US dollars deposited in banks outside the United States, had developed and there was a burgeoning trade in currency. The Bank's participation in this market represented a big change in direction. By then there were many of these new kinds of transactions, which were not Australian trade-related. In the 1950s the first test of a transaction would have been: is it related to Australian, New Zealand or Fijian business? If not, then we don't do it. Whereas in the 1970s it was, if it is business we'll do it.

In about 1950 we competed keenly, but not keenly enough, with the ANZ for the Russian wool trade finance. The Russians were emerging wool buyers who, like other eastern European countries, wanted to buy on credit. Our business was built on a solid foundation of trust. We used to approve export credit lines for buyers often on little more than a 'gentleman's agreement', agreements which were then honoured without fail. They were big names, old and long established in the wool business, and of course they were all names prominently displayed as buyers in every wool auction room in Australia and New Zealand. The business was profitable, highly competitive and of course highly prized, and woe betide any officer guilty of a mistake in servicing the buyers' requirements. Senior managers would drop everything to go to Roubaix in France or Basle, or anywhere, to express an apology or to put things right.

It was in this trading environment that requests started to mount for wool export finance to the eastern European countries, and to the Bank for Foreign Trade in Moscow. The London office was naturally anxious to promote trade to these countries but the Bank remained cautious about extending credit to state-owned trading entities in the then communist bloc. It is interesting that although there was no formal country risk and credit assessment unit in the Bank, somebody in Sydney must have had at the back of his or her mind that a centrally planned economy, albeit sovereign risk, should not have unlimited credit even for wool or sheep skins. And so the answer for a big Russian credit ultimately was, 'No more'. The result was dramatic. The Russians closed the door on the Bank, and it remained closed for many years. Not surprisingly there was considerable frost in the relationship between the London office and the British and Foreign Department in Sydney from that event.

The ANZ had a ball as the Russians became more established and more respected buyers of wool. The Russians had long memories and it was only by making a series of visits, consuming much vodka, and making up-front offers, that we re-established ourselves. About the only comfort we could get was a rumour that the ANZ had to fly an officer to the Suez Canal (the final point before the port of destination in eastern Europe, and beyond recall) to be prepared to take possession of a shipment of wool bound for Russia because the credit was late in arriving. To the chagrin of our officers, the credit arrived in time.

The Bank's business strategy did not operate along the lines of 'loss leaders'. But it was prepared to be an aggressive bidder for foreign exchange transactions or export-import transactions because there were big margins under fixed rates of exchange. In those days Australia was a part of what was then known as the sterling area. In my inexperience with currencies and foreign exchange, I wrote a letter once using the term 'Sterling currency' and earned a sharp rebuke from one of my English colleagues – 'Listen, boy, this is not a currency, this is Sterling'. As we drifted from the mother country, we began to denominate our trade in US dollars. With a fixed exchange rate, the margins were fixed and were generous to the Bank. The Bank was then able to bid aggressively on other terms. Finance to wool growers and to wool buyers was provided at concessional rates, and those rates would generally be agreed between banks and with the Reserve Bank of Australia.

We were dealing with Australia's principal export, and advances to wool buyers were separately recorded in statistics to focus attention on other advances which were strictly controlled.

In hindsight, I wonder whether the losses we may have incurred in the early days of the Russian wool trade would equal the losses we did in fact incur by losing trade finance and perhaps contingent business to the ANZ. I believe we recovered our competitive position with the ANZ in the international arena, but their staying power has easily outclassed the Bank in more recent years.

China was also a major source of wool business for the Wales, even though Australia had no diplomatic relationship from the time of the revolution until Gough Whitlam came to power in 1972. In the 1950s Australian wool accounted for nearly 100 per cent of our total exports to China, a figure which remained until the end of the 1950s when Australian exports broadened to include iron and steel and more wheat.

After the People's Republic of China was established and Mao Zedong assumed leadership, the Bank of New South Wales continued to do business with the Bank of China. In the aftermath of the 1949 revolution the branches of the Bank of China in London, Hong Kong and Singapore continued, whereas the branches in Sydney and New York transferred with the Chiang Kai-shek government. The Wales was always concerned to nurture and preserve its foreign bank relationships, and when faced with the dilemma of dealing with balances held from the Bank of China at that time, it solved the problem by paying the balances due to both parties. As a result, the relationship with the Bank of China in Sydney was preserved, as was the relationship with the continuing London branch. The Bank of China readily understood the explanation that we were bankers not politicians.

Managing the export business with China from London presented no problem, because the Wales was just around the corner from the Bank of China. While we had a strong and friendly relationship with the Bank of China, their Letters of Credit were so long, so complex and so detailed that the technical people in the Letter of Credit section in London looked for a strong drink after processing a credit from the Bank of China.

When Australia and China eventually agreed to normalise

diplomatic relations in early 1973, I was touched by an invitation to me and my colleagues from the senior management of the Bank of China to join them for a celebratory lunch in Soho. It was a long lunch with many toasts to the future friendship of our two countries and our two banks.

In 1956, I attended the seven week 'Senior Course' at the Midland Bank's Staff College in Oxted in Surrey, the first overseas banker to be invited. I then attended the International Banking Summer School in Bavaria in 1957 while Molly visited the Isle of Skye to check out her McKinnon ancestors.

As the first overseas banker to be invited to attend the 'Senior Course' at the Midland Bank Staff College, I was keen to compare banking practices between our two countries. I had ample opportunity to do so. At the College we had some very good tutors who stimulated our appetites for learning and created enthusiasm. We were highly motivated students; we taught ourselves, and probably each other. As it was a residential college, we worked a fairly long day and often carried on our discussions well into the evening. I kept a detailed set of notes which I later used when I was appointed to organise the Wales Residential Staff Training College in Sydney. A sensitive host, the Midland Bank had arranged for my roommate to be the Accountant of their wool branch in Bradford. Such was their interpretation of the interests of an Australian banker of the time.

The fundamentals of banking did not differ widely between Britain and Australia. They are universal to western-style banking. At the Midland Bank College I had an opportunity to think about banking practices in depth, and I was guided by them during my long career. I believe the basic lending principles still hold good today. I remembered the principles of lending with the aid of a mnemonic P-A-R-S-E-R, which indelibly imprinted them on my memory. Each stage represents a hurdle to be cleared before the next stage is considered and before the loan is ultimately approved. They are:

P for PERSONAL. Is the personal element satisfactory? Are the borrowers people of integrity or have they been found unreliable?

A for AMOUNT AND PURPOSE. Is the amount adequate and appropriate for the purpose for which the loan is sought?

R for REPAYMENT. The lender should be satisfied that the cash flow of the borrower is adequate to support the loan or that there are other sources of repayment.

S for SECURITY. It is worth noting that security ranks for consideration only after the first three tests have been passed.

E for EXPEDIENCE. In local parlance, this might well be interpreted to mean 'Are there collateral advantages in the approval of this loan?' In the 1990s E would also mean ENVIRONMENTAL IMPACT.

R for REMUNERATION. Obviously there is no point in making the loan if there is not a positive impact on the bank's profit. The banker at the coal face is best able to assess the value, present and potential, of a particular relationship, but he must be required to operate within parameters which satisfy the Bank's goals for return on assets (immediate and potential).

These principles went into my knapsack of good advice. Now, in reflecting on my banking career, it seems to me that many banks, not just the Bank with which I was associated for so long, occasionally forgot these time-honoured basic principles. With all of these prescriptions in mind bankers should not have gone wrong, but they did and will probably continue to do so given the propensity for humans to forget history or to ignore the checks and balances for their own ends.

The topic at the Banking Summer School was 'Relations between the central banks and the commercial banks'. The Deutsche Bundesbank (the German central bank) had recently been formed, with heavy emphasis on its independence. Dr Malcolm Hill, my Australian colleague from the Commonwealth Bank, who later became Secretary and Adviser to the Governor of the Reserve Bank, spoke with great emotion about the absurd concept of a central bank totally independent of its political masters. Then, as now, it is a subject which excites comment from the academic community, business and government. It still creates unresolved and perhaps unresolvable tensions between the regulators and regulated. Are we any nearer to resolving these tensions?

Those taking part were all aged about thirty to thirty-five. Participation in the school left a very strong impression on me; I met a number of people with whom I remained in contact for the next twenty or thirty years, people such as Jeremy Morse of the Bank of England, who was Head of the Committee of Twenty to discuss global exchange rate management, and who later became Chairman of the Lloyds Bank, and Bill Rae, one of the principals of Brown Brothers in New York.

The Russians were there, and were never seen independently of each other. Along with my London colleagues, I was still smarting from the view that Sydney had mishandled the Russian wool business, and here we were face to face with the Russians and other people from central Europe. Some interesting stories were related at the school about how for them vodka was a big part of business: in early morning calls instead of getting a cup of coffee, it was often a glass of vodka.

I remembered this lesson very well, and it stood me in good stead on my first visit to Moscow in 1974 to represent the Bank on the occasion of the tenth anniversary of the Comecon Bank (the byname of the International Bank for Economic Co-operation), the IMF of the communist bloc. It was a major celebration, attended by bankers from all over the world. The major event was a luncheon which started at 1.30 p.m. and finished well after 5.00 p.m., with unlimited quantities of Russian champagne and vodka. Some of my colleagues had great difficulty in leaving the lunch, not only because of the vodka and champagne but also because it was so cold. It was 20 below – a mild winter, they said. I'd like to think I was a bit more cautious than my colleagues. That night we were scheduled to attend a performance of the Bolshoi Ballet, and I can remember one of the long-lunchers being threatened by his wife, 'If you go to sleep, I will spear you with this,' – the 'this' being a long hat pin.

Business changed dramatically between my two postings in London. From 1955 to 1958 the whole London office revolved around the trade of physical goods, and the Berkeley Square office dealt with travel and Australian visitors. We opened the travel branch out of loyalty to our Australian customers, many of whom were wealthy graziers and usually stayed for twelve months. People spoke of the Berkeley Square branch fondly – almost as a club or a home away from home. In fact, there was a staff canteen in the basement and there are anecdotes of travellers who found their way there, taking advantage of the low-cost meals. One day a fellow who had his lunch in the canteen remarked to the staff that it was the best lunch he had ever had for a shilling; he was a wealthy grazier from Queensland. We treated such incidents with good humour.

One afternoon the staff in Berkeley Square, who had been flat out all day serving Australian visitors, closed the doors at 3.00 p.m. but one customer remained unaware that the Bank had closed. The innocent customer, who thought himself a rarity in a country so far from home, went to the teller's counter to present his credentials. In the normally tense and busy atmosphere of the banking chamber, it was usual for the tellers to relax for a few minutes after the doors closed, and before they started to balance the day's work. This customer introduced himself to the teller and, with the usual Australian openness and enthusiasm, said: 'I've just arrived from – ' (some country town or other in Australia), as two to three hundred others did every day. The teller welcomed him warmly, shook his hand, and then called loudly to his colleagues, 'Hey fellas, here's a customer who has just arrived from Australia.' You can imagine the customer's surprise at such a warm welcome, unconscious as he was of the understated English humour at his expense.

The branch was a meeting place. The ship would arrive at Tilbury on Tuesday, and people who had travelled together all the way from Sydney to London made their fond farewells at the dock-side. Having left the ship, they usually found their accommodation, and perhaps because they were homesick or needed currency, their next port of call was the Bank, where they all met up again the following day. There were glorious reunions.

For the staff of the Berkeley Square branch, however, it was chaos when a ship arrived, and even more chaotic when there were two ships in one week. As well as attending to their banking requirements, passengers who were our customers usually collected their mail which we held for them. There were ornate writing desks; it was like banking in a boudoir. The branch was a residence of the last century: it was William Pitt the Younger's house at one stage. The offices of the senior managers were located in former bedrooms, all handsomely decorated. The building had all sorts of features, beautiful reception rooms, tapestries on the walls, valuable paintings. But it was certainly not designed to be a banking chamber.

In the immediate post-war years, the pace of business was slower and time permitted the Manager to retreat to The Running Footman at 11.30 a.m. daily to partake of some liquid refreshment. The Bank's messenger was instructed to tell customers inquiring after the Manager that he was with the Bank's solicitor. The Manager's dignity and cover were blown one day when a customer was overheard to remark, 'Bank's solicitor, my arse, he's around at the Footman.'

Because there was so much mail for Berkeley Square branch from a relatively small post office in the West End, all of the mail from overseas, readily identified by the airmail stickers, was sorted into the Berkeley Square branch mail bag. After the Bank messengers went to collect these big bags of mail, their next task was to sort the mail which actually belonged to us and send back the rest. Readdressing and returning lost mail was an onerous task.

One thing I remember particularly were the yellow boxes of slides. There used to be hundreds of these boxes coming in the mail. People would collect the slides they had taken on their previous trip to Europe. They used to spend time in London, save their money, go to the Continent, come back, pick up their mail and then sit on the stairs in the Bank, or wherever they could sit, and hold their slides up to the light for a first look.

After the establishment of a savings bank service in 1956, many visitors arrived requiring not only a cheque account but also a savings account. We had to calculate interest on savings accounts, we had a high turnover of accounts, and all of this was compounded by the age of jet travel. This additional service added to the already busy atmosphere.

Whereas in the pre-jumbo jet era we would have had

hundreds of customers, in the 1970s we had thousands of customers opening their accounts and collecting their mail. By this time lack of space had forced us to close Berkeley Square and move to custom-built premises in Sackville Street, but the premises were still inadequate for the volume of business and associated activities. The visitors, in greater numbers, were still sitting on stairways reading mail. Fellows were walking outside with sandwich boards using the Bank's flow of customers to advertise backpack travel or other forms of budget travel in competition with the Bank. It was ironic: here was the Bank spending its large advertising budget on the travel section and here was the low-cost alternative opposition using us as the best spot in which they could advertise. It was very different from what I had seen twenty years before.

My second posting, in 1972-74, was as Chief Manager, UK and Europe, and I could not help but feel haunted to some extent by past disappointments. Here I was, over forty-eight years of age, with over thirty years service before I received my first command in the Bank, and yet it was such an important one, and so far away from home. Until then it seemed that I had always been the bridesmaid – assistant or deputy to someone or other. To add to the irony, I did not then realise that it was to be less than five years before I moved into the top job. It all came with a rush, and reinforced the views I had been developing about the need for more planning in all aspects of the Bank's operations. When I became the chief executive officer, my frustrations about the lack of planning generally, and particularly career planning and the power of the personnel department, led me to make radical changes in that area.

The closure of Sackville Street was my biggest single headache when I returned in 1972. Even now my former colleagues and friends speak of this branch with a great deal of affection, and they regret the decision to close it. Yet not only were the premises no longer large enough to cope, but we also suffered from very high staff turnover. The Heath Government's pay freeze, initiated in late 1972, compounded that problem. Coping with the resulting industrial relations difficulties was another major task. All the banks were in the same predicament, the ANZ particularly because it also had a large travel department.

It was in this troubled climate that I decided that I had to find a way to close the branch. It was difficult because I was so emotionally involved. I was conscious of the history of the branch, and the high regard in which it was held by countless Australians and New Zealanders. The last thing I wanted to do was to close it down. But I was acutely conscious of the high cost of running it, and the losses we were incurring. The Travel Department was originally intended as a public relations exercise, and the Bank was prepared to spend money on 'high net worth' people who travelled. The facilities in London were so superior that we gained a lot of goodwill and customers over the years. By 1972, the Sackville Street branch was still very popular, but it just could not cope. The whole exercise deteriorated. In the last year of its operation the Bank lost over £1 million in running the travel branch in London. Its closure marked the end of a remarkable era reflecting the Bank's commitment to an old-fashioned standard of service in London.

By the early 1970s the Eurodollar market was reaching a stage of maturity. Between late 1973 and 1974 oil prices quadrupled. Nearly all, if not all, of the oil producing export countries (OPEC) producers deposited their surplus funds in Triple-A rated banks, creating a great discontinuity in financial markets. In the non-oil producing countries, escalating current account and domestic budget deficits, arising from increased expenditure on imported fuels, had to be financed if global trade and commerce were not to be seriously disrupted. The international banks, confronted with a sharply expanding short-term deposit base of so-called petrodollars, stepped into the breach to use the petrodollars to finance the more open-ended deficits accruing in the oil importing countries. Unsound though it may seem in the blinding clarity of hindsight, was there an alternative? Naturally the Bank of New South Wales had moved from having one foreign exchange dealer, who merely bought and sold what was necessary to settle the trade transactions initiated by Australia, to a dealing department with five or six dealers.

However, we were slower to take on profitable business generated by the growing number of syndicated recycling loans. We were getting offers from syndicate leaders to participate in syndicated loans. When I arrived in London most of our responses to these requests were negative. The Bank's reputation as a leader was not enhanced; it was overly conservative and other bankers tended to be switched off. While I was there we had an invitation from the Western American Bank Europe, in which the Midland Bank had a majority interest. A consortium of banks was common in those days. Partnership Pacific had three Banks; the Western American Bank Europe was led by the Midland Bank and the Bank of Tokyo with most of the banks in the western United States.

In 1973 the Western American Bank Europe consortium had secured a mandate to raise a billion US dollars for the Great Electricity Council of Britain. In inviting various banks to join them in the loan, the consortium informed us that we had been given a notional allocation of $US50 million. The margin was very fine; I think it was 0.75 per cent. I hadn't been long in the job, but the boys in London said, 'Let's go for it. This is the way to get our name on the map.' The loan was risk free because it was guaranteed by the British Government. When it was submitted to Sydney, Sydney was horrified. $US50 million. Where are the dollars to come from?

I used to send telexes to R.J. Blackwell, General Manager, Administration (second in the Bank's hierarchy) on the subject of getting into the Eurodollar market. Chinks in the door come in useful; my sources tell me that on receiving this lengthy telex, Blackwell spent some time going through it, finally picked up his pen and wrote at the bottom 'My Goodness!' When he subsequently travelled to London to meet all the senior managers, he dispensed with the preliminary pleasantries, having come all the way from Australia, of 'Good morning, it is nice to be here,' and immediately said, 'Where are you going to get the dollars from to maintain your business?' To say that my troops were visibly demotivated would be an understatement.

Ultimately, approval came back for the Great Electricity Council Loan for $US25 million. In the event, the loan was heavily oversubscribed, and because of our friendship with the Midland, we got into the top of the three tiers with our $US25 million participation. That put us into the league of international banks. The invitations subsequently came flooding in.

Our participation was a deliberate attempt to become more international in our lending. We had the capacity; we had age, tradition, strength and respect. My view was that we should be making use of it. At the time, one of my banking friends in London responded to my comment that we had some unused capacity by saying, 'Unused capacity it is not. It is neglect.'

The banks participating in the Great Electricity Council syndication were criticised by some of the more pocket conscious banks on the basis that a 0.75 per cent margin did not pay for the capital. They were probably correct, it didn't. There were no compulsory capital ratio requirements. If one operated on the basis of, say, five per cent capital ratio requirement, one would probably have needed a margin of about one per cent just to service the capital. But the Wales had surplus capital and it wanted to get into the market, so there was a temptation to take on loans at margins too fine to service capital. To some extent I let the marketing side of me take over when we departed from the 1950s way of doing business and participated in the Great Electricity Council Loan.

I have often thought that the industrial unrest in the finance sector brought about by the British pay freeze in the 1970s should be a classic case study in industrial relations literature, and it was to be my lot to grapple with that problem in 1972.

From its early beginnings in London, the Bank had the support of an Advisory Board. In 1972, with my predecessor nearing the end of his career and probably for other reasons not available to me, the relationship between him and the Board had changed. The Chairman, Sir John Prideaux, had written to Sir Robert Norman, the Chief General Manager in Sydney:

> . . . On Bank of New South Wales affairs, I have been a little perplexed. This is probably due to the fact that I have not been giving sufficient time and thought to the problem, but as you will know, my hours are pretty full. In fact in many ways I feel that in the not too distant future I should be writing to the Chairman suggesting that it was about time I relinquished the assignment. You know what a wrench that would be because for the past twenty years, it has been an important part of my banking life . . . One would like the London Advisory Board to be able to make a fresh start on the right lines when the new appointment is made and clearly we shall be most interested to hear who it is likely to

be, although I don't imagine any of us will know him . . .

Sir Robert was quick to reply:

> . . . I must say that your letter of 5th April, 1972 caused me to hasten with the appointment of a successor. We will get Bob White to London as soon as we can . . .

As this implies I had more than an industrial relations problem to contend with on my arrival. The Bank was indeed fortunate to have in London an Advisory Board of such high calibre. It comprised the Chairman of the National Westminster Bank, the Deputy Chairman of Barclays Bank, the Chief Executive of P&O, a director of each of the two merchant banks, Kleinwort Benson and Schroders, and I found no difficulty in establishing a mutually beneficial relationship with all of them. Each was particularly helpful with background and advice on a range of matters, especially the industrial relations problem.

In the unsettled atmosphere prior to the Heath Government's pay freeze, businesses and workers rushed to beat the announcement. Shortly before the announcement on 6 November, four car manufacturers announced price increases, and some one million workers obtained pay increases. The Heath government's solution did not work, and in my view worsened the situation for many employers and employees. The numerous new banks opening at that time were looking for experienced staff, and because they had no record, they could entice employees from existing banks, or they could meet the market for pay and conditions. In contrast, the established banks such as ourselves could not meet the market, and we had difficulty in retaining our existing staff since we could not give pay rises.

Dealing with the resulting problems was a hell of a business. From my experience in personnel management in Victoria, I had become a consensus type of manager, to the extent that I believed in personal relationships and thought the confrontationist approach was useless. (My style of management, then deemed appropriate, was later regarded with some disrespect in the movement away from the team approach in staff relations.) But the problems in London, brought about by entrenched work and management practices and exacerbated by the pay freeze, tested every idea that I had developed on the subject, and gave me new insights into human relations.

I had inherited a union crisis because my predecessor did not believe in unions. As part of the Heath Government's industrial relations policy, somewhat akin to enterprise bargaining, employees were required to organise and discuss contracts of employment.

Just prior to my arrival, our staff were really not well organised, so they sought presentations from two unions – the National Union of Bank Employees and the ASTMS, the Association for Scientific and Technical Management Staffs. They opted for the second one. This rankled with the City, because ASTMS was concerned about the unionisation of people who traditionally had not been organised. The City wanted to inhibit its growth, and for our old and respected bank to be negotiating with ASTMS was a matter of some surprise and considerable comment.

I was told that my predecessor's riposte to the staff was, 'Now that you have a union, you will fight for everything you get.' In retrospect, and in my working with them, I found ASTMS a good union for the staff to join. They were sophisticated, and basically we were a good employer. The staff were discontented largely because of a lack of communication. We had good conditions of service, better than the English banks, and I got on very well with the staff. In fact, I had worked with many of them during my first time in London. During my welcoming remarks to the staff, I made the deliberate comment that at last I could find out if the management was as bad as we used to think. We had to maintain a margin in pay and conditions because that was the only way we could stay alive in the competitive environment of the major banking capital of the world.

Conditions were very difficult during the pay freeze, not only for employees, who were not allowed to receive pay rises, but also for employers. The only way to get a pay rise was to change jobs, and many of our good people left to join one of the new foreign banks, because newcomers were not affected by the freeze. Our staff also had an adverse view of Sydney; they felt that they were not understood, and I knew that it was a problem to overcome. I could see that many of the reasons for their problems lay with our management style. Traditionally, the senior managers were all Australian and many of them had not been to London before. It was only in the 1970s that English people began to move up in the London office hierarchy although our English staff weren't much better at managing. Because they had not moved out of the London office, they had limited horizons.

When we appointed an English staff member to the position of Accountant, a position which until that time was held by an Australian, one of the older English staff commented to me: 'At least with the Australian bastards, we only had them for three years but with this so-and-so we've got him forever.' It used to fascinate me that some of the routine letters written to large city branches in Australia about following the correct procedures were written as if the recipient Australian branch was way out there in the back blocks of a remote colony, with precious little knowledge about anything.

Our industrial relations problems were a great concern to the other banks' senior management. I was offered the full facilities of Barclays' and National Westminster's industrial relations departments. Their motivation in making these facilities available to the Wales was probably to lessen the chances for this monster – the union – to expand.

When I went to London in 1972 the crisis already existed. To some extent I had a mandate to fix it up, which gave me room to move. Confronted by this unknown union, one of my first responsibilities was to negotiate in effect what we might now call an enterprise agreement or contract. We talked about this. Our concluding arrangement, after lengthy discussions, was that I would recommend to Sydney a certain percentage increase across the board.

Sydney immediately responded by asking what the others were doing, particularly the major British banks. I replied that I had not bothered to consult them even though there was a lot of negotiation in progress in the City. I wanted to establish our goodwill in the new relationship by being in the forefront. Imagine my dismay with the reply, 'We don't want to become the pacesetter.' I again wrote – by telex – something along the lines, 'Here we are in this great city, in a country which probably has 500 000 bank officers, and we have a staff of about 350; it is drawing the long bow to say that we could become the pacesetter.' The response was irrelevant because we were overtaken by events. I could not take much comfort from the adversarial system of Australian industrial relations. I had a point of view as to how things should work, and I had to follow my own path. I worked in an atmosphere of questioning the system, and in doing so I often came up against the entrenched power of the remote human resource department.

The head of our branch of ASTMS union was an ex-policeman. He had an interesting background, because he was an Englishman who had migrated to Australia, joined the Bank after a friend introduced him, had quite a varied career in a number of branches, and gained a good grasp of the working environment in both countries. When some family problem arose, he applied to go back to London. This was granted. Because of his Australian experience and his experiences as a migrant, he was appointed as Officer-in-Charge of the Migrant Advisory Department, and ultimately became President of the Bank of New South Wales branch of the union. As our negotiations progressed, I cultivated him. I went to Blackpool with him to the Trade Union Congress, and was nearly blackballed by the City as a result.

It emerged that he was having great difficulty in gaining access at the right level in pursuit of his migrant business activities, particularly to the Australian authorities in Australia House, the Agents-General's officers for Victoria and New South Wales and also to New Zealand House. We both thought that if he were called Manager, Migrant Services instead of Officer-in-Charge it might help, because officials were always more inclined to receive a manager. It wasn't a question of pay, it was a logical request and I recommended (all requests had to be filtered through Sydney) that he be appointed as Manager, Migrant Services.

The reply from Sydney was that this was not possible because it would set a 'precedent' – they had a precedent book. I was quite aggressive in those days, I suppose, and replied that I understood what had been said, but that this was London and the particular function was quite different from any other function. There was no danger of a 'precedent', and I asked to have the matter reconsidered. If this were not possible, could I please have a real explanation. I received a reply that it was against the Bank's policy.

I felt that this was a demonstration of the continuing over-centralisation of authority in the Bank, notwithstanding that the business was growing and diversifying. The experience was to influence me in the reforms introduced following my appointment as chief executive in 1977. I believed in more power to the line administration, and I was therefore more 'hands-on' because I had an emerging industrial crisis to solve. The pay freeze was having serious effects on staffing. The stayers, who were financially disadvantaged by the pay freeze, remained as a matter of loyalty to the organisation. I felt I should try to do something in their interests.

Before we had gone very far in resolving the crisis, the union said they wanted me to address a general meeting of the staff. I was advised by the local Australians not to do this, but having more or less committed myself I decided to do it. The union leader was pleased. It enhanced his importance, and he offered to give me all of the questions in advance – I could not believe my luck. The tone of the meeting was first class. It was a big step forward.

One of the questions was from a forthright woman in a senior position in the travel department. She was one of about six travel officers who arranged travel for executives and influential people coming from Australia. She got up and said that there were three women and two men, or vice versa, and the women were paid less than the men. What was the logic: the two jobs were the same? I said that there was no logic and that I would have it fixed immediately. Although the restrictions imposed by the pay freeze were tough, I could do that because I didn't think that the pay freeze covered this problem.

The personnel manager gave me heaps because I had put him in a difficult position. As the representative of the human resources area in Sydney, he was now obliged to implement a policy contrary to the one laid down in Sydney. As a result of the general meeting with the staff, I really found out what was happening on the shop floor. I was prepared to sit down and talk about it, probably a unique occurrence in the London office. Our attitudes to human relations were akin to telling a toddler to do something and when it asks 'Why?' replying 'Because I said so.' It may work for some three year olds, but this style of management does not work well with adults, as the Bank has found over and over, much to its chagrin.

Early in the morning of 7 December 1973, only about 18 months after my arrival, I received a cable advising me to return to Sydney because I had been appointed General Manager, which placed me on a level immediately below Sir Robert Norman who was then the Bank's Chief General Manager. My immediate reaction was that there had been a mistake in the transmission because, at best, I expected that my return to Australia would be as an Assistant General Manager. Whom should I ask, or to whom could I talk? While I was contemplating what to do, I had a call from the Chairman of the London Board of the Bank, who, fortunately, had been advised separately. I waited until midday before calling my executive team together to inform them. John Chatterton, who was from Australia and in charge of personnel couldn't resist voicing his incredulous reaction, 'You mean Assistant General Manager?' I must be tolerant, because he did not finish up in Boulia or the back of Bourke.

I didn't feel the same sense of excitement with this move as I had when I received the news in Melbourne of my first move to London a little over 18 years earlier. Molly did not lose her voice this time. She loved London, and could not mask her disappointment, and in many respects it was a disappointment which I shared.

It had been a wonderful experience which had expanded my horizon, which had given me great satisfaction and which had given me confidence to return to higher responsibilities in Australia free of any anxiety.

It is difficult to describe the pleasure I derived from being in what I and most others regarded as the centre of world finance. There were more American Banks in London than there were in New York. The Bank of England letterhead said just that, and no one asked where it was. There were merchant banks like Rothschild and Warburg which did not even display a brass plaque, let alone a sign, on the outside of the building. The big four: Barclays,

Lloyds, National Westminster and Midland (no longer the largest because of currency changes) still dominated the world banking scene. It was enjoyable developing relationships in the City where formality and friendship mingled to provide a network of lasting value.

Overwhelmingly, the greatest satisfaction from my last term in London arose from the personal relationships which developed. And paramount in these was the loyalty I was privileged to enjoy from the staff, with whom I had shared many difficulties in my relatively short term of twenty months as their Chief Manager.

On my retirement from the Bank's service fifteen years later, they still remembered, with a never-to-be-forgotten farewell in the Merchant Taylors' Hall behind the Bank's old premises on Threadneedle Street.

STAYING ON TOP

6

The story of banking in the Menzies era concerns the often troubled relationship between the trading banks and the Commonwealth Bank, in its capacity of both central banker and competitor. It is about the gradual relaxation of government restrictions on banking. Last, it is about the growth of non-bank financial intermediaries at the expense of the trading banks. By initiating or participating in many of the new financial market developments, the Wales continued to position itself as leader of the private trading banks – to 'stay on top' – an objective not attained without a struggle.

During my activities in the nationalisation campaign, I had become interested in the linkages between government policy and 'shop floor banking'. But I was too junior to participate in strategic planning decisions or too busy with the day-to-day routine to develop a fuller understanding of them. Also, I had always felt some disadvantage in the absence of tertiary education, which motivated me to use every opportunity to learn more economics. As the years passed and as I progressed in my career, I believe I succeeded in understanding the linkages between economic development and banking.

The post-war immigration program was one of the outstanding features of Australian government policy, and directly benefited banking business. In 1949-50 some 185 000 permanent settlers arrived in Australia, an extremely large total in relation to the 1950s population of about 8 million, or by any comparison with today. The number of settlers continued to average over 100 000 per year for at least a decade – all potential Bank of New South Wales customers. In a labour-starved economy, the contribution of the newly arrived settlers to our economic development was undoubted. Estimates show that migrants formed as much as 80 per cent of the increase in the male work force between 1947 and 1961. The government intended to maintain an immigration target which would result in a population growth of 3 per cent per annum.[1]

The Wales staff used to visit British provincial cities in a mobile office to conduct migrant evenings, usually in conjunction with Australian or New Zealand immigration officers, and often accompanied by furniture removalists. The purpose of these visits was to extol the virtues of life in Australia or New Zealand. We offered information on the countries in the form of booklets and pamphlets, and we publicised our banking facilities. We reaped the benefits of the immigration program, as many of our earliest customers for housing loans were newly arrived immigrants who often worked several jobs or pooled family resources to save enough money for the deposit on a house. They were some of the best customers. They often paid off their loans well in advance, and, when they traded up in the housing market, we refinanced their new home loans.

Our manager at St Albans, Victoria, told me a typical story of one of his experiences in arranging a housing loan for the head of an extended migrant family. There was difficulty with the repayment arrangement – the manager was seeking repayments of a minimum of £500, whereas the borrower felt that he could not possibly go above £400. The argument finally dissolved when the manager discovered that the borrower was talking in terms of weekly repayments. These same customers, many of whom went into business, became trading bank customers and were another source of profit.

As people resumed their war-interrupted lives, or resettled in their new country, they required capital to finance their houses and consumer durables to fill them. As the population and commerce expanded, the demand for public finance to build the roads, bridges, schools and hospitals also increased. For example, the 1949-50 Commonwealth budget provided for an increase in public works expenditure of 42 per cent.[2] With the switch from wartime to domestic production, manufacturers found their capital requirements changing from working capital to investment capital. In my view, investment spending, so fundamental to economic growth, was often blocked by rigid controls on bank lending and deposit gathering.

The central bank controlled the level and direction of credit and advances. These controls influenced the level of short-term economic activity, and they facilitated longer term goals such as price stabilisation. As bankers, we were faced with an excess demand for capital, and were often frustrated because we were unable to satisfy the needs of well-qualified customers who came to us with viable and profitable business propositions. Permission had to be sought from the Commonwealth Bank for loans for specified purposes, and the story had to be put up carefully to protect the identity of the borrower. A typical submission of the day would discuss, for example, a company established in 1947 by two ex-servicemen in a large country town wanting to borrow £10 000 to build a new factory to make valves. Other details about costs, contribution prospects, and repayments were, of course, required; then some central bank bureaucrat would deliberate on the result. That this was all happening in 1950, only a little over forty years ago, is almost unbelievable.

Prior to 1953, the Commonwealth Bank was seen to enjoy advantages over the private trading banks with the continued integration of the savings, trading and central bank functions; freedom from commonwealth and state taxes enjoyed by the General Banking Division; and the special treatment of the General Banking Division, which did not have to meet Special Account calls. The Wales referred to this special treatment as 'unfair competition'.

The Banking legislation of 1953 partly resolved our criticisms. The Commonwealth Trading Bank was created out of the General Banking Division and was then required to follow the Special Account provisions of the Banking Act. From many accounts of banking history, and to the disappointment of some general managers, it appears that substantive reform of banking was not a priority of the Menzies Government. News reports of the day suggest that the Bank of New South Wales remained dissatisfied with the changes and that the government, in turn, regarded S.J. Gandon, General Manager of the Wales, as 'rigid, uncompromising and extreme'.

With the threat of nationalisation fresh in their minds, the

Sydney and Melbourne based banks buried their differences to form the Australian Bankers' Association (ABA), with the Chairmanship to rotate between the two cities on an annual basis. The Association then proceeded to establish a Research Directorate.

The propaganda unabashedly used the now somewhat quaint term 'free enterprise banking'. In conjunction with the Research Directorate our object was to build up community feeling for the private banks. I remember the advertisements by the ABA Research Directorate in the early days of television. One theme was a horse race, with the commentator describing how the various horses were struggling to get into the competition, the horses being the banks. In retrospect, it was somewhat naive. We published literature which spelt out the merits of free enterprise banking, and explained at the same time how, through a system of controls and regulation not of our own making, the banks could not do certain things. During the various liquidity squeezes imposed by the central bank, we were blamed for the central bank's and government's actions, and it was obvious we had a challenge to minimise the damage to our reputation.

The appropriate role of the Commonwealth Bank continued to be a contentious issue. The private banks, assisted by the ABA, under the campaign slogan of 'Unfair Competition', continued to lobby for separation of the central bank and the commercial arms of the Commonwealth Bank until 1960, when they finally attained their objective and the Reserve Bank of Australia was created.

The Bank of New South Wales' documents of the time reveal the depth of feeling against controls on interest rates and advances and the method in which they were administered. They were sources of continued disputes between the Wales and the central bank. The Wales had no doubt that a 'stop/go' lending policy, not of its own making, disrupted commercial relations and resulted in a loss of goodwill and bank profits. After 1959 the Special Account system was replaced by the system of Statutory Reserve Deposits (SRDs), leading to a little more flexibility. Banks were allocated a maximum amount they were allowed to lend, say £9 million per week in new lending. It was up to the banks to allocate these funds, but not infrequently the central bank issued directives on the sectors to which the money should be lent.

As a bank officer dealing with the public, I used to dread the not infrequent times when commercial customers came in to see me to ask for a loan, and I had to refuse because we had reached our quota or the request was outside the policy. In the mid-1960s, when I was Assistant Manager, Sydney Office, a longstanding and reliable customer, a Post Office employee, approached me for a loan to buy a new motor vehicle. There was no problem with security because his home was free of debt, but the qualitative policy of the day precluded the use of bank finance for motor vehicles. The borrower had a strong aversion to the use of hire purchase finance at about twice the cost, and I had so much sympathy with him that I actually contemplated telling him to come back tomorrow and ask for a loan for some extensions to his house to which I could agree. Of course I did not, and thus the finance companies continued to grow.

Even though some of the more onerous controls on trading banks were eventually dismantled, it was some time before the banks introduced new financial products. The mechanisms of banking in the 1950s and 1960s were relatively simple. Deposits could be taken on current accounts, on which no interest rate was paid. Deposits were also collected in fixed term accounts bearing interest on a minimum of three months to a maximum of two years. Loans were by way of overdraft, legally payable on demand, and there were no term loans. The overdraft system diminished the effectiveness of the special accounts and SRDs over time. There were two elements of central bank control. The first, called the 'limits outstanding', comprised existing limits at the beginning of the month, plus the new limits granted by banks less the run-off of old limits during the month. The second element was called the 'actual advances outstanding'.

Over the years monetary policy continued to be blunted or thwarted as the non-bank financial intermediaries developed new products not bound by Reserve Bank requirements. Nevertheless, despite the sometime lack of success with discretionary monetary policy, hindsight leads me to the view that a system of 'free banking' may well have been inappropriate in the developing Australia of the 1950s-70s.

In all fairness, while the tough regulatory environment imposed by the central bank was a major source of tension, there were benefits in the close association with the central bank which gradually evolved. The general managers of the trading banks used to meet as a group once a month with the Governor of the Commonwealth Bank, and later the Governor of the Reserve Bank. Minutes of these meetings reveal lively and frank discussions about the economy and banking practices. I believe the central bank was sympathetic – we all had similar problems with the Advance Policy, and it required finesse to manage our liquidity within tight constraints. I was sorry when these group meetings were discontinued, following the introduction of trade practices legislation, and with deregulation. Although they did continue informally, on a one-to-one basis, when senior officers of the Wales walked up the hill or across the road to be sounded out on various issues; and occasionally it was the other way around. Perhaps if we had continued to meet formally some of the disasters of the post-deregulation era could have been avoided.

In the early 1950s, the Wales also had to contend with another threat arising from the expansion of the Commonwealth Bank. With its directive to develop its general banking business, the Commonwealth Bank aggressively expanded its branch and agency network, grew its deposit base, and diversified its asset base in the Savings Bank. This expansion gave the trading banks a run for their money. Comparative figures prepared by the Wales' Chief Accountant show that in 1945 the share of deposits held by the General Banking Division of the Commonwealth Bank was 8.4 per cent (not very different from its 1925 share of 8.1 per cent). By 1955 this share had increased to 12.7 per cent. During the same period, the Wales' share of deposits slid from 26.1 per cent to 24.2 per cent. The three-year period 1952 to 1955 saw a spectacular increase in the Commonwealth Trading Bank's deposits of 63 per cent and the Savings Bank's by 19 per cent, while the Wales' deposits grew by only 16 per cent.

There was great consternation among the Wales' senior management. This was an unacceptable trend. We had enjoyed a paramount position in the trading bank hierarchy, and 'staying on top' was our principal aim. The Wales also worried about its future customer base. By virtue of its savings bank network in many schools, the Commonwealth Bank enjoyed a growing influence upon the younger generation. In those days, before banks raised deposits through wholesale markets, the focus was on the younger generation as the future of the Bank's deposit base. Our thinking was that if we got a young person signed up with the Wales, that person was probably our customer for life.

The benefits from linkages between the Savings and Trading Banks were marked. As the Wales' strategy documents show, the Commonwealth Trading Bank made the greatest progress in the three states where its Savings Bank was the strongest. In Queensland, Western Australia and New South Wales, where there were no state savings banks, it increased its deposits by over 50 per cent in the four years to 1955. The Wales was also concerned that the resulting high level of liquidity enjoyed by the Commonwealth Trading Bank was enabling it 'to take good commercial advance business from other banks'. A further cause for apprehension was that the public would find it convenient to do all its cheque account and savings account banking under one roof – that of the Commonwealth Bank.

The consequences of this new competition went to the heart of the goal to stay on top. In 1955 the Wales, in one of its strategy documents, concluded, 'So long as we are unable to provide a complete banking and savings bank service we must remain at a disadvantage and run the danger of watching our relative size diminish. If we do nothing to combat the rise of the Commonwealth Trading Bank, and the experience of the past three years is repeated, *we shall be only the second trading bank after 1962.*' Not content with this prospect, the Wales once again examined the feasibility of opening a savings bank.

On reflection, diversification was probably the only course of action the Bank of New South Wales could have taken in its struggle to stay ahead. Other competitors were those who benefited from regulation – the non-bank financial institutions such as finance companies, building societies, and credit unions. The Wales was determined to stay on top and consequently broadened its customer base by establishing a savings bank and moving more heavily into consumer finance; became more involved in longer-term lending to the corporate sector; and participated in the evolving money markets.

Cognisant of the fact that its diversification plans required a high level of market intelligence and skilled staff, the Bank allocated funds for the appropriate research unit and staff training colleges. It continued to lobby the government and the central bank individually and through the newly formed Australian Bankers' Association, its efforts contributing to the long process of financial market deregulation.

It was during my first posting to London that, in 1956, the Wales established a savings bank. I was sorry not to have participated in the process of setting it up. The activities of the Savings Bank ran parallel to the Trading Bank – every Trading Bank branch became a branch of the Savings Bank. The same tellers handled the transactions, the only things which differed were the stationery, the rules and the use of a passbook retained by the customer. Initially, we decided not to open in South Australia, and delayed opening in Tasmania. The Bank of New South Wales was the first trading bank to obtain government approval to open a savings bank; the ANZ quickly followed and managed to open on the same day.

In granting the licence, the government imposed stringent conditions. Interest rates were controlled and changing them required consultation with the government and the Reserve Bank. We also operated at a distinct disadvantage in the home loan market because the Commonwealth Bank, in its central banking function, had stipulated a maximum rate for housing loans; whereas permanent building societies were able to offer higher interest rates on deposits and could also lend for housing on more favourable terms than we could.

A further condition imposed on us required that we lodge 70 per cent of the deposits raised by the Savings Bank with the federal government in the form of government securities. We could lend only 30 per cent of the deposits raised to home buyers and to schools; in banking parlance this was the '70/30 ratio'. The lower level of free assets available to us for home loans was another source of contention, and we continued to press for an increase. Until then, apart from the State Bank of Victoria, there had been no significant bank lending for housing. Even the Commonwealth

Bank was not a major player in housing finance – home loans were made mostly through building societies.

In the lead up to the opening of the Savings Bank, we surveyed our own staff and found they were ready for it. The Savings Bank provided a new opportunity to build up our deposit base; the staff recognised opportunities for themselves. They saw the advantages of obtaining deposits from new customers as well as retaining customers who might otherwise drift to the Commonwealth Savings Bank. Managers were of the opinion that the Wales missed out on profits from 'business they never saw'.

Until 1970 there was only one kind of savings bank account – the passbook account, paying a low rate of interest. This was followed by the Investment Account, which was the first move beyond the traditional passbook account, and offered substantially higher rates of interest on a minimum balance of $500 and three months notice of withdrawal. From then on, we fine tuned savings bank accounts. We used to conduct laborious exercises on a fully operational basis to determine how much it cost the Trading Bank to provide savings bank services. It was a genuine exercise conducted partly to satisfy the Tax Commissioner and partly to track the success of this new venture. Our success was more than we could have anticipated: we thought we would take in deposits of about £10 million after two years, but we achieved our target in about five months.

In 1976, the twentieth anniversary of the Savings Bank, it had $2 billion in deposits. The Trading Bank, in contrast, having been in business for over one hundred years, had $5.6 billion. It used to gall me when some of our own staff occasionally disparaged savings bank business as 'less sexy' than corporate business. Nevertheless, at the outset the Wales was a bit nervous about earning too much profit, and decided to keep published savings bank profits as low as possible by ensuring that the Trading Bank was paid for its service. The decision to keep published profits low was taken to deflect possible adverse public relations and undesirable political attention. At the time management was also mindful that very low profits could lead to uninformed criticism of the Bank and/or critical examination to ascertain whether anything was being hidden.

From the beginning we marketed the Savings Bank enthusiastically both to the staff and to customers, and I believe this was the major reason why we were so successful so quickly. Marketing in general, let alone aggressive marketing, made a distinct contrast with the banking behaviour of my early days at Echuca, when it was considered 'ungentlemanly' to tout for business. Even a low key comment such as, 'Why don't you call in on me' would have been cause for reproach. Our aim was to get every trading bank customer to open a savings account and, as a result, marketing fever took over. In order to get the staff committed, managers used to travel to the various branches to explain the mechanisms and the benefits. Such was the pace of country life that one visiting manager found himself arriving at a remote branch which had shut for lunch. We continued to have key savings bank drives, awarding prizes such as overseas trips to officers who brought in the largest number of new accounts or accounts with the highest balances.

By maintaining close community associations, branch managers were able to secure school bank accounts from independent schools. The emphasis was on attracting people who had deposits with long-term potential to grow. Hence we did not levy fees on the small saver; we distributed money boxes, and were quite willing to count the pennies of small children. One minor disaster occurred when we used Donald Duck as a motif. The money boxes were designed so money could not be got out. The tellers had to chop off poor Donald's head to get access to the coins, and small children used to cry.

Partly as a result of its manager's unbridled enthusiasm, the Manly NSW branch was the first branch to achieve £1 million in deposits. A young telephone technician was called in to repair this manager's telephone one day. On returning from lunch the manager discovered the technician under his desk. 'Are you a customer of this Bank?' the manager asked good-naturedly. 'No one leaves my office unless he opens an account.' The result – another account. The manager was also reputed to have tested the queues at the local branch of the Commonwealth Savings Bank.

One of the busiest and most successful branches was the Wynyard branch, until recently located next to the busy Sydney railway station. People coming to and from work used the branch because it was one of the few that opened at 8.00 a.m. and closed late in the afternoon. Savings activity on Saturday morning was so great that we had problems in coping with the volume. In those days bank officers worked a five-and-a-half-day week. They were the last of the semi-professional white collar class to work on Saturday for the next twenty-five years or so. We felt a little disadvantaged. I can remember getting on the bus to go to work on Saturday morning, and feeling that I was the lone figure while everyone else was in the garden. The end result of this marketing effort was that we stayed on top of our competitors; we retained our prime position in the market.

Even with the success of the savings banks, and the gradual relaxation of the more onerous controls on advances, there was still a gap between the demand for funds and the supply of available funds for lending. Because of this shortfall, it was natural that non-bank financial intermediaries (NBFIs), such as intercompany markets, finance companies and building societies, flourished outside the regulatory umbrella.

The growth of NBFIs was, in my view, the third major threat to the Bank of New South Wales. All trading banks, as they lost market share, perceived themselves to be under a shadow. In the 1960s, if a trading bank raised a deposit of $100, over 30 per cent of that deposit was frozen to satisfy the central bank's liquidity and SRD requirements. NBFIs had no such requirement, and their relative freedom from regulation was to their advantage. The banks' share of financial assets declined from 57.6 per cent in 1948 to 46.7 per cent in 1960.

In its submission to the Committee of Economic Enquiry (the Vernon Report) in May 1965, the Australian Bankers' Association stressed the importance of banks as a source of credit; it also stressed the constraints under which they operated. As the Association noted, 'The relative decline in the importance of the banking sector has gone too far, and monetary and fiscal policies should recognise the important role the banking system can play in planned national development.'[3]

In addition to opening the Savings Bank, the Wales diversified into hire purchase, the emerging short-term money market, and term lending. Not unexpectedly hire purchase, or finance companies, a feature of Australian life since the arrival of Ford and General Motors in the 1920s, came into their own in the consumer boom of the 1950s. Finance companies' shares of financial assets rose from 1.0 per cent in 1948 to 7.4 per cent in 1960. The Australian Hire Purchase and Finance Conference estimated that between 1950 and 1960 about 40 per cent of all new cars, 70 per cent of used cars and 75 per cent of household appliances were sold under hire purchase contracts.[4] The Wales was determined to get a bigger piece of the action.

In 1953, the English Scottish & Australian Bank led with its wholly owned subsidiary, ESANDA. In July 1957, the Wales followed by converting the £4 million overdraft of Australian Guarantee Corporation (AGC) to a 40 per cent equity holding, a share which progressively increased. Under the agreement between the Bank of New South Wales and AGC, the AGC Board was left to manage its own affairs, the exception being that AGC would ratify any major financial or policy changes with the Wales. This gave us the ability to broaden our range of facilities to the public, and interestingly, to use AGC as a means of writing long-term loans. This last advantage may have been seen as one way to counter the influence of the Commonwealth Bank's Industrial Finance Department and Mortgage Bank (later called the Commonwealth Development Bank) which specialised in providing longer-term development finance otherwise not 'available on reasonable or suitable conditions'.[5]

As the economy grew in the 1960s, the official controls over banking became more burdensome, if not threatening. The trading banks were not permitted to pay interest on short-term deposits and that limited their capacity to meet the increasing demand for loans. Customers began to borrow and lend to each other; to illustrate the absurdity, the banks often acted as the broker at no cost merely to maintain the goodwill of their customers. The unregulated finance companies were major beneficiaries and soon they were joined by the merchant banks, the money market dealers and others all of whom expanded their share of total financial assets at the expense of the once dominant banks.

The banks' overdraft system, based on the establishment of limits against which customers could draw at their discretion, was,

My original home in Conargo, as it was when I lived there.

In 1938, I moved to the Hay War Memorial High School.

Holding the cup, I led the school debating team from Hay against Albury High School in 1939. *Photo: Albury Border Morning Mail*

My promotions in the army were anything but meteoric.

I submitted my application for a job to the local branch in Hay, in 1939.

My first car in 1954 – a 1936 model Oldsmobile.

Our wedding day – 3 June 1950, Daylesford, Victoria.

As I started high school in Deniliquin in 1935, I watched in fascination the construction of four new banks.

Chifley ignores the signal of Premier Cain's defeat.
Melbourne *Herald, 12 November, 1947.*
Photo: La Trobe Collection, State Library of Victoria

The Darwin branch of the Bank taken after the first air raid on Darwin in 1942.

In 1956 we established a Savings Bank.

The doors of our old Gundagai branch now protect the Gundagai Museum.

A joint venture with Kuwait Investment Company and Industrial Bank of Japan begins in 1976 in Kuwait City.

The Bank opens in Tokyo – 1985.

surprisingly, another instrument used to overcome the restraints of regulation: innovative customers discovered they could lend and borrow between themselves with greater ease if there was an unused overdraft limit. One of my old colleagues used to refer to the unused limits as the Bank's idle machinery. The Reserve Bank and the banks themselves had to make careful assessments of the uncertainties associated with this time-bomb ticking away; what would be the impact if all limits were suddenly fully drawn? Although this was not likely, there was much pondering over the utilisation ratio and what was a normal ratio at any given time – when companies paid their annual tax for example. It is little wonder that a charge for unused limits followed.

The control mentality was in conflict with the unsatisfied demands of a growing economy and, those driving it were slow to recognise that lenders and borrowers will always find a way around barriers. The non-bank sector therefore continued to grow until there was a realisation that controls were becoming less effective simply because the regulated sector was contracting. To preserve the concept of regulation and in response to economic and political pressures, a number of devices were developed in the 1960s, within the banking system, like the Term Loan Fund, the Farm Development Loan Fund and many others – none of which have survived into the 1990s.

I don't doubt that these facilities achieved much good for the community, and I accepted the logic of some form of control. Nevertheless, I felt at that time that an element of farce had crept into the regulatory framework; many controls on banks had outlived their usefulness. They were not working, and finance was granted elsewhere. Deregulation of the financial markets did not come soon enough.

In order to stay on top, we continually looked for the main chance. We diversified, we knew when to take the jump, but we also knew when to hold back. Amalgamations with other banks were the thing, and as far back as the 1960s we ran files on all the banks; but the one that fitted the best was the Commercial Bank of Australia. In 1962 we saw the advantages of a union to provide a wider deposit base and potential profit growth, but nothing came of it. In 1970 we made an offer. There were lots of discussions, but again we were not successful. Their superannuation fund was unfunded, and we were concerned about the level of reserves as well as the level of bad and doubtful debts. In addition, the management of the Commercial Bank was against it and, although some people in the Wales were keen to make a hostile bid, we were not united. We held back for another eleven years, and probably paid a lot more as a result.

Following my return from London in 1958, and as a result of my activities associated with staff training including the course with the Midland Bank, I was posted to Sydney and was given the task of developing a program of senior training. After a couple of trial courses the Bank purchased a large property in the northern Sydney suburb of Wahroonga at the end of 1960 for conversion to a residential staff college and I was appointed to take charge. This was an invaluable experience for me as it put me in touch with senior management who were regular visitors and with the many officers who attended the courses.

After I had finished my term at the Staff College, I was appointed General Manager's Accountant, a position which was in effect personal assistant to the chief executive, and one I was to occupy from late 1961 until early 1964. I was particularly fortunate to hold this position because it brought me into close contact with the upper echelons of the Bank; with top policy makers; with senior staff of the Reserve Bank, and with the Board which continued to meet twice a week in the boardroom on the first floor at 341 George Street. The first floor could only be described as spectacular with its abundance of golden Italian marble. I, like every other newcomer to the floor, felt that I had to walk its considerable length on tip-toe to avoid the echo of footsteps which might disturb those who wielded such power in those marble-enclosed offices.

As an aside, the job also entailed the Sydney secretarial duties of the Australian Bankers' Association, which was, and still is, located in Melbourne. This familiarised me with the functioning of the industry in the pre-deregulation era, and it also gave me an insight into the considerable resources which all the banks devoted to the Australian Bankers' Association. The Association consisted of a number of committees which usually met on a monthly basis. At the bottom of the pile were the Chief Accountants' Committee, which looked after the domestic operations of the banks, set the charges and agreed on various other practices; and the Exchange Officers' Committee, which looked after the international operations of the banks, again setting the charges and agreeing the practices. These two committees reported to the General Committee comprising the deputy chief executives. That committee, in turn, reported to the Council comprising the chief executives which met once a month and conferred with the Governor of the Reserve Bank.

The consensus among the banks on charges and interest rates, often in consultation with the Reserve Bank, made life comfortable; it is now a relic of the past. It was during this period that the growing use of cheque accounts, and increasing costs, put the spotlight on the nice, gentle, unfair approach to charges for keeping cheque accounts – five shillings a half year whether it be for CSR or for people like Bob White. A fancy new system of charges was introduced, based on the number of cheques drawn and the number of cheques deposited, with a rebate for credit balance maintained. The system was developed within the Australian Bankers' Association and announced by the boss of the Bank of New South Wales, R.J. Abercrombie, in his capacity as Chairman of the ABA, to a press conference at the Bank in Sydney in 1964. Of course there was some flak about the cast-iron uniformity of the system, or as some of the so-called radicals said, 'in the absence of competition', but that is how things were done thirty years ago.

In 1964 I returned to Sydney Office, this time as Assistant Manager 'A'. The Sydney Office, the original office of the Bank opened on 8 April 1817, was controlled by a Chief Manager, a Manager, two Deputy Managers and four Assistant Managers who looked after a large, active and diverse business. It was an exciting place with a staff of 600 and front line banking at its best. The managers were located on the mezzanine floor with lots of mahogany and atmosphere. It was, as the Chief Manager told me, 'One of the few institutions where the inmates had to work for a living.' It was the banker to any company of size in Sydney, and had customers from all over the state.

And, of course, it was also the banker to the New South Wales Government. On the fifth floor a special space was allocated to the Government Department where there were specially appointed government tellers to handle the government's business. Because the Bank was banker to the railways and to the Department of Main Roads, it was the principal source of coin in Sydney as it accumulated coins from the Harbour Bridge tolls and railway fares.

The Sydney Office was also the home of the Chief Cashier who was responsible for the cash distribution requirements of the Bank throughout the state of New South Wales. Heavily armoured cash trucks travelled in and out of the loading bay at the rear of the building. Placing great value on its independence, the Bank of New South Wales in those days declined to participate in a centralised cash marshalling and delivery system engineered by the Reserve Bank. There was a revolver range on the roof where officers were trained in the handling of the pistols held in each branch wherever cash was kept.

The banking chamber, arguably one of the best of its kind in the world, rang to the clatter of ledger machines as forty machinists posted the ledger accounts of the thousands of customers who maintained their accounts at the Sydney Office. At 3 o'clock every afternoon an imposing bronze door closed off the banking chamber to the customers, until one day the hydraulic system failed and the door dropped deep below coming to rest in the Tank Stream, as the legend put it, and from which it has never been recovered. Why spoil the legend by pointing out that the Tank Stream, Sydney's original source of fresh water, flows on the other side of George Street and underneath the General Post Office? Long gone are many of those symbols of pride which characterised the Bank opened by Governor Macquarie.

In 1965 I became Assistant Chief Manager for New Zealand. Because New Zealand was a much more rigidly controlled economy than Australia, this new position gave me a clear insight into the interaction between government, banks and the economy.

Molly and I found life extremely difficult in New Zealand, which at that time was undergoing a severe shortage of foreign exchange, reflected in an overall shortage of imported goods and of housing. The banking system was closely regulated, and there was strict credit control with a heavy bias to lending for exports as well as rigid controls over deposits. I was not disappointed therefore when the news of my appointment back to Sydney as Deputy Chief Accountant came a little over a year after I had arrived in New Zealand. The only downside was facing up to the task of selling and buying yet another house.

My principal responsibilities as Deputy Chief Accountant were connected with the Australian Bankers' Association, serving a term as Chairman of the Chief Accountants' Committee. In 1969 I was appointed to yet another term on the unattached staff, which I found extremely disappointing, feeling like the bridesmaid never destined to be the bride. During that time I relieved the Manager Adelaide, on a couple of occasions, and I was assigned to investigate the rising level of activity in the money markets of the day.

The emergence of another stock exchange boom in 1968 was associated largely with important mineral discoveries in 1967-68 – that boom was to become much more intense in 1969. Australian investors, then as now, were always quick to respond to the implications of significant mineral discoveries. The cash surpluses arising from the new share issues were freely available for short-term investment on intercompany money markets, and the Bank was becoming concerned about the level of activity which was obviously bypassing the banking system. I was not able to reach any conclusions in the course of my investigation because it was obvious that free funds would continue to bypass the banking system so long as there were substantial penalties on the banks by way of compulsory liquidity ratios and Statutory Reserve Deposits. At that time, when I was appointed Manager of Sydney Office, I did not expect to be thrust into the middle of this activity. Whilst I was pleased to be back in my old favourite Sydney Office, and to be back again in contact with the customers, I did not expect that I was to begin probably the most difficult, and perhaps the most worrying, time of my career.

By February 1970 the Sydney Stock Exchange was out of control. The Rae Report reported share sales from the four major stock exchanges in Australia had risen from $505 million in 1966 to $3443 million.[6] In those days securities markets operated on paper-backed systems, and sales and purchases therefore involved the transfer of share certificates through the medium of a broker's office from a seller to a buyer, after registration through the share register of the particular company concerned. It does not require much imagination to identify all the potential bottlenecks.

In practical terms a bank, in its capacity as banker to the stockbroker, was involved in a system which enabled a broker to buy shares on behalf of his client on the stock exchange, thus incurring an obligation to settle the transaction before midday of the following day or face suspension. The broker's only hope of survival in the choked-up system of the day was to draw on his free liquidity, which soon became exhausted, or to overdraw on his bank overdraft. If the banker applied normal banking criteria and refused payment of his cheques, the broker would face suspension and the system would be reduced to chaos.

I remember one particular frustrating experience involving a broker customer, shares in Queensland Mines, a uranium mining company which was subject to a government regulation limiting the extent of its foreign ownership to 15 per cent; a Canadian investor buying shares in Queensland Mines and the Bank's Investment Division acting as the buying agent and custodian for the Canadian buyer. The broker had purchased the shares on the stock exchange and was required to issue a cheque for, say, $500 000 before he was able to produce the share certificates, registered in the name of the Canadian purchaser, for reimbursement by the Bank's Investment Division.

The share register at Queensland Mines was, as were other share registers, so far in arrears that it was unable to register the shares immediately because it was unable to calculate the extent of its foreign ownership. The broker took the obvious way out, from his point of view, by calling me on the telephone to explain the impasse, adding that the Bank itself was the problem in not providing the funds to enable him to settle with the exchange and forewarning me that he would draw a cheque for $500 000 on his overdraft. The conversation was a little heated, as many of my other conversations with brokers were at the time, and he ended by saying that he would be drawing the cheque and that I could do what I liked. I told him that, if he did draw the cheque, I would 'stiffen' it, but I probably used some other less polite language. The end of the story was that he drew the cheque and I paid it, not wanting the Bank to be involved in a lengthy and difficult court case which would undoubtedly follow his suspension from the stock exchange to discover where the true responsibility lay.

I was surprised, although I should not have been, to find that so many responsible citizens were caught up in the euphoria of that stock exchange boom. This may be a reflection of the gambling instinct in many of us, but I suspect that it was also a reflection of the greed. I remember one customer, a senior member of the business community, who overdrew his account to an excess of $2500 without arrangements, and later, following correspondence which was not answered, had allowed the debt to increase to something in excess of $4000. My first letter in October 1970 remained unanswered, and I had occasion to write again some months later when the excess had risen to $4340 as a result of a further cheque in favour of stockbrokers.

As a guide to the size of the debt, it was equivalent to a third of his annual salary. I was never able to understand what lay behind this kind of conduct – was it arrogance, or was it reluctance to be brought to account for plans gone astray? Perhaps I should have dishonoured his cheques and thus put an end to the business career then in the making.

One of the early star performers of the boom was Endurance Mining, whose shares increased tenfold in the first quarter of 1969. But that was to be relatively insignificant alongside *the* star performance of Poseidon NL, a mining company based in Adelaide. That company, along with many others, enjoyed popularity on the stock exchanges throughout the latter part of 1969, when the shares were ranging from $1 up to $2. As the drilling reports became more favourable, the share price began to increase quite sharply to $5.80 on 29 September, and up to $7 on 30 September. On 2 October it was $17.70, and by 17 October up to $19, rising to $36 at the end of October. Escalation to that point was modest, because by January/February 1970 the price was to soar through $200 per share.

On my appointment to Sydney Office in February 1970, I was to discover that I had a close interest in what had happened to the Poseidon share price. I had a stockbroker customer with an overdraft in excess of $300 000 which had arisen, I was informed, from a mishandled order to buy Poseidon shares. The order had come from a Melbourne stockbroker to his Sydney agent by telex, instructing the Sydney broker to purchase 50 000 shares in Poseidon at a price limit of, say, $50. The Sydney broker went on the market, executed the order within the price limit, sent a reply to the Melbourne broker by telex to the effect that the order had been fulfilled within the price stated.

Several weeks later, when the paper pile in the two brokers' offices had been reduced to the stage where the transaction could be processed, it was discovered that the order had been fulfilled only to the extent of 5000, and not 50 000, shares. In a state of panic, particularly as the Poseidon share price had increased so rapidly and so substantially, the Sydney broker went on the market immediately to purchase the other 45 000 shares, but had to pay a huge excess over the price limit set initially, so frightened was he of the continuing rising price. His friendly banker paid the cheque, the Poseidon price ultimately collapsed, and so too did the Sydney broker.

The manner in which rumours spread about share price expectations was unbelievable. I had a customer, an actuary, who had been caught to the extent of $80 000 to purchase scrip which was subsequently almost valueless. In seeking assistance to cover his situation, he explained that his wife had been speaking on the telephone to a relative in Scotland, who in turn had been speaking to a geologist in Perth, who in turn had been speaking to someone else in the know, and on the basis of that information, had committed himself to a substantial purchase of shares.

I felt that I had been landed with a hell of a problem, and wondered why it was me. In my portfolio were a number of mining companies which had issued prospectuses, and had raised substantial cash, on exploration prospects which were little more than fictitious. These prospectuses could be cleared through the regulatory system, which was obviously not geared to ask the right questions or to impose the right sanctions. However, it was necessary for the issuer to seek the Bank's consent to name the Bank as its banker in the prospectus. I thought I had the answer one day by refusing to sign the Bank's consent to be named in one such prospectus. I quickly found myself on the receiving end of legal advice that I had no option but to sign such a consent, because the fact of the matter was that the company had already opened an account with the Bank and was merely stating the fact in its prospectus. Thus I found myself saddled with even more of these companies.

As the prospectus money came in, it was released when the share certificates were issued and the funds were immediately invested in the various money markets operating in the city at the time, sometimes on a secured basis and sometimes on an unsecured basis. With large cheques floating through the system it became even more necessary to ensure that no processing errors occurred. The Bank's computerised ledger system had been operating only for a few years, and it was not unusual for cheques and deposits to be processed out of sequence.

As a sign of my growing concern, I began to count to myself the number of people with whom I had become associated who should probably be in gaol. Some were subsequently to go there. Perhaps it was inevitable that I found myself one day hauled up before an official enquiry into the mishandling of funds by one of these companies, and I found it a most unpleasant experience, particularly as I was accused of being 'supine'. This was not surprising, because I had earlier determined that I would have as little to do with these people as I possibly could. I was firm in my mind that I would not lend them any money, but that was not sufficient to stay out of trouble, as these experts organised various complex round-robins of transactions to achieve their various objectives.

About a year after my appointment, one of the most significant collapses of the time occurred when the shares of Mineral Securities Australia Limited (Minsec) were suspended by the stock exchange. Formed in 1965 as a mining house, during its five years of existence the company expanded at a rapid rate to become a substantial operator in the markets. At its peak in 1970 Minsec was said to be in control of the production of more than twenty per cent of the world's rutile and, through a subsidiary, it was the second largest producer of tin and wolfram in Australia. It controlled the company which held the largest share in the Robe River project, and that project rested on the biggest iron ore contract ever signed.

It would be an over-simplification to say that the outstanding growth achieved by Minsec, and its subsequent collapse, were the result of the closely and tightly regulated banking system. The facts are, however, that bank money was not available for much of its expansion and as a result the company was enticed into borrowings of a non-bank character in the short-term money markets which flourished because of bank regulation. With a share portfolio on one side of the balance sheet, financed by short-term money market borrowings on the other side, this had to be an accident waiting to happen – it is fundamentally unsound to borrow short and invest long, particularly in risk assets.

When its shares were suddenly suspended in February 1971, there were wide fears that there would be serious repercussions throughout the money markets. This was even more serious because certain of Minsec's large creditors were associated with broking firms. So great were these fears that the then Prime Minister telephoned Sir Robert Norman, the chief executive of the Bank of New South Wales, to discuss courses of protective action, and as a result Sir Robert convened a meeting of senior business executives to consider rescue arrangements to limit the fallout. I remember being at a meeting a few days later in the office of the Chairman of the Sydney Stock Exchange, when the story was related that it was then impossible to secure independent legal advice in the city of Sydney, since every major law firm and every prominent barrister were already committed to one or other of the participants in the Minsec collapse.

I look back on that part of my career as one which I would rather forget. Ironically, I passed up three opportunities which would have had me avoid it – two from headhunters and one from the Bank to return to New Zealand as Chief Manager. I turned down the position of Chief Manager, New Zealand, largely because I did not want to return so soon and we were still renovating the house we had purchased only three years earlier with a big overdraft after our first posting. In addition, I had only been three months in my current appointment as Manager of the Sydney Office, arguably one of the most important and active account management portfolios in the Bank. Coming to grips with one of those jobs, particularly in a mining boom, was somewhat traumatic, not only for the manager concerned, but also for the customers. I could not believe that another change would be contemplated in such a short time but, nevertheless, my refusal to go back to New Zealand was not well received in those more conservative days, and I was summoned to meet the head of the Bank to explain myself. My request to be excused from the move was accepted. The episode left me with a lasting impression that it was counter-productive to move managers after such a short term. Apart from the officer concerned, the impact on the customer was disruptive.

There was obviously not much sympathy in the higher echelons of the Bank for the stock exchange and brokers in the situation of the 1969-70 period, as I discovered when I prepared a long submission to my masters in 1970 strongly recommending that the banks should enter into detailed discussions with the stock exchange to compare notes and to devise a better system for handling such situations. The reply was a long time coming, and told me that the management of stockbrokers' accounts should be treated no differently from the management of any other account. My fellow bank managers of the day and I felt locked in by the rigidity of the system, and I certainly felt deeply the responsibility we had in managing the stockbrokers' accounts to avoid their suspension or default.

Some of the brokers were so besieged by paper and pressure that they neglected to follow up on the collection of amounts owing from their clients, many of whom should more rightly have been at the Randwick Racecourse. One of our managers had actually succeeded in obtaining a list of debtors from one of his stockbroker customers, and I was amazed to find this document somewhat akin to the old overdrawn account returns used by the Bank in the 1950s, although the remarks were considerably less sophisticated. As a sign of the desperation facing all of us at that time, this broker had inserted a comment alongside many of his debts, 'Shot through'.

In retrospect, it would be an exercise in futility to level criticisms at any of the players in that unfortunate episode. Those charged with regulation probably lacked the powers to control the losses, while those at the centre, the stock exchange and its broker members, had a responsibility to provide a market. In the conditions of the day the market might well be criticised for overtrading, but I think it would have attracted much stronger criticism had it not responded to the market forces which so quickly intensified in 1969.

The Senate Select Committee on Securities and Exchange reported some time later, and most of its findings and recommendations have been accommodated by subsequent developments. I emerged from that experience with a lasting respect for the much-criticised Chairman of the Sydney Stock Exchange, the late Jim Cooper, who approached the crisis with total dedication and integrity and who was to remain a friend until his death in 1993. I believe that the Bank, too, emerged with an enhanced reputation for balance and tolerance in a difficult situation.

As I look back, with the formation of the Australian Stock Exchange and its much more sophisticated approach, we are light years ahead in the area of general supervision. Likewise, the formation of the Australian Securities Commission has been a big step forward. However, I think we have introduced such a degree of complexity in the whole approach to corporate governance that the time has now arrived when there should be a rationalisation or simplification to make supervision and the extraction of appropriate penalties a much speedier and more effective process. What cannot and probably never will be controlled is people's intense desire to bypass the system to make a quick buck. Those involved in the securities industry can now be thankful that electronic data processing, not available in 1970, has speeded up the settlement and done away with the clumsiness previously associated with the movement of paper in securities transactions.

At the end of this era of many successes and some disasters, the Bank adapted to changing financial markets, setting the pace with new banking products and new technology. It was the most profitable bank with the largest market share of all banks. It stayed on top. My career and the careers of my contemporaries were built around the achievement of that goal.

A HIGHLY UNORTHODOX REQUEST

7

It was December 1972, and I had been in London a little less than six months when the news came through that the long, unbroken period of Liberal-Country Party government in Australia had ended. The newly elected Prime Minister was Gough Whitlam. Of such interest was the news in London that I interrupted the proceedings of the London board meeting to telephone Russell Prowse, the Bank's executive in charge of public relations in Sydney to get an update on the election results and reactions. The Liberal-Country Party majority of seven became a majority of nine for the Australian Labor Party.

Whitlam and his Deputy, Lance Barnard, shared all the cabinet posts for the balance of the year, pending the election of a full Cabinet in the new year. The two Ministers became active immediately, and the *Sydney Morning Herald* began to run a column headed 'What The Government Did Today'. The earliest measures of interest to the banking community were a revaluation of the Australian dollar on 23 December 1972, and the strengthening of restrictions on overseas borrowings for terms in excess of two years. The revaluation of the Australian dollar reflected the healthy state of Australia's balance of payments at the time, and the additional measures to control overseas borrowing were also designed to limit the volume of capital inflow, which, as the Treasurer said in February 1973, had led to a build up of domestic liquidity to a dangerously excessive level.

The first year of the Whitlam Government was a good one for Australia, with high returns from agricultural and mineral exports. It was a good year for the Bank, too, with profit up from $23 million to $36 million. But there were signposts of caution ahead, in the form of a blow-out in government expenditure and widespread gains in labour market conditions. There was surely a warning when the Reserve Bank lifted the maximum overdraft rate from 7 per cent to 9.5 per cent in September 1973, the highest rate since 1890.

Having, sadly, reached the end of our term in London, Molly and I arrived back in Sydney on the morning of Saturday, 23 February 1974. As I passed through the immigration barrier at the airport, I was identified from my passport by an immigration official who told me there had been a startling development in the Bank's boardroom on the previous day. I could not get to a newspaper quickly enough to satisfy my curiosity. Sir John Dunlop, one of the nine directors of the Bank, had resigned over a dispute concerning his membership of the board of the Australian Industry Development Corporation (AIDC). This body, a wholly-owned government financing organisation set up by the previous government to provide finance for industry, had its charter expanded by the Whitlam Government to enable it to participate in the ownership of businesses.

The ghost of socialism was still alive in the memories of those who were around during the nationalisation threat of 1947, and, as one might expect, government-owned financing authorities with tax privileges were always regarded with a great deal of suspicion by the banks. The AIDC was no exception, because it was able to offer more favourable terms than the commercial banks. However, with its expanded charter, the AIDC attracted far more vehement criticism, and Sir John ultimately was obliged to choose between his board memberships.

As I took up my new post, I wondered whether Sir John's difficulties were a portent of gloom. Naturally bankers are keen to write the new business arising from buoyant economic activity but I was concerned about overheating and the effect it would have on the management of the Bank and its business prospects. Throughout 1974, I watched the economy slide and the Bank's business begin to dry up.

There was a major dispute with the Australian Bank Officials' Association. Bank officers in New South Wales and Victoria were refusing to handle business cheques as part of their campaign for a 25 per cent wage increase. In Victoria the Association had threatened to prosecute the Bank in the Industrial Court for docking salaries of members who took part in the ban on business cheques between 29 January and 4 February 1974. At the meeting between the banks and the Reserve Bank on 26 March 1974, it was disclosed that bank advances had skyrocketed by 38.8 per cent in the twelve months and, as a result, bank liquidity was under extreme pressure, thus putting a brake on new lending. As well, the political situation was unstable, with differences between the Senate and the House of Representatives. We soon found ourselves in the middle of another election campaign, concluding in May 1974 with the re-election of the Whitlam Government with a slightly smaller majority.

At the meeting on 1 July between the banks and the Reserve Bank, there was talk of buoyant spending with a heavy flow of imports, earnings and prices rising at unacceptable rates and financial institutions still experiencing liquidity problems. Imports, in fact, were at a level 20 per cent above the total for the previous three months, and 70 per cent higher than in the same period of the previous year. By the end of July 1974, the Consumer Price Index was 14.4 per cent higher than in 1973, the largest rise since the 1952 June quarter. Quarrels continued with the Australian Bank Officials' Association, this time on the question of the employment of part-time staff. The Association argued that part-time workers would destroy the career nature of banking, or clog up additional training grounds for permanent staff, whereas the Bank was concerned to provide adequate staff to service peak periods, particularly during lunch hours.

Because of my recent sojourn in London, and its importance as a financial centre, I kept closely in touch with my successor to monitor developments there, and to monitor reactions to the oil crisis which had begun in 1973. Prior to my departure from London, a lengthy coal miners' strike had compounded the effects of the oil price hike on the British economy so severely that power and petrol were rationed in the closing weeks of 1973. I had sat at my desk in the heart of London, the financial centre of the world, with no light other than what I could squeeze from a small table lamp fired by a cartridge of gas. When Molly and I went for our Christmas holiday to Cheltenham in the west of England we had taken a two-gallon can of petrol in the boot of our little Wolseley to cover the return journey.

Later in 1974 strains began to surface in the international financial markets as they struggled to cope with the delicate and difficult task of transferring vast amounts of the wealth of the western world to the oil producing nations.

The size and nature of most of the oil producers' economies were such that only a small portion of the transfer could be made in the form of goods and services. The oil producers wanted to avoid all risks, including possibilities of expropriation and nationalisation, and so they opted principally to place their new-found surplus wealth on short-term deposit with a limited number of first class banks. Massive and continuing balance of payments deficits in the oil importing countries seemed to be the inescapable outcome, while governments and official instrumentalities left the burden of solving this crisis of imbalance largely to the private sector and the banks.

Heavy losses by some banks had already occurred, and doubts began to arise about the ability of the Eurocurrency system to cope with the task of recycling the surpluses of the oil producers, estimated to be in the range of $US55/65 000 million. There was no authority to regulate this relatively new Eurocurrency and no lender of last resort. Mutual confidence between banks, essential to the smooth running of any international system, began to decline, particularly after the collapse of Bankhaus Herstatt. The West German central bank closed Herstatt on the afternoon of 26 June 1974. Herstatt had purchased DM55 million from Hill Samuel for £9 million, but the payment in US dollars was frozen when Herstatt was suddenly closed. Chase, the New York bankers to Herstatt, estimated that outstanding claims could amount to $US1000 million, whereas the Herstatt account had a balance of only $US156 million.

At a meeting with the Governor of the Reserve Bank on 30 July, the chief executive officers of the banks were advised of his concern about the recent crashes of overseas banks, and suggested we should be watching carefully our offshore operations. Heavy losses had been reported by United California Bank, West Deutsche Landesbank in Germany, Franklin National Bank of New York and Union Bank of Switzerland. Additionally, the US National Bank of San Diego and the Herstatt Bank were closed. On the local scene, the Balance of Payments deficit of $678 million for the 1973-74 year was the largest for twenty-two years and a considerable contrast to the $981 million surplus in 1972-73. Share prices on the Sydney Stock Exchange continued to plunge during July. The All Ordinaries Index fell 15 per cent to 330.25. Interest rates were in double digits with the general rate for bank loans in excess of $50 000 at 12.5 per cent. The maximum rate for loans under $50 000 was 11.5 per cent.

Under the arrangements of the day, the banks were required to maintain 18 per cent of their deposits in the form of Prescribed Liquid Assets (in other words, cash and government securities). If a bank was unable to maintain its liquidity ratio at 18 per cent, it was obliged to borrow from the Reserve Bank, usually at a penal rate of interest, to restore its liquidity to 18 per cent. During the crisis which occurred in 1974, it was believed that all banks, with the possible exception of the Commonwealth Bank, were borrowing from the Reserve Bank to maintain the minimum liquidity requirement. It was a matter of great consternation at the Wales that we too had to borrow, because we had always steadfastly avoided the indignity of Reserve Bank borrowing, and we believed that we were the only major bank, apart from the Commonwealth Bank, to have avoided borrowing until that time.

As the year progressed, imports continued to rise rapidly, further draining bank liquidity. The trade deficit for August was the largest monthly deficit recorded in Australia for almost twenty-three years. Of course there were major international problems in the aftermath of the oil shock of 1973, but with the abundance of our energy resources, Australia should have been faring better than most other countries outside the oil cartel. Trying to put aside the natural political leanings I had nurtured since the bank nationalisation crisis of 1947-49, I was uncomfortable with the quality of the Whitlam Government's management of the economy.

The Bank of New South Wales was not heavily committed internationally in 1974, but we had staked a position in the Euro-currency markets to protect our future role, since it was inevitable that Australia would become a substantial borrower to finance the development of its huge mineral and energy resources. The collapse of Herstatt had created a wave of nervousness that pervaded all banks, but particularly those in the middle to lower range category. All of us were on edge to avoid the publicity of even the faintest smell of a problem.

The London *Economist*, 20 July 1974, raised doubts about the ability of the Eurodollar market to handle the recycling of the huge surpluses from 'the haves', the oil producers, to the 'have nots', the oil importers. It offered the view that the 'commercial banks are not well fitted to lend King Faisal's short-term money on medium term to the would be international borrowers in direst straits'. It was obvious that the strains being put on the commercial banking system were making it really 'creak'.[1]

The *National Times* following detailed research into recent bank statistics revealed that: '. . . the trading banks as a whole have gone "into" the Reserve Bank to the tune of around $270 million.'[2]

The newspaper was proud of the fact that it had unearthed information which the banks considered should be a secret. The other purpose of the article was to demonstrate that the banks were not likely to be making new loans ahead of the need to repay their substantial borrowings from the Reserve Bank.

Our London Manager wrote to me on 29 August 1974, 'I know everybody is concerned about our ability to raise funds but we have experienced no difficulty and unless events in Australia cause serious adverse publicity we feel we can continue to raise what is likely to be wanted.'[3]

Perhaps it was just as well that I did not know what was yet to come on the Australian scene.

At its September meeting with the banks, the Reserve Bank reported that average weekly earnings rose by 6 per cent in the June quarter, compared with 3.6 per cent for the previous quarter. The increase for the 1973-74 year as a whole was 16.3 per cent compared with 9.1 per cent for 1972-73. The deposits of the major trading banks declined for the fifth consecutive month by a record $374 million. The total of all lending fell by $103 million and total loans were 79 per cent of deposits compared with 68 per cent a year earlier. That ratio was the highest we had seen since the great depression of the 1930s. Savings bank deposits fell by an estimated $93 million compared with an increase of $147 million twelve months previously.

An added cause of our gloom was the decline in the Bank's share price. On 20 September 1974 it was $3.30 compared with $7.20 a year earlier. It was too much for John Valder, the Chairman of the Sydney Stock Exchange. As the Bank's share price headed down towards $3.00 at the end of the second week in October 1974, in a high profile gesture, he announced that he had purchased a parcel of shares as an act of faith. I could have kissed him! The other listed bank shares followed a similar trend although the extent of the decline for our Bank was greater than the others.

The Whitlam Government's second Budget, brought down in August 1974, provided for a 32 per cent increase in spending for the 1974-75 year, against a background of its expected increase of only 2 per cent in the real gross domestic product, and an unquantified expectation of price increases. The Bank's own Economic Department commented on 20 September 1974 that the Treasurer had virtually abdicated from any pretence of trying to curb inflation by budgetary policy, and had fallen back to a reliance on the operations of the Prices Justification Tribunal (PJT), with the sinister admonition that, 'The Government expects the principal burden of restraint to fall on upper income groups, particularly through the impact on profits of the operations of the PJT.'[4] It was generally accepted that the government did not have the power to control prices, and the idea behind the PJT was to establish a tribunal capable of delivering a 'public lash' to any company increasing prices beyond a level considered justified by the tribunal.

I became even more disheartened when, on 4 October 1974, a special meeting was called at the Reserve Bank to talk about relatively long-term objectives, that is, over a period of months, rather than days, to use the Deputy Governor's words. He spoke of big swings and major corrective actions, with difficulty in predicting the timing necessary for corrections to take effect. He also said we were now faced with an excessively tight liquidity situation, rising unemployment, a feeling of insecurity in the fringe banking system and widespread apprehension among the public.

The Australian dollar had been devalued by 12 per cent on 25 September. Instances were beginning to arise where building societies were requiring assistance because of run-off in their deposits. Various options of increasing or strengthening bank liquidity were discussed, with yet another reduction in Statutory Reserve Deposits held with the Reserve Bank, the eighth in 17 weeks, reflecting the continuing severity of the downturn in bank liquidity. This was not a credit squeeze, it was a credit drought.

The savings banks were also suffering a run-down in deposits and, as a result, lending for housing almost dried up. The Reserve Bank responded by reducing the proportion of savings bank deposits required to be held in government securities. As a further and much more dramatic response, the Reserve Bank took the unusual step of asking the savings banks if they could raise their new lending in the three or four months immediately ahead by bringing forward some part of the loans which they would otherwise have been planning to make in the June and September quarters of the following year. To assist the savings banks in meeting this request, the government enacted legislation which allowed it to lend $150 million to the banks for on-lending for housing. I don't recall such a dramatic step having been taken previously.

The Reserve Bank meeting at the end of October 1974 further signalled that the economy was on a downward spiral. Wages and prices continued to rise rapidly; there was a marked downturn in demand; production was slowing; unemployment was rising steeply; overseas reserves continued to fall; the Consumer Price Index rose by 5.4 per cent for the September quarter compared with 4.1 per cent for the June quarter, bringing the yearly increase to 16.3 per cent. Over 1973-74 award wage rates had increased by an alarming 25 per cent for males and by 35 per cent for females, and were still increasing. The move towards equal pay accounts for this difference in rates of increase. Liquidity in the banking system had improved and there were no banks borrowing from the Reserve Bank. Is it any wonder I had feelings of gloom? Around the floor we all had an unspoken sense of foreboding.

By mid-November, not only did we have growing concern about the level of our deposits, but also we were worried by mounting evidence that we were losing deposit share. In 1971, our share of the major trading bank deposits remained fairly steady at 24.5 per cent, in 1972 it was 25 per cent and 1973, 24.5 per cent. However, as 1974 progressed we dropped to 23.47 per cent in

August and further to 23.28 per cent in September. Part of our difficulties lay in our management of Certificates of Deposit.

In March 1969 banks were given authority to issue Certificates of Deposit to raise deposits from wholesale depositors at market rates of interest. This was the first time in the post-war period that the banks had been given freedom to bid for deposits on the open market. That freedom was restricted to individual deposits in excess of $100 000. In August 1973, Certificates of Deposit represented only 3.9 per cent of the total deposits of the banking system. By February 1974, that proportion had reached 11 per cent and by July 1974, 22.2 per cent. We had not been as successful as our competitors in the use of this new instrument in the particularly tight conditions prevailing in mid-1974. Interest rates paid for Certificates of Deposit were around 5.5 per cent in 1970 when they were first used, and that rate jumped to peaks in excess of 17 per cent by June 1974.

In November it was reported that Frank Crean, the Treasurer, had changed portfolios with Dr Cairns while the Budget that was technically his was still being debated by Parliament. Cairns now had to bear the actual responsibility for economic management instead of pontificating from the sidelines as the de facto Treasurer. To add to the woes of the day, the government, with strong disagreement in its own ranks, introduced legislation on 20 November 1974 to appropriate an additional $200 million to finance continued purchases of wool by the Australian Wool Corporation with the floor price unchanged at 250¢ per kilogram. The Wool Corporation had stockpiled over 800 000 bales of wool. Whatever else I have learnt in my banking career, I know that history does in fact repeat itself. The price for average quality wool at 258¢ per kilogram in November 1974 was 114¢ lower than a year earlier. Almost twenty years later, the wool price was less than 500¢ per kilogram in the wake of a floor price of 850¢ per kilogram and peak sales in excess of 1100¢ per kilogram.

At the conclusion of an exceedingly difficult year, the Bank earned a net profit of $34 million, down by $2 million on the previous year. The next year opened with a little less gloom from the Bank's point of view. Liquidity was looking better and, in early January, we were already looking at some reduction in interest rates as well as increased lending. Some of the improvement came from the government; its spending was beginning to pump additional funds into the system, although it created a deficit of $654 million, the largest on record.

The pendulum began to swing to the political arena. Billy (later Sir Billy) Snedden, the Leader of the Opposition, began to look less secure, and he was defeated at a party meeting on 21 March 1975, when Malcolm Fraser became the new Leader of the Liberal Party. Whitlam and his government, while enjoying the shift of the spotlight to the opposition, continued to experience difficulties. There was wide controversy about the appointment of Senator Murphy to the High Court, and the newly elected Treasurer attracted renewed attention with the revival of the 'Morosi controversy'. A more serious problem for Whitlam arose with the resignation of the Labor-appointed Speaker of the House, the Hon. J.F. Cope, who had been under pressure because of a ruling unfavourable to one of his government colleagues. The Premier of New South Wales, Tom Lewis, decided to depart from a longstanding convention in Australian politics that casual Senate vacancies were always filled with a new senator of the same party; he appointed Senator Bunton following Senator Murphy's resignation.

The year of 1975 has undoubtedly gone down in history as a year which established new traditions in Australian politics. A major contributor to this new standard was Rex Connor, the Minister for Minerals and Energy from Wollongong. In his book, *The Unmaking of Gough,* Paul Kelly describes Connor:

> . . . not just a big man physically; he was a man of genuine stature, a man who generated an aura, characterised by his drab suits, big braces, granite-like countenance, quick mind, pithy speech, a predilection to reel off statistics like a machine gun and whose old-fashioned style contrasted sharply with a radical espousal of modern and sometimes impractical schemes such as converting coal and natural gas to oil.[5]

I first heard the name Rex Connor during my last year in London, when the Bank was working hard in conjunction with two other banks to put together a financing package to enable the Australian Gaslight Company to construct a pipeline from Moomba in South

Australia to Sydney and other provincial centres in New South Wales. This project was an exciting one, and was proceeding satisfactorily until the election of the Labor Government and the appointment of Rex Connor. Within a couple of months of the 1972 election victory, the Cabinet approved Connor's Pipeline Authority, and the necessary legislation was passed to allow it to take over the proposed pipeline project from Moomba. The pipeline proposal was but a small part of an overall grand plan to increase public ownership of mineral resources, and when one considers the potential mineral wealth in Australia in 1973, it was indeed a grand plan. However, it was a plan which could only be executed with substantial financial support, and at that time the only source of financial support of that magnitude was overseas. And so it was that Rex Connor began work on raising the necessary and substantial loan funds. In this search he appeared to have full support from his colleagues in the government.

In the aftermath of the oil boom, bankers throughout the world became familiar with the activities of a variety of money brokers offering millions, if not billions of dollars, often at ridiculously low interest rates. Unsolicited telex messages would frequently arrive on the desks of chief executives of prominent companies submitting offers, designed to attract a response on an official letterhead which would then be used by the money broker to seek out the funds. I received calls from responsible businessmen talking about offers of this kind, and enquiring about their availability, so authentic were they in their form of presentation. My advice always was to despatch these offers to the waste paper basket and to avoid any form of acknowledgement, because this would provide the so-called broker with a mechanism to establish his credentials.

In this climate, it was not surprising that the anxious borrowers in Canberra soon discovered a Pakistani money broker, Tirath Khemlani, the Manager of Dalamal & Sons (Commodity) Limited, based in London.

The events which followed make a fantastic story of efforts by Rex Connor and by Jim Cairns to raise huge sums of money offshore using the services of Khemlani and George Harris, a Melbourne business friend of Dr Cairns and President of the Carlton

Football Club. Letters were issued to these gentlemen in a form open to interpretation as a mandate from the Australian Government or, at least, as an agency arrangement which could involve the government in the payment of substantial commissions. In December 1974 an Executive Council minute was signed by four Ministers, in the absence of the Governor-General, authorising a borrowing for temporary purposes of $US4 thousand million. It is interesting that the authority was for a borrowing for temporary purposes, because borrowings for other than temporary purposes required the authority of the Loan Council, and since that would have involved State Premiers it was almost certain that the necessary authority would have been refused.

The direct involvement of the two ministers in a loan raising activity running into billions of dollars continued into 1975 with predictable lack of success, and with equally predictable embarrassment to the government. I was concerned that these highly unorthodox activities might not only damage Australia's reputation in the international financial markets, but might have an adverse impact on the Bank as one of Australia's leading financial institutions. Australia had long-established and valued relationships with leading banks and investment houses in New York and Europe, which had for decades satisfactorily handled Australia's foreign loan requirements, and it was extraordinary that their expertise and their rock solid names should have been abandoned in favour of Khemlani and Harris. Early in June 1975 Cairns was replaced as Treasurer by Bill Hayden in a Cabinet reshuffle and the government's difficulties were intensified when the former Deputy Prime Minister, Lance Barnard, retired from politics, giving rise to a by-election in his Tasmanian seat of Bass. Labor suffered a massive defeat in that by-election. I was in Shepparton, Victoria, on 2 July 1975, to attend a Managers' Conference when I heard that Cairns had been sacked from the Ministry. This announcement went forth with all the drama associated with yet another nail in the government's coffin. Only a week later the government was obliged to recall Parliament for a special one-day sitting to conduct a post-mortem into the whole loans affair. Once again the series of unfortunate events of the previous seven or eight months were hung out to be aired in the full glare of publicity.

In the run up to the first Hayden Budget, due in August 1975, it would not be idle to speculate that the relatively new Leader of the Opposition, Malcolm Fraser, was rejoicing that almost every day added grist to his mill, but that grist was not of much use unless he could engineer an election. Until then he had been appropriately cautious by asserting that 'reprehensible circumstances' would be needed before the opposition would block Supply to force an election. Some were saying that those reprehensible circumstances were already in the making. I believe there was a sense of relief when Bill Hayden was appointed Treasurer, because he had already earned a considerable degree of respect for his performance as a minister. It was generally accepted that the process of developing the 1975-76 Budget had been efficient and responsible compared to the process followed a year earlier. The government finally presented a Budget which enjoyed relative acceptance, given the difficult economic circumstances.

In the immediate post-Budget period, we began to witness an interesting battle of tactics. Whitlam came out with comments to the effect that a Prime Minister is entitled to remain in office so long as he has a majority on the floor of the lower house. If he was to remain in office, there seemed to be two alternative tactics. The first would be to tough it out, in the hope that the opposition would weaken, or else he could go for a half-Senate election in the hope that he could win a majority in an interim Senate. Legislation had earlier been passed to extend Senate representation to the two Territories, the Australian Capital Territory and the Northern Territory. Although that was under challenge in the High Court, a challenge which proved unsuccessful, the Labor Party hoped that a half-Senate election would bring it four additional Senators from the two territories. There was also argument on the question of the Senate's power to reject Supply Bills and, naturally, opinions from the government and the opposition differed on this question. There was another complication when the Queensland Labor Senator Bert Milliner died. Like the New South Wales Government, the Queensland Government departed from the tradition of appointing the Labor Party's nominee to fill the vacancy. That move added to the likelihood that a half-Senate election might not produce the majority Whitlam would need if his strategy were to be successful.

Meanwhile, there were divisions in the opposition camp on the question of the principle of withholding Supply, and also on the departures from the convention in filling casual vacancies in the Senate.

On 18 October 1975, the Chief General Manager of the Bank, Sir Robert Norman, departed for an extended overseas visit, and I became Acting Chief General Manager. It was my 52nd birthday, and little did I realise that I was about to become a part of one of the most serious crises of my career.

On 4 November, I received a call from the Australian Bankers' Association Chairman's Sydney Representative, Geoffrey Bowen (later Sir Geoffrey), the chief executive officer of the Commercial Banking Company of Sydney. The Governor of the Reserve Bank, Harry Knight (later Sir Harold), had advised him that a question was to be raised in the House on that day on the subject of bank loans to public servants when the government's Supply had run out. He advised that the answer from the government would be to the effect that the banks would be looking after their own customers. Bowen said that he had taken the opportunity of saying to Knight that the banks would not welcome any possibility of being asked or being directed to assist. The Governor made it clear that the matter must always be for the banks' own decision. Knight said that the Prime Minister and the Deputy Prime Minister had given assurances that nothing of an illegal nature would be done.

On that same day, I, along with the chief executives of the other banks, received a telex from the Treasurer, Bill Hayden. The telex read as follows:

> You probably know that in Parliament today the Prime Minister indicated that the Government is seeking the co-operation of the Trading Banks in the provision of credit for its employees and suppliers for moneys that the Government will owe them but will be unable to pay them if the Appropriation Bills are not passed this month. In saying this the Prime Minister referred to the Government's expectation that the banks would co-operate in relieving in this manner the hardship that will face the persons concerned if the Government is unable to pay them.
>
> To follow up the matter it is proposed to convene a meeting

> at the Treasury, Canberra, at 10am on Thursday, 6 November and I should be grateful if your bank could be represented at the meeting.
>
> The meeting will be chaired by Mr. J. H. Garrett, Deputy Secretary of the Treasury, and will be attended by representatives of Attorney-General's Department and Department of the Prime Minister and Cabinet.
>
> The purpose of the meeting will be to discuss possible administrative arrangements for facilitating the provision of loans by the banks to employees and other creditors of the Government in the event that funds are not available to the Government to enable them to be paid beyond around the end of this month.
>
> I trust that it will be possible for your bank to be suitably represented at the meeting. You might be good enough to arrange for Mr. Garrett to be advised of the name(s) of your bank's representative(s).[6]

The next day I met with my executive colleagues, and it was decided that I should not attend the meeting and that we should instead send the Assistant General Manager (Finance), E.C. Tait. Tait had earlier been the Chief Accountant of the Bank, and was well experienced in the operational side of the Bank's activities.

At the meeting at the Treasury on 6 November 1975 the government was represented by four officers from Treasury, three from Prime Minister and Cabinet, four from Attorney-General's Department and two from the Reserve Bank of Australia. Representatives were present from the ANZ Bank, Commercial Bank of Australia, Commercial Banking Company of Sydney, Commonwealth Trading Bank, Bank of Adelaide, Bank of New South Wales, National Bank of Australasia, Rural Bank of New South Wales and State Bank of South Australia.

The meeting opened with statements to the effect that the government would soon run out of money. There was sufficient money to pay wages and salaries until the end of November, but there would not be money to pay wages and salaries in December, the first pay day being 11 December. Details were available as to the requirements for wages and salaries, but no details were available of sums due to other creditors of the government and certain authorities, being contractors, suppliers, etc.

The government was seeking the co-operation of the banks to look after government employees and other creditors. It was confident that trading banks would be happy to assist in meeting hardship caused by the blockage of Supply by making bank loan arrangements. The arrangements which were proposed were to facilitate matters both for the administrative machinery of the banks and the government.

A paper was produced outlining 'The Scheme'. It involved the issuing by the government of a certificate stating:

(a) In the case of employees that a specified sum was owing to the employee by way of net salary, that is gross salary and pay and allowances, less PAYE taxation and superannuation and payments under garnishees. 'The Scheme' proposed that each employee would execute a loan agreement with a bank, whereby the bank would lend to the employee an amount equal to the net salary and the employee would agree to pay interest thereon. The employee would then assign the debt due from the government to the bank. To complete the legal assignment each bank, would by schedule, notify the government of the assignment of the debt. The government would then acknowledge receipt of such notice. The Prime Minister would then make a statement promising to pay the interest on behalf of the employee. This would have required a separate Appropriation Bill to be passed, when the government was able to do so.

(b) In the case of suppliers, what amount would be due to a supplier? That debt would similarly be assigned to the bank with notice to be given by way of schedule to complete the assignment. It was realised, because of the probability of prior existing charges and the difficulty and expense of registering assignments of book debts either under the Companies Act or the Instruments Act, that this procedure would not be as complete as was the proposal for employees. It was also realised that the banks would continue to charge commercial rates of interest to suppliers and that the rate of interest payable by the government would probably be less.[7]

We realised in both cases that if and when the government honoured the moral obligation which it would accept by its statement as to payment of interest, that the interest would be received by the banks not on their own behalf but on behalf of their customers who were obliged to pay interest to the banks. It will be obvious, given the complexity and uniqueness of 'The Scheme' being proposed, that many of the issues involved remained unresolved. There were, for example, questions relating to the ability of public servants and members of the defence forces to assign salary, to the problem of minors and bankrupts, to the probability of large scale fraud and the uncertainty of the government's ability to provide an indemnity.

One of the paramount concerns of the banks was the government's inability to put a figure on the sum due to suppliers. The banks had in mind that the continuing blockage of Supply would not only affect public servants and suppliers to the Commonwealth and its authorities, but also a lot of customers. In considering any assistance the banks could offer, the magnitude of demands on banks for assistance from these categories would have to be considered. Payments to State Governments would not be affected by the blockage of the Supply Bills, as there were no payments due until February or March 1976. However, there were problems regarding some payments due to local government councils and it was accepted that these would not be paid until the Appropriation Bills were passed.

We reiterated our two major concerns: first the ultimate sum required of the banks under 'The Scheme', and, second, our broader customer responsibilities outside those related to the public servants and suppliers. We expressed strong reluctance to enter into any arrangements which would have restricted our ability to help other existing customers. The Reserve Bank representatives explained that adequate liquidity should be maintained to meet the immediate needs of the economy. It so happened that liquidity levels at that time were perhaps the highest in history, but there were concerns among those present that the total sum required, if the impasse continued, was unknown. Neither the size of the money flow affected, nor the length of time, were known. The Governor of the Reserve Bank had earlier told bank chief executives that it was expected that if Supply was blocked, $800 million net per month would cease to flow into the banking system. The Reserve Bank's policy would be to keep liquidity at levels to suit the needs of the economy and, of course, bank liquidity would be closely watched.

Our concerns as bank representatives were not allayed when the Reserve Bank representatives added that it would be slow to provide funds until there was a need, and that it would resist any proposal whereby it had to equal dollar for dollar the amounts lent by banks pursuant to 'The Scheme'. At that time there were in effect quantitative controls over bank lending, and the Reserve Bank representatives stressed that there should be no new lending beyond the levels recorded early in 1975, and stated that there would be no change in this basic lending policy. After further debate, no commitment was available from the Reserve Bank to cover the unforeseen future. We then made it clear that one condition, if the banks entered into 'The Scheme', would be that they would require a firm understanding from the Reserve Bank as to how funds would be made available to cover the situation, and as to what would be the cost to the banks of providing these funds. It was not possible at that meeting to resolve the question of the rate of interest, reimbursement for stamp duty, and other costs including the administrative costs. If a common rate of interest were agreed as well as a flat fee, the question of a clearance or authorisation from the Trade Practices Commission would arise.

In summing up our concerns, the bank representatives felt that adoption of 'The Scheme' for all intents and purposes would mean that the banks were cashing pieces of paper for government salaries, and would thereby be virtually cashing government cheques. We realised that legally this would not be so, because the government's certificates of indebtedness would not be cashed; rather, loans would be made to individuals. We put the same point in legal phraseology by asking whether 'The Scheme' looked at as a whole, taking into account such things as government indemnity, the bulk collation of loans, and the bulk repayment not only of principal but also of interest on behalf of the employees, could be properly characterised either as a loan to the government or the provision of an alternative paying facility for government employees.

Immediate steps were taken to secure legal advice on the position in which the Bank was placed. Before that process could be properly put in hand, I was concerned to receive another telex message from the Treasurer late on Friday, 7 November, the day following the Canberra meeting. The Treasurer, in that telex message, said that his officers had reported on the outcome of the meeting with the representatives. The telex message concluded in the following terms:

> I understand that the banks will be advising me, as quickly as possible on their position regarding participation in the proposals discussed at yesterday's meeting. For reasons outlined at the meeting there is an urgent need to press ahead with contingency arrangements, and I do hope that the banks will find it possible to provide their advice with a minimum of delay.[8]

In view of the urgency, the banks replied to this latter message independently. My own reply, on Monday, 10 November, was in the following terms:

> We reply to your telex message dated 7th November addressed to the Chief General Manager. Your message does not seem to reflect an appreciation of the difficulties inherent in 'The Scheme' submitted by the Government to the banks on Thursday last and which were foreshadowed by our representatives at the meeting. We therefore felt we should let you have an interim indication of this Bank's position.
>
> The scheme raises questions upon which we have sought independent legal advice and we shall advise you of our position as soon as we have determined our legal and other responsibilities.
>
> In the meantime we feel constrained to say that the legal advice we have received to date suggests that there are serious obstacles. In the light of various public statements which have been made in relation to the Government's scheme and since we are aware of some public concern, particularly from our depositors, we are considering whether we should issue a statement to clarify our own position. We feel we should advise you to this effect.[9]

My colleague from the Commercial Banking Company of

Sydney replied in much stronger terms. He was worried that there was not in fact a proposal before the banks other than a scheme which had been placed before us for decision which still incorporated assumptions of quite doubtful legality, and which apparently ignored community reactions. He also referred to reactions from depositors, the restrictions under the Trade Practices Legislation relating to any agreement with competitors on 'The Scheme' and charges, and, finally, he sought an assurance beyond all doubt that his directors, officers and the bank itself would not be implicated in any way under criminal legislation or any more obscure legislation. He offered to continue to examine the many facets of 'The Scheme' and to advise when all relevant information was available. As the Commercial Banking Company was the only other bank in Sydney, it was natural that we conferred frequently. Although we agreed in principle we did not compare notes, or seek to agree, on the precise detail of our responses to the Treasurer.

On 10 November I also received a message from the Treasury representative at the 6 November meeting, to provide further advice on the application of s45 of the Trade Practices Act. A procedure was suggested that each bank agreeing in principle to participate in 'The Scheme' might individually advise the Treasury of interest rates and any other charges that would be acceptable to it. This would enable the government to consider the basis of interest rates and any other charges on which it would reimburse participating banks upon funds becoming legally available; in other words, when it could get legislation through the Senate. There should be no collaboration between banks, but the government would in due course announce the basis on which it would be prepared to reimburse, subject to the passing of appropriate legislation. This would be expressed as a maximum; individual banks could charge less if they so desired. Should a bank charge more than the maximum on loans made by it under 'The Scheme', only the lesser amount would be reimbursed to it by the government.

By this time various legal opinions were becoming available and were being analysed. At that stage, some difference of approach had emerged between the Melbourne-based banks and the Sydney-based banks. The legal advice I had received indicated that, apart from questions of obtaining an effective assignment, some of which could probably be resolved, the proposals generally fell down on the question of the necessity of the government providing the interest and charges payable to the bank. Aside from the question of the government's own powers, the proposals were being put forward in such a way that the government expected its employees to accept primary responsibility for interest and charges in order to receive the pay to which they were entitled.

The Chairman of the Australian Bankers' Association, following receipt of the legal opinion given to us, telephoned to say that the opinion appeared to miss certain important points. He said that the reaction in Melbourne to the views expressed was that interest and charges were to be paid to the banks on behalf of the customers. In other words, it was being argued that the payments for interest and charges were to be made to the customers through the bank. The fine point of difference in the government's plan was that the payments to reimburse interest and charges were not to be made to the bank. The government was not accepting the legal obligation, then, only making a promise to attempt to get approval to pay. On the question of funding, the impression the Chairman was getting in Melbourne from their Counsel was that the banks need not be greatly worried about illegality. I was not able to take the call from the Chairman, and a member of my staff in relaying it to me had commented, 'A little bit of pussy-footing in Melbourne, I would judge.'

Over the five or six days preceding Tuesday, 11 November, I had been involved in a frantic round of telephone conversations with the other banks, with lawyers, and with the Chairman of our own Bank. There was evidence of disquiet from a number of customers, and it was obvious there would be a substantial volume of customer discontent or protest, whether the Bank participated in 'The Scheme' or not. I had decided to send a message to all Chief Managers of the Bank so that all States would be informed. The message was sent in the following terms:

> Representatives of all trading banks attended a meeting in Canberra yesterday at the request of the Treasurer to discuss possible lines of assistance if the deadlock over supply to the Government continues. A confidential proposal has been submitted to the banks and this is

> currently being considered. At this stage there is no suggestion of undue pressure from the Government. The discussions were purely of an exploratory nature. We shall give you more details as soon as we are able. This information may be of assistance to you in dealing with extravagant or unfounded fears of customers and others. We regret we are unable to provide you with any further details at this stage and I feel sure you will appreciate the need for strict confidentiality and avoidance of public controversy.[10]

Early on the morning of Tuesday, 11 November, I received from our solicitors a detailed and lengthy opinion from a Queen's Counsel which confirmed that, in his opinion, the Bank should not accept 'The Scheme' proposed by the Australian Government for reasons which in all substantial respects followed the earlier advice from our solicitors. On that same morning I received a further telex from the Chairman of the Australian Bankers' Association in Melbourne reporting that the opinion of Counsel to the Australian Bankers' Association had been received.

Bank representatives had arranged to meet again in Melbourne on the morning of Tuesday, 11 November, and the opinion of Counsel to the ABA would be tabled before that meeting.

As that morning dawned, I was becoming more worried. The front page of the *Australian Financial Review*, hours before the Melbourne meeting of bank representatives, scheduled for that morning, splashed right across the front page, a headline which said: BANKS BACK GOVERNMENT CREDIT SCHEME. The somewhat lengthy comments which followed did not really reflect the substance of the headline, but they did, to some extent, highlight the differences in the approaches of the various banks. Was there some covert pressure being applied?

To add to my anxiety, I was getting strong messages from the President, the late Sir John Cadwallader, that it was the Board's wish that we should look at means of making available our legal opinions to the Governor-General. On the other hand, the message from Melbourne seemed to be, according to my jottings, 'look after our own affairs and co-operate provided it is legal'. All sorts of rumours were circulating that the Governor-General was about to step in.

I felt lonely as I walked around my desk several times,

contemplating how I should act next. It would have been easy for me to deal with the request for funding assistance as a professional banker and to decline it for the variety of valid reasons which had been brought forward. However, the customer submitting the request in this case was no less a party than the government itself, and that was a good and sufficient reason for second thoughts.

It was one thing to decline the request for financial assistance, but it was another thing to provide, on my own initiative, our legal opinions to the only higher authority in the land. That step certainly called for sober reflection. After all, the outcome might well be withdrawal of the Prime Minister's commission, and that was not the sort of stuff in which professional bankers should normally become embroiled. As I continued to contemplate the situation which confronted me, my conclusions could not help but be influenced by the government's poor economic performance, particularly in the loans affair.

The government's request was at least highly unorthodox; it presented enormous practical difficulties associated with the cashing of countless pieces of paper, the validity of which could not readily be verified; it involved the Bank in a huge financial commitment, not capable of precise measurement, nor was the potential impact on the Bank's ability to look after the continuing needs of its other customers capable of being measured; the security for the Bank's outlay was not clear cut; finally, recovery of the amounts outlaid, together with interest and charges, lacked the kind of certainty usually required by a prudent banker.

In the end, motivated by both the national interest and the risks for the Bank, I summoned the Bank's Secretary and asked him to book himself on the first available flight to Canberra. I then arranged for the Bank's Canberra-based solicitors to receive our legal opinions from the Bank's Secretary and to take the necessary steps to make them available to the Official Secretary at Government House. It was approaching midday on 11 November.

In the middle of these deliberations, I had a telephone call from Tait, attending the meeting of bank representatives in Melbourne, to advise me that the ABA banks, plus the Rural Bank of New South Wales, did not want to participate in 'The Scheme'. It was proposed to recommend that the Chairman of the ABA, the late Tom Bell of the National Bank of Australasia, should advise the Treasurer in the following terms:

> Representatives of the following banks met in Melbourne today to consider basic principles of 'The Scheme' suggested by government officials at the Canberra meeting on Thursday in the light of further consideration and legal opinion which was obtained at their request by the Australian Bankers' Association. The meeting ... sought a common approach to 'The Scheme'. Legal opinions obtained by some banks were tabled. All opinions were adverse to 'The Scheme' in at least some aspects and additionally doubts were apparent in significant areas. As a consequence, the meeting found insurmountable difficulties in 'The Scheme' and it was agreed that each representative would report to his Chief Executive who would advise you of his bank's attitude as soon as practicable. In subsequent discussion member banks of the Australian Bankers' Association reaffirmed the Chairman's press statement of Wednesday, 5 November, and will do all they can to ease any financial difficulties faced by their customers.[11]

This was not a final draft as the bank representatives had decided to reconvene after lunch for further consideration.

On that same day, 11 November, I had a long-standing commitment to entertain senior executives from Mitsui & Company to lunch at the Bank, and I absented myself from my office at around 1.00 p.m. Early in the lunch I received a message that I was required urgently. I excused myself, and returned to my office to be informed that the Governor-General had terminated the Prime Minister's commission, and had commissioned the Leader of the Opposition to form a new caretaker government until an election could be held. Later I was able to listen to the radio rebroadcast of the House of Representatives, where Whitlam, in his capacity then as the Member for Werriwa, was proposing a 'Vote of No Confidence' in the newly appointed caretaker Prime Minister, Fraser. The Senate reconvened hastily to approve Supply, and the Parliament was prorogued. The Official Secretary to the Governor-General read a proclamation on the front steps of the Parliament dissolving both houses of Parliament.

In the afternoon, the Chairman of the Bankers' Association issued a public statement to the effect that the proposals made by the former government to the banks in the previous week, following careful consideration by the banks individually, could not be accepted in totality, because of significant legal constraints and other implications that could arise from following the course suggested. The statement contained reassurances that the banks were prepared to the best of their ability to stand by those of their customers who were public servants or suppliers to the government. The concluding paragraph of the statement said that the banks had also sought to ensure that banker-customer relationships and proper banking procedures had been fully preserved.[12]

The following day, we were greeted by a variety of headlines in the morning newspapers. The *Financial Review* had relegated the subject to page five with a heading much less prominent than the one of the previous day. The message on this occasion was 'BANKS REFUSED AID FOR WHITLAM GOVERNMENT'. The *Australian* headline said 'BANKERS' REFUSAL LED TO PM'S DOWNFALL'.

The Chairman of the Australian Bankers' Association issued a further statement to say that in fairness to the former government, the Treasurer and to the banks, he must correct two wrong impressions being made. The former government had not requested the banks to provide money for it to spend, nor to lend money to it. The sole request had concerned the possibility of banks making temporary loans to civil servants as individuals and to private contractors whose bills might be unpaid. He added that the second incorrect suggestion was that the banks had refused to make any such loans. In clarification he reaffirmed the substance of the statement released on the previous day, referring to the legal restraints which precluded the banks from accepting in total the proposed basis for loans as originally suggested by the former government.[13] The most important clarification of the Chairman's message was to remind all that the banks had neither rejected nor approved the government's scheme. When Supply was passed, the Melbourne meeting of bank representatives considering the proposal was still in progress.

From my own point of view, I received a letter from our Canberra solicitors to advise me that the opinions made available to them were delivered to the Official Secretary of the Governor-General on Wednesday, 12 November 1975. The opinions I had worried about so much had arrived after the event.

And so it was, by a twist of fate, that as Acting Chief Executive Officer of the Bank of New South Wales, I found myself once again contending with the political intentions of a Labor Government, which, even with the best of motives, seemed to have missed the mark. Economic confusion, followed by the public scandal of the Loans Affair and ultimately the deadlock between the Senate and the House of Representatives over Supply, convinced me that the government was not governing. The main difference for me between 1947 and 1975 was that I was no longer a foot soldier in 'the battle for the banks'. I had been thrust into a position of responsibility: to assess and respond to a highly unorthodox request by the Labor Government, to assist it to circumvent the Senate's deferral of supply.

In the twenty years since, I have reflected on whether I was perhaps too biased, and, in all honesty, I think not. In 1975 I was very much a product of my generation and social background. I regarded the Labor Government as a vehicle of socialism, and some of the actions of the Whitlam Government reaffirmed that view, which is, of course, not valid of more recent Labor Governments.

Regrettably the country was facing a monumental crisis. The government was running out of money and there seemed to be little possibility of obtaining funds through the Appropriation Bills before the Senate. The banks were being asked to participate in a scheme that was poorly thought out, unrealistic and possibly open to legal challenge. Since the certificates of indebtedness would form the documentation of a loan, there would have been a degree of recording by the banks to complete the process, and there was also the problem of authentication to eliminate the risk of forgery. Although it was only twenty years ago, we were in another technological age. We had only limited data processing facilities, and would have had to process manually much of the paper for 160 000 public servants plus members of the defence forces.

When I was informed that Whitlam's commission had been terminated and that a caretaker government had been appointed until an election could be held, I was immensely relieved.

On 13 December, the people of Australia exercised their own judgment, which was clearly in favour of the Liberal-Country Party Coalition. Labor lost 29 seats in the House of Representatives and its 65-62 majority became a 36-91 deficit.

During the December 1975 election campaign, and in the twenty years since, some people have regarded the Governor-General's decision of 11 November as a defence of the Constitution, while others have claimed the Constitution had been violated. Critics of Sir John Kerr have argued that he acted too soon: that Supply had not run out; that the Senate had not voted to refuse Supply; that it was possible that Liberal Senators would cross the floor to give the majority to the government; or that Fraser may have weakened in his resolve to force an election. Having regard to the stakes involved, those who argued that the Governor-General acted too soon because Supply had not run out must surely have been advocating a type of brinkmanship outside the bounds of responsible behaviour. For my part, I did not criticise the Governor-General and still hold the view that he took the appropriate course of action.

However unsettling the events of 1975, they did not lead to a fragmentation of our society and the present federal structure seems to work well enough. Nevertheless, it is inevitable that the Constitution and the structure of government we have now will not last forever, and we would be foolish as a nation if we thought it could. More recently, the appropriate form of government; the role, if any, of the Governor-General; the structure of the Constitution; and the very processes of government have once again come under scrutiny. By having regard to what happened in 1975, we need to be careful in devising alternative arrangements that will accommodate the kind of crisis we faced then. It is no good sticking our heads in the sand and saying that it will not happen again, because it could.

As financial intermediaries, banks occupy a special place in the fabric of Australian society. They have collective fiduciary responsibilities to their customers and to the broader community. It is arguable that 'The Scheme' as presented in 1975 would have been prejudicial to the interests of all banks. It was not in the interests of the broader community, and I don't think it would have assisted in breaking the deadlock between the Senate and the House because it would have been an operational nightmare if not impracticable; and some aspects of 'The Scheme' may have been open to legal challenge. Ultimately the system of checks and balances under our Constitution permitted the deadlock to be broken. It is in our interests in reviewing our Constitution to ensure that any future constitutional changes do not weaken that system. Regardless of what form of government eventually emerges, the banks will, no doubt, contribute to yet another chapter in Australia's political history.

8 THE SLUMBERING GIANT

Over the years I have often reflected on the crucial strengths a good manager needs in a modern financial corporation, or any other corporation for that matter. If I had to choose one particular strength I would say that it is the ability to recognise and read the signposts. No modern manager, however clever, can know all the answers; instead he or she should know what the signposts are. In the 1970s I believed the two major signposts were the emergence of the so-called 'global economy', and the pressures for deregulating the international financial markets which inevitably would flow into Australia.

I was convinced that we in Australia could not lower a boom gate across the entrance to Sydney harbour and carry on as if the rest of the world did not exist, although there were some who did, and still do, think along those lines.

The laws and regulations which defined national boundaries, limited international capital flows and foreign investment and, to some extent, sheltered the domestic banking industry, were becoming less relevant. Global financial competition was expanding rapidly; by the end of the 1970s, more and more foreign-owned banks had set up shop in Australia disguised as non-bank financial institutions. In March 1978 the International Division of the Bank reported that there were sixty-two non-bank financial institutions in Australia with foreign bank shareholders, and that there were seventy-five foreign banks with representative offices. To put that in perspective, Australia had at that time only fifteen banks, comprising eight with federal licences, five state banks and two foreigners, the Bank of New Zealand and the Banque Nationale de Paris.

One problem was that the Wales did not have, but needed, a forward plan and a clearly defined corporate philosophy. A second problem was that we were too bureaucratic, and the bureaucracy had become too slow in moving to cope with the changing scene.

Prior to the establishment of the Corporate Banking Division in 1974, the cumbersome system of approving business transactions for our large corporate customers was irksome, embarrassing and sometimes worked against us. The state managers had always been responsible for servicing corporate customers, but their authority ended at state boundaries, and thus the Bank's overall corporate customer relationships were fragmented. There were too many links in the chain and, in addition, where a customer was operating in several states, it was often difficult to take a wider view of their activities and fully service all their needs. There were two or three large customers based outside New South Wales who felt obliged by the system to present themselves to the chief executive in Sydney with their annual results and an indication of their forward requirements. They were received with courtesy and listened to with interest, but politely reminded that, of course, the formal submission of their needs would, as usual, be awaited from their state Chief Manager.

In keeping with the established practice, when the opportunity arose of getting a profitable slice of the business of a large Melbourne-based Commonwealth Bank customer, it was arranged that the manager of the Melbourne Office would make contact. He put up a proposal which, having been agreed with the company, then went to the Chief Manager of the state who modified it to suit his own assessment but did not inform the Melbourne Office, leaving it and the customer unaware that the proposal had been modified. Such was their perception of the standing of the Bank, the fact that the modification of the original proposal might prejudice the new business opportunity probably did not even occur to them. The proposal then went to Sydney where it was changed again and thus finally to the Board which approved it in its changed form. In those days when up to five or six people reviewed a lending proposal, usually independently of each other, the red ink flowed freely with comments and appendices tacked onto documents with what often amounted to amendments to amendments, whether or not they were necessary, effective or efficient. I knew the chief executive of the company in this potted case history, and he separately informed me of the obvious reasons why we did not get the business.

The concept of a Corporate Banking Division was that it would establish a total relationship with our major corporate customers, so that we could develop a better understanding of their overall needs and plans. We had a lot to protect, in that the Bank had a relationship with probably seventy of the top one hundred companies in Australia. To illustrate our sense of vulnerability, a survey of companies in the late 1970s had disclosed that our principal competition for corporate customers was not the ANZ Bank, as we had suspected, but Citibank, and that was before Citibank had been granted a licence to operate as a bank in Australia. In a two-way relationship, we could suggest things we could do for the company, and if the company wanted assistance from us, it had a direct conduit to the Board. After the focus of the banking relationship went from the state administration to the Corporate Banking Division located in Sydney, the state managers felt their powers were being whittled away.

While we were adjusting our strategy, there were ructions as the bureaucracy campaigned against the change. Why should there be a change, the argument went; the system had served us well for the last hundred and fifty years. Rather than looking back, they should have been looking forward and asking whether the system would serve us as well over the next hundred and fifty years.

I used to smile to myself when a large proposal was having a dream run right up to the top of the Bank; the red ink appendages would say: 'I support' – 'I too support' – 'and I'. In my younger days in the General Manager's Office, I was tempted to add: 'me too'. If a younger, more aggressive manager were to step out of line, the reply from the bureaucracy would take on a more authoritative, impersonal tone with phrases such as: '*The* Bank has decided that . . .' or '*The* Bank's policy does not permit . . .' I speak from experience in saying that such phrases are off-putting. In my later career, I used to ask myself, 'Where does the future of the Bank lie when it is awash in red ink?'

On 22 April 1977, I assumed the position of Chief General

Manager and from that moment the future was my problem. The rapidity of my rise suggested that I was not always the front contender for the job. There were still no agreed career plans in those days, and, of course, we did not lobby for jobs. There were several jobs near the top which interested me, with a preference to be the chief of one of the interstate divisions, and I was fortunate in having a broad base of experience. In 1965, my appointment to the position of Assistant Chief Manager, New Zealand was regarded as a good training ground, because it provided an opportunity for managers to operate their own bank in a separate economy and deal with their own central bank.

Since I had turned down the offer in 1970 to return to New Zealand as Chief Manager, I settled in to what I thought would then be a long term as Manager Sydney Office, but alas, another change came only a year later. Managing a state division was also a good way to qualify for the more senior management positions, and I really wanted to run my own state division. At the end of 1971, when the opportunity came to relieve the Chief Manager for Western Australia for several months, I thought: This is just the sort of job I want – away from Head Office and a chance to make relatively independent decisions.

My London appointment followed, and when I was appointed from there to the number two position in the Bank, it seemed that only a major accident would stop me from getting the top job. Life was more simple then. In contrast to the appointment of my successors, my appointment as the chief executive officer was made without fuss or controversy, and I considered that the support I received from my colleagues and from the Board enabled me to be decisive from the beginning. That gave me added confidence to pursue the rather far-reaching plans which had been evolving in my mind in conjunction with the late Lionel Conway, then Chief Manager Research and Planning.

In the period preceding and immediately following my appointment, I worked closely with him in reviewing all aspects of the Bank's operations and management practices, and in identifying those issues which should be addressed by the new regime. Lionel looked at the Bank as it existed. He brought the obvious into view, and his conclusions were informative and sobering. With the growth of the Australian economy and the resulting growth of the Bank, especially in transaction banking, our management methods were not good enough to take advantage of new opportunities. We were too slow and inflexible. The changing environment placed greater demands on branch managers in coping with staff problems, in marketing the wider range of products against the wider range of competition and in developing the credit assessment skills necessary to preserve the quality of the Bank's growing balance sheet.

Staffing problems ranked high on the list, with difficulties partly a result of our outmoded recruitment policies, and partly as a result of over-full employment. The Bank was slow to recognise the implications of a changed regime where school leavers were either attracted by the easier availability of tertiary education or the wider choice of jobs offered by over-full employment. The Bank was no longer a first choice, but it progressed slowly in hiring staff with tertiary education, which was where the best leadership potential was likely to be from then on. Our training facilities were not producing enough people to fill the important positions becoming available, even though we had introduced internal staff training in the 1950s and senior training with the establishment of Mahratta, our residential staff college, in 1960.

Although we offered incentives for part-time external study, we turned our backs on university-trained staff until mid-1971. When we did implement a graduate recruitment program, it assumed a low profile in the Bank, and our recruiting target of twenty-five graduates seemed extraordinarily modest in a nationally operating bank employing 25 000 people. The integration of graduates, the fast tracking of their early careers, and in some cases their inflated expectations, caused tensions in our traditional staff structure, and as a result our graduate wastage was high.

With young recruits now becoming tellers more rapidly, and at a younger age, we found that many did not have a sufficiently high level of skills. As students found it easier to undertake tertiary education, and with banking becoming more complex, we faced the challenge of preparing school leavers for duties hitherto carried out by more experienced people.

In addition, we were wasting the talents of many of our

women staff through the restrictive and discriminatory work practices. The dictum of equal pay for work of equal value was giving way to equal pay but not to equal opportunity. In 1976, there were 276 people at management level in head office. We had 'weakened' to the point where five of them were women (less than 2 per cent), two each in the Economic Department and Investment Division and the other in Catering; none in the mainstream of banking.

Under the Board, the bureaucracy was alive and well, with a Chief General Manager, supported by two General Managers, presiding over the head office. There were twelve Assistant General Managers, sometimes impolitely referred to as the twelve apostles, with responsibilities for: Operations, Finance, General, Branch Banking, Loans and Advances, Staff, Development and Marketing, Economic Department, International Business, Investment Management, New South Wales Division and Victorian Division.

The reporting lines and areas of accountability provided potential for overlap, and discouraged independent thinking. These deficiencies cascaded down the line to frustrate promotion of the Bank's services, communication and understanding of some of the fundamentals of banking, including the interaction of revenue, expenses, profit and service.

The outcome of Lionel Conway's research contained few surprises. In earlier years Lionel and I had belonged to an informal discussion group of 'angry young men'. We met, usually once a month, for dinner and talked about the problems and opportunities in the Bank, and how we would resolve them given the chance. I remember one expression frequently used following a typical bout of criticism, 'Thank God it's a good business.' Although it was some years before I was within talking distance of the Board, the discussion group was an important part of my development. It helped me to think about and identify the broader economic and social signposts and to consolidate my ideas on management and possible changes I would make if I ever had the opportunity.

When I assumed the post of Chief General Manager, I was well aware of the Bank's internal difficulties, and conscious that if we were to arrest the decline of traditional banking, and above all preserve our status as the Number One Bank, we would have to make major changes to our thinking. Although the problems were serious, they were not insurmountable. I saw this as a great opportunity to improve things. The Bank had many strengths on which it could capitalise, the basics of which were officer loyalty and their high degree of trust in each other. I calculated that we had the customer base and the basic core of people, but we needed a new management system and a strategy to take the Bank forward. Our task was to remove the following obstacles: an entrenched bureaucracy; the lack of forward planning; and the lack of a defined corporate philosophy.

We set out to define our corporate philosophy. It was a team effort, and there was much discussion of our priorities and how we should rank profits and service. The ANZ and the National challenged us in the profit stakes, but with less regard for service. The Commonwealth Bank challenged our deposit share without a high regard for profit. At the Wales, the Top Team argued over whether we should be service-driven or profit-driven. There was no doubt that our two free-enterprise competitors were profit-driven, but I had the view that while earning sufficient profits was a critical objective, it could be best achieved by putting our customers at the top – if we could deliver with a high degree of service a product our customers wanted, then profits would be a natural outcome, assuming, of course, that we were cost efficient.

The need for change was not readily accepted, and I remember exercising some strong persuasion in our various planning meetings. It was frustrating to hear some senior managers say, 'But we have always done it this way.' It appeared to me that some had not yet grasped the magnitude of the changes which were taking place in global financial markets. In fairness to those concerned, the high expectations of the Fraser Government had not been delivered by 1977, and the promised inquiry into the financial system had not materialised.

The Bank's *Annual Report* for 1977 set out the corporate philosophy which was to guide our future activities. That philosophy was well accepted by the shareholders and financial markets, and incorporated the following elements: to maintain our leadership in the financial markets of Australia and the South West Pacific; to provide the best in friendly and proficient service in all aspects of our business; to acknowledge our social responsibilities and our special role in the economic life of the community by absolute integrity, efficiency and good corporate citizenship; to be a good employer and to foster the career development and well-being of all members of our staff; to earn sufficient profits to achieve a fair return on investment for our proprietors, and to ensure long-term stability and growth of the Bank of New South Wales Group.

The new objectives would involve redirecting our focus from the old goal of 25 per cent of the major trading bank deposits to our share of total financial market intermediation – about 10 per cent of the market.

I was determined that we should begin to think in 'group' terms, not just in the context of the Bank, and that we should focus on our customer base and its needs, including our potential customers in Australia and overseas. I saw banking as a people-oriented business and realised that our staff were our most important asset. In embarking on the program of organisational change, we set a number of ambitious goals: to improve our people management skills, our relations with the union, the quality of our staff and our communications with them.

I was much inspired by a report from Western Australia, attributed to a senior officer of the National Bank, that the Wales was like 'a slumbering giant', an appropriate simile, and I was determined to wake it up. In order to do so, I needed a catalyst.

That catalyst was Bill Reddin, a British-born Canadian consultant who specialised in organisational change strategy. Bill Reddin had done some work for the Australian Institute of Management, of which I was a board member. Geoff Thompson, who had succeeded Lionel Conway as Chief Manager Research and Planning, had seen him at work with the Institute, and believed strongly that he was the man for us. Reddin's style was to diagnose and assist us with our program of change. The novelty in his approach, in contrast to other management consultancy firms we had investigated, was that we would find the solutions ourselves – not he. I cannot over emphasise how novel this approach was. We already knew that other banks had used more expensive management consultants, who moved in easily but who were more difficult to move out. Of one case I knew, the newly arrived consultants asked for the thirty most promising officers of the bank to be seconded to them, and this reinforced my view that obtainable solutions usually lie within. I believed that a commitment to change must come from everyone concerned with the process, and that a sounder approach was to involve people from day one in the analytical and decision-making machinery.

I arranged to meet Bill Reddin on 18 October 1978 during a visit to London to discuss my plans generally. In answer to his specific question as to what was my principal objective, I said I wanted 'to unfreeze' the organisation. As a result of my recommendation, the Bank recruited Reddin in 1978, and over the next two years we committed ourselves to the principles of organisational development and change.

The core of Reddin's approach was a focus on managerial productivity – 'managerial effectiveness' – using the process called Management By Objectives. In broad terms, managerial effectiveness means devolving more power from the centre to the line; defining the job in terms of outputs not inputs; making sure that the staff have the skills to do the job, and building staff commitment to Management By Objectives. The focus on outputs forced managers away from job descriptions built on inputs or abstracts. 'Keep the customers happy' or 'Oil the machine every hour' were unacceptable definitions, which gave way to 'Increase loans and deposits by x per cent by 30 September next' or 'Zero machine breakdowns by September', both of which were outputs and measurable. Reddin said that if it is not measurable, forget it, because no one will know.

The Reddin approach fitted well with my personal philosophy regarding people. My experiences in people management, particularly in the army and in London, led me to favour a consensus approach. I was a team man, and I believed then, and still do, in participatory decision making. In spite of the difficulties we were experiencing with our staff, we were fortunate because we had a large pool of good people, and good people are a scarce resource. Therefore the best ideas for the Bank probably already lay within. It was also my perception that we were good at research and analysis, but not as good at using the information to implement changes. I was confident that we had a fair degree of unused managerial capacity, and that these unused talents could be a major force for change, growth and expansion in new directions – the talents needed for waking the slumbering giant.

The exercise we were about to embark upon was budgeted to cost about $1 million, and, following a detailed presentation of our intentions, the Board's approval was forthcoming. I would be less than honest if I were to say that the Board embraced the idea with warm enthusiasm, but no obstacles were raised until Reddin suggested that the Board itself become directly involved in the process. That idea was not acceptable, and I had a sense of discomfort when I invited Reddin to present his first preliminary report directly to the Board. For some unaccountable reason, the chemistry was not right. I came to the conclusion that the Board did not wish to expose itself to a process which might lead to some unpredictable, if not uncontrollable, change in its activities. In 1977 our Board operated within the traditional mode established by years of practice, and while it may have been appropriate for the management of the Bank to expose itself to a major review under the close surveillance of the Board, there was no good reason for such a review at the Board level.

Committing $1 million to a management change program was a risky venture, particularly as this approach was relatively novel compared to the programs which had been used elsewhere in Australia. But when I considered the threat to the Bank's profitability from our competitors, I felt it was better to take the risk. I really did not have any reservations at all, and maybe I didn't realise the dimensions of the risk. However, the more I got into it, the more committed I became, because I could see the benefits. The atmosphere at subsequent staff meetings, such as the one to discuss the Bank restructure, had to be seen to be believed. It was magic.

In his initial assessment of the Bank, Reddin commented that the level of trust and candour was amongst the highest he had seen at the start of a management change program. That level of trust helped to increase candour, which was so essential to the process of change. And candour there was! The young people who had been through the Reddin program were immensely refreshing. We organised 'interventions', a series of issues-based meetings. At one such intervention, the Structure Conference in 1979, a young woman from Taree branch employed under the antiquated title of Signing Officer related a story of how one day a customer asked her why she was called Signing Officer. She told us how difficult it had been to answer the customer's question, and then announced, in a forthright manner, 'My God, what does it mean!' Such a statement to one's seniors would have been unthinkable in the past. People who had not been to Management Effectiveness Seminars were sometimes nonplussed when they spoke to people who had, because they had become so candid in speaking their minds. It became important to get everyone through this cultural rejuvenation quickly. We had the people and we had to reassure them that we valued them as people not resources.

The atmosphere in the Bank was lively. With one-third of the managers directly involved in the process, their enthusiasm was contagious, spreading to the remaining two-thirds. The push for change really came from the younger generation of men and women. There was no returning to the old way of doing things, no bureaucratic prop. The managers' Effectiveness Areas were set down and the buck stopped with them. They were accountable. From time to time I attended some of the feedback sessions, and I found the comments a quite useful barometer; for example, one manager remarked how important it was that the staff be considered as people not as 'hands'. The Bank was turned on its head.

It would also be fair to say that when an organisation takes such a directional turn, those involved in the process experience a period of uncertainty. It was very much a generational change, and the introduction of Management By Objectives created a new pressure of accountability which some older managers found difficult to accept. There was also my determination to reduce the frequency of manager movement, and this required a look ahead to plan future career progression. The inevitable result was to limit future movements of older managers, and to accelerate the promotion of younger managers with sufficient years left to introduce greater stability at the customer interface. There was a perception that the new policy was directed to the promotion of younger managers more rapidly to key positions, and led others to conclude that they had no further prospects and that perhaps they were simply not up to the new demands and extended responsibility.

I had a great deal of sympathy for them. In some instances they had spent many years working in a bureaucracy which minimised their decision-making authority and did not reward initiative, and they felt they could no longer continue their commitment to the Bank under the new management system. These managers sought early retirement or, in fewer cases, resigned. Also because of changes to the superannuation program, initiated during the panic of the attempted nationalisation of the banks in 1947, retirement at age fifty-five was not all that unattractive. On the whole, though, there seemed to be less bad feeling concerning those retirements and resignations, where they did occur, than with those in recent times. Notwithstanding the dramatic change, the Bank did not at that time depart from its lifetime employment philosophy, and therefore there were no retrenchments.

I didn't expect it to be all calm sailing, and I wasn't blind to some of the healthy cynicism, doubts and resistance to organisational change. Nevertheless, I am convinced that without the Reddin program the Wales would not have been able to restructure itself so smoothly, and it would not have implemented a successful merger with the Commercial Bank of Australia. That had, after all, been tried before without success.

The next step was to implement a new organisational structure, because without it the motivation to continue change might well have been lost. The reorganisation of our management structure in 1980 was one of the most important outcomes of the Reddin program. In contrast to the pre-Reddin days, and more recent times, the new structure was not imposed on the network as a fait accompli. Instead, eighty Reddin-trained officers in various grades of seniority and from right across the Bank were invited to Noah's Northside Gardens Motel, North Sydney, for a weekend meeting commencing on 17 March 1979. As we gathered together that Saturday morning my assistant ordered me back to my room to remove my tie, so strong was the concentration on informality and the team approach.

Working in small teams, those attending developed the organisational structure they wanted. The tone of the meetings was dynamic, and the debates were sometimes heated, but at the end of three days they reached a consensus. In exploring the process to develop a new organisational structure, one of my senior colleagues voiced strong reservations. 'What if,' he said, 'this produces a new structure which is not acceptable to the Bank?' I felt confident in replying, 'If this procedure of a number of small teams drawn from a wide cross-section of eighty of the Bank's most capable officers interacting with each other, produces a consensus plan which is unacceptable to the Top Team of the Bank, it is we, the Top Team, who should rethink our position.' The end result was all that could be desired with a structure which achieved most of our objectives including: moving power from staff to line positions; removing a layer of top management which permitted line general managers to report direct to the CEO; reducing the numbers in the Top Team; moving responsibility downward to as close to the action as possible; becoming more customer oriented and concentrating more on strategy and planning.

One minor setback was the delay in implementing the new structure in order to accommodate the Board's wish for the orderly retirement of the senior executives whose jobs disappeared in the new structure. In the context of social change in banking, both for employees and for customers, the people priorities of the early 1980s were in sharp contrast to those of the early 1990s when thousands of bank officers were declared redundant, in many cases with less than twenty-four hours notice, in the interests of greater efficiency and often with dubious or contradictory assurances of better service for the customers. In the early 1980s the staff could see the benefits to come, and I felt we had achieved a major goal – we had awoken the slumbering giant with a positive impact on staff morale.

Our actions were well-timed, because on 18 January 1979 the Liberal Treasurer, John Howard, announced the establishment of a Committee to inquire into the Australian financial system. The result of that inquiry, which later became known as the Campbell Report after its Chairman, the late Sir Keith Campbell, was one of the most far reaching documents to influence Australian financial markets. The Wales was ready to meet the new challenge head on.

Fortified and reinvigorated by its new structure, corporate philosophy and business strategy, the Wales proceeded with one of the most far-reaching strategic decisions in its history. It decided once again to consider the possibility of a merger with another bank. Financial market development suggested that the banks were ripe for rationalisation. Following the absorption of the Bank of Adelaide by the ANZ, five private banks remained: the Wales, the ANZ, the National, the Commercial Bank of Australia and the Commercial Banking Company of Sydney. The Wales and the ANZ were the biggest. Having acquired the Queensland National Bank, the National ranked third with strong bases in Victoria and in Queensland. The other two banks were relatively smaller and considered to be vulnerable in the event of any rationalisation which might follow deregulation. We considered that size was our best defence against competition from the anticipated licensing of foreign banks, and our fear was that any combination of the existing banks which excluded us could threaten our leadership.

In 1980 our Mergers and Acquisitions Task Force, having considered and rejected a number of alternative strategies chose three options to be presented to the Board: to be a relatively small, but profitable, bank with our main focus on Australia and New Zealand; to become more internationally oriented and become a world ranked bank by establishing an overseas link or to become stronger in the domestic market by increasing our market share and then expanding to international banking.

The last option implied merging with another bank, the most favoured being the Commercial Bank of Australia, and this was the option favoured by the Board.

Although I was proud of the name, the Bank of New South Wales, it had seemed inappropriate to me during my London years, and even less appropriate in 1981. The Top Team agreed, and so it was that, not for the first time, we began the exercise of examining our name for the purposes of our international representation, and to overcome some of the bias in other states as well as New Zealand. Because Australia was a closed market to foreign banks, we were not permitted abroad to open branches, not being able to offer reciprocity. The only option for us in Hong Kong, for example, was as a licensed deposit taker. We were anxious to take that option, but then found that we were not able to link it with our name – Bank of New South Wales – because a deposit taker could not use the word 'bank' in its name. We wanted a new point of reference which would enable us to look to the future and not to the past. Ultimately, a name change was seen also as a tactical advantage in our approach to the Commercial Bank – a demonstration of our commitment to a 'merger' in contrast to a 'takeover'.

Founded in 1866, the Commercial Bank was a relatively small bank with limited points of representation, but it had a strong base in Victoria where it was headquartered. With financial market deregulation soon likely, the Commercial Bank had serious doubts about its long term viability, and its detailed strategic analysis concluded that a change of direction was necessary. It could expand further throughout Australia, or become a small, specialised bank leading the market with specialised products. Although the Wales had been unsuccessful in an earlier attempt to acquire the Commercial Bank in 1970, the prospect of success was much stronger in 1980.

Having set our sights on the Commercial Bank, we prepared a basic document for the Board outlining our view of the future banking industry, stressing the threats of rationalisation. This venture, if it were well-crafted, could provide the opportunity to create a new bank with a new name. But the document contained little detail, and certainly was not in the nature of an offer. That document was presented to a special briefing of the Wales' Board in August 1980, and was enthusiastically supported.

Foremost in our thinking was the preservation of the entity of the Bank of New South Wales because of its unique status as Australia's first bank, incorporated under its own act of the NSW Parliament. The only way this could be achieved would be for the Bank of New South Wales to acquire the shares of the Commercial Bank under the Companies Act by the issue of a Part A Statement, an offer to the shareholders to purchase their shares – in effect, a takeover. The code name for this project was 'Bermuda', named after Bill Reddin's place of business.

If the merger were consummated, the Commercial Bank would bring 191 new points of representation, few enough so the combined bank would not be unduly large, and we would have about 30 per cent of trading bank deposits, or about 20 per cent of savings and trading bank deposits combined. With more deposit and capital resources at our command, we would be able to increase our participation in individual lending projects. We believed that the Commercial Bank was about to embark on a new equipment program, and that if we merged in the near future, we would achieve economies and systems compatibility. Most importantly, the Commercial Bank merger would strengthen our business in all states, notably in Victoria and South Australia where we would almost double in size.

At the time I felt there might be significant obstacles to the merger: objections by the government and the public to increased financial concentration, and that we might be pipped at the post by other banks merging first, or by the ANZ outbidding us. However, I thought that with careful attention, these obstacles could be overcome. The Commercial Bank was the best fit for us.

Using the expertise of David Block and his associate Peter Mason as our strategic advisers, and Allen Allen and Hemsley as legal advisers, we worked secretly and quickly. From October 1980, we quietly bought shares in the Commercial Bank through a wholly owned subsidiary of the Wales. The senior management of the Commercial Bank were aware that shares were being purchased, but did not know the buyer was the Wales. By the beginning of 1981, about two months before our formal discussions with the Commercial Bank, the Wales had acquired 2.5 per cent of its capital through the share purchases. As the timing of our move became more important, I noted in my diary: 'Why Act Now: overhang decisions; pension fund; profit sharing; capital expenditure (duplication); Senate goes in June; 1983? Election.'

Conscious of the need to avoid any move which could be construed as an offer, the Chairman and I travelled to Melbourne and presented the basic document to our counterparts in the Commercial Bank. Their Managing Director was away, and his Deputy remarked almost in disbelief on our willingness to change our name. Having considered our document, some days later they advised that they were not interested in pursuing the discussion further.

A few days after we were rebuffed, the Chairman of the ANZ, Sir Ian McLennan, invited Stephen Kimpton, Chairman of the Commercial Bank, to lunch. Sir Ian expressed the ANZ's interest in having talks with the Commercial Bank, and provided

Kimpton with a piece of paper which apparently set out some terms and conditions as a basis for further discussion.

In analysing that piece of paper, the Commercial Bank considered that the approach was a signal which in effect constituted price-sensitive information. The Commercial Bank therefore felt obliged to make a public statement to that effect that same day; having planned our move some time earlier, and having opened a dialogue, we were taken completely by surprise. But we were positioned to take the next step.

The name change and the offer to work together to create a new bank was preferred by the Commercial Bank over the more aggressive approach of the ANZ. In the Commercial Bank Board minutes of 14 May 1981, the directors commented that, 'the ANZ proposal represented a takeover with little or no regard for Commercial Bank staff.' The pressure was then on us to come forward with terms and conditions which were better than those offered by the ANZ. We felt that we were the preferred partner, but we were in a rather delicate situation.

With the ANZ's offer for the Commercial Bank and National Bank's offer for the Commercial Banking Company of Sydney both making the headlines, the Wales was represented in the press as slow and almost certain to miss out. In the *Age* in April 1981, Terry McCrann, an influential financial journalist, opined that the federal government would not permit two mergers and the reduction to three major banks. The Commercial Bank merger, he wrote, meant that, 'the last chance for many years was at hand for any bank to undertake a major lift in assets through a merger.' He echoed our fear exactly. However, market forces prevailed: the government did not move to halt the rationalisation process, and the National Bank made a successful bid for the Commercial Banking Company of Sydney as did the Wales for the Commercial Bank of Australia.

In the pressure to succeed, our advisers suggested the aggressive approach, which was to call on the Chairman of the Commercial Bank on Friday evening and demand a response by Monday. I rejected this because of my long and friendly relationship with its Managing Director, the late David Dobbie. We had served our respective banks in London at the same time as

Chief Managers, and we had been reasonably close neighbours. We had a great deal of respect for each other and I was anxious for a friendly, rather than a hostile, marriage. The Wales' Board accepted the less aggressive, co-operative approach which we followed. We tried to come up with the right price in the first instance to avoid haggling, and when the Board finally determined our best offer, we proceeded on the gentlemanly route. Press speculation was rife in the course of this difficult period; moreover I had to fulfil a long standing commitment to address the Australian Society of Accountants at Surfers Paradise on Saturday, 9 May 1981. I was so pressed for time that I flew in by a chartered aircraft, delivered my address, and left immediately to return to Sydney. There were many awkward questions from the audience which I was naturally anxious to escape.

On Thursday, 14 May 1981, Ian Matheson, my deputy, Graham McCorkell, the Chief Accountant, Geoff Thompson and I travelled to Melbourne for a final presentation of our proposition, and waited patiently at the Commercial Bank head office while its Board deliberated. Late in the afternoon, we were told that we had been successful and the Board invited us for a drink to celebrate. The period of suspense which followed gradually faded when the ANZ did not come back with a counter offer.

Perhaps we paid too much, but, had we missed out, the cost to the Wales' standing in the market would have been substantial. During the day, many Commercial Bank staff gathered at the front door of its head office to protest against the ANZ. Their concern was understandable, as the ANZ, it was quipped, 'did not take prisoners'. We seemed to be in favour at both levels. I advised our Chairman, waiting in Sydney, 'mission accomplished' and I later enjoyed the headline 'The Gentlemen of the Wales' in an article by Vicki Smiles, Financial Editor of the *Sydney Morning Herald*. The target date for the merger was 1 October 1982 – a little over sixteen months to complete an enormous task.

Although the Commercial Bank officers had indicated their support, I was aware that the successful integration of the two banks rested on that support, and that their resistance to becoming officers of a new bank could upset our target date. Their concerns had merits: the Wales was a rival and much bigger; a shift to

Sydney from Melbourne for the key executives concerned would entail considerable upheaval and expense, given Sydney's higher real estate prices; and their career prospects might be diminished, particularly in the areas of dual branch representation. At the time there were nearly 500 dual points of representation.

The threat of redundancy, although not real, was on the minds of staff in both banks. We were conscious of the rumour mill. It was only fair that each person wanted to know what would happen to him or her, so we tried wherever possible to give people facts as they came to hand. We signed a 'non-redundancy' undertaking whereby no Commercial Bank employee would lose employment because of the closure of redundant facilities. We offered early retirement with attractive benefits to those people who chose to resign. We also offered employees of both banks the choice of remaining in the existing pension fund or joining a new fund which had been set up by the Wales.

We were also conscious of customer loyalty, and that some Commercial Bank customers might switch banks. Our customers, in particular small businesses, which had a high level of awareness of the merger, were worried that they would lose valued personal service. Lastly, we were mindful that we would need the confidence of the financial markets and the Bank's proprietors.

We placed a ban on the use of the term 'takeover' because we felt it would be perceived as unfriendly – the antithesis of the image we wanted to project. In summary, we approached the merger in a spirit of goodwill and fair play with an emphasis on harmony and a focus on the benefits from the merger.

During the process of changing our name, the Bank engaged Pieter Huveneers, a highly respected practitioner in names and logos. Our thinking was that Australia was no longer an extension of Europe and that our fortunes were bound up with the future of the western Pacific. During the selection process, we considered geographic names, rejecting the 'Wales' because of its connotation of an entirely different country, to people outside Australia and New Zealand. The solid, respected name of the Commercial Bank of Australia was also rejected because it was geographically limiting, and because the word 'commercial' no longer reflected its broad base and functions.

Huveneers had a strong view that selection should not be attempted through long discussions between senior executive teams or boards of directors. The need for absolute secrecy was paramount if we were to reserve the chosen name and ensure it remained available throughout Australia and a host of other countries throughout the world. A meeting of the Board was designated as the one which would make the choice. Huveneers' plan was to reveal a panel of names secretly to the Chairman and me a day or so before the designated Board meeting. Thus the process would be something in the nature of a fait accompli, unless the Board chose to adjourn for more choices or further discussion.

Finally, we chose a constructed name because we wanted a different, concise and attractive alternative. The Board agreed to Westpac, which offered the advantages of retaining the red W logo – a logo which was readily identifiable to 77 per cent of the Bank of New South Wales' home market. The commercial value of the symbol could not be overlooked; it was eye catching, it identified the company and the public had a positive attitude to it.

The Board was less than excited about the new name, which attracted public debate on its merits or otherwise. The controversy was invaluable in publicising the name at home. For example, one writer quipped that he could not decide if Westpac was a charity package from Western Australia or a Swan Brewery promotion. Another wrote, 'If some Americans believe the Bank of New South Wales is centred in Cardiff, will they not think Westpac(k) is based in Karachi?' To other critics I used to say, 'You should have seen the other names the Board rejected.' In devising his suggestions Huveneers faced an unenviable task to find an appropriate name not already reserved somewhere in the world.

Although the Commercial Bank staff protested that retention of the logo breached the 'new look' undertaking, the name change was probably the most important ingredient in the recipe for success. The name, Westpac, was a new banner for the staff of both banks. It added reality to the creation of a new bank, and it helped to dispel prejudices or divisions based on earlier loyalties.

The logistics of harmonising two distinctly different systems were onerous; our October 1982 deadline was short and, in spite of our best efforts, we made some mistakes. Banks are systems driven, and we failed to recognise the extent to which this was the case. The Commercial Bank staff, as members of the smaller partner, were under great pressure to conform to the Wales systems and procedures. The plan to use the best of the systems of the two banks from day one of the merger proved impossible, leading to delays in the provision of some essential information to Head Office.

We were too anxious to make it all happen quickly. We made elaborate plans to destroy all material using the former names. I learnt from this plan to make sure of the flow of the new before the old is destroyed.

Last, having paid such a lot of money for our increased market share, I issued an edict that we must make sure we retained it. Thanks to the Reddin program we had much more aggressive managers and a new group of managers. The combination of all those factors quickly resulted in some questionable new business, and consequently our bad debts rose. However, that trend was quickly brought under control. Although the ultimate costs were greater than initially anticipated, and we should have been more mindful of the loan portfolio from the outset, looking back there was no better alternative.

On the positive side, the new, moderately priced Westpac wardrobe was also important in establishing a new and common identity for the staff. From the designers, Adele Weiss said, 'This is not a uniform, it is a wardrobe which they will be proud to wear.' And proud they were – the acceptance ratio greatly exceeded our forecasts. The half-day road shows throughout the network were not only a successful medium from which to launch the wardrobe, but were also a 'pep rally'. We emphasised staff participation by choosing five men and fifteen women at each location to model the wardrobe. They had a lot of fun preparing for the two and-a-half-hour roadshows, and the spontaneous applause at the end of each was a great morale booster. The wardrobe and the roadshows were, in my view, two masterstrokes which helped to win the acceptance of the staff.

In many respects the merger was a 'non-event' because, in spite of the complications, it proceeded smoothly. We increased our market share; we became more profit and customer oriented; we established a strong presence in the Asia-Pacific region and in the US. We rationalised the branch network and established ourselves as a leader in technology. We delivered better services to our customers and, after a short term of depressed prices, to our shareholders. The name 'Westpac' became established and respected in the public mind, and helped to unify the staff. Indeed, many officers who have joined Westpac since the merger have no other frame of reference.

Because of its many successes, I am tempted to crow about the achievements of the organisational change program. However, there were areas in which we were not as successful as we might have been, and the flow-on effects tainted the Bank's performance.

In spite of my best efforts, I did not succeed completely in controlling the power of the personnel function, and the consequences were major industrial relations problems in 1986.

Second, Reddin encouraged lateral recruitment, often on three-year contracts, short-term by traditional Bank standards, as a way of filling gaps in expertise. Although they were few in number, the people contracted were in key positions, and some of them played a major part in the Bank's development. They were a new breed of managers who were hard drivers and achievers. But their commitment was, understandably, short-term; or their sights were set on different goal posts or they developed their own agendas. There is no doubt that the Bank benefited immensely from their expertise, but their efforts created cultural conflicts in the organisation – not always to its advantage. The newcomers came from a background where it appeared that peer group loyalty and trust were not as dominant as they were in the Wales.

Many people in positions of power seek to enhance their own status; in the 1980s a drive to self-aggrandisement began to emerge. And so it was that the planning area, although exceedingly successful, became too big and too powerful. Initially, Management By Objectives was a practical way of forcing managers to become more accountable, but when quarterly reporting was introduced, many managers commented that the attendant paper work was as cumbersome as the bureaucratic system it was supposed to have replaced. The argument had some foundation, but I could not help thinking that some managers might have felt some discomfort in assessing their subordinates or in being assessed themselves. More importantly, quarterly reporting was a subtle exercise in accruing power by the planners. Instead of a performance planning system or Management By Objectives with appropriate measurements, we found ourselves confronted with terms like 'management system', which implied broader horizons beyond formal planning and measurement of performance. As the Bank proceeded with its expansion program the planners, whose task it was to develop strategy, could not resist the temptation to become involved in its implementation, thus blurring one of the checks and balances and leading to some acquisitions beyond the boundaries of the agreed strategy.

Our decision to promote younger managers provoked the criticism that we allowed a lot of expertise 'to walk out the door'. It is true that our experienced managers were street-smart and understood the importance of the credit function. While not contenders for the top jobs, they were often a moderating influence. Did we go too far? I don't believe we did. On balance, and with the blinding clarity of hindsight, the credit problems which subsequently were so destructive to the Bank were more the result of an overly aggressive marketing thrust, coinciding with the frenzied business environment of the late 1980s associated with deregulation of financial markets.

By now the merger of the Bank of New South Wales and the Commercial Bank of Australia is well and truly part of Australian financial history. The methods employed in the Reddin change program, the subsequent execution of the merger with the Commercial Bank of Australia, and the results achieved so impressed Dr David Zenoff, a leading teacher of management studies, that he arranged for a three-part case study to be developed for use by IMEDE, Lausanne, Switzerland.[1] The Reddin method was a new way of doing things; it strengthened the checks and balances which are crucial to a financial organisation. In the final analysis, however, it was up to the senior managers to steer the Bank through the turbulent market.

Only vestiges of Reddin's influence survived in the years following my retirement as Managing Director when the doctrine of 'Directional Management' was espoused. Any management change program can be diverted from its course. I call this the 3-P syndrome: People, Power and Politics. Any one or more of the 3-Ps can in some circumstances corrupt the best systems. There will always be people who will override those systems for their own ends.

THE SEE-SAW OF POLITICS

9

Traditionally bankers are pessimists. This is because those asking for loans are always optimists. At the beginning of the 1980s, though, many of my banking colleagues and I had a sense of great optimism and little notion of what was to happen during the decade. Little did we anticipate the international debt crisis which, by 1983, would see some twenty-eight countries struggling with, or trying to avoid, debt rescheduling. On the contrary, the second oil price shock of the late 1970s offered even better prospects for the abundant Australian energy resources. We were unique, unlike Britain or the US, in that we had such huge resources in the areas that mattered – coal and gas. Australia had a stable government and I was confident at the time that our policy makers had a high level of skills and a high sense of responsibility. I was to be sorely disappointed.

I remember the fanfare accompanying the release of a report, *Major Manufacturing and Mining Investment Projects*, in 1980, by the Department of Industry and Commerce which listed the resources projects in the pipeline. The report showed that 306 projects, mainly in coal, oil and gas, and base metals, totalling some $33 billion, were committed or at the stage of final feasibility. A further 149 projects valued at $41.75 billion were at a preliminary stage of investigation. We began to see headlines about our forthcoming embarrassment of riches.

In the banking industry, we did not question the assumption that the forecast export earnings from minerals would be good for Australia. The Bank was developing more sophisticated products and management tools so that we could get a piece of the action. Since the amounts of capital required for these projects would be large, and well beyond the reach of Australian dollar financing, the Bank took advantage of the opportunity offered by the Eurodollar markets. It would all be good business. The major resources projects, because they were entirely different from traditional banking in that there was a 'project risk' attached to them, required more careful consideration than the traditional corporate loans. They were not credit or country risks in the normally accepted sense, so we had to undertake very detailed studies of the reserves and the technicalities associated with the completion of each project, as well as of the availability of contracts to buy the outputs, whether gas, coal or some other resource. To boost our expertise in the minerals and mining industries, the Bank set up a unit with a geologist and a minerals economist, and, as a result, we were able to write a lot of sound business without loss.

When some people pointed out the downsides of the gung-ho resources policy they were dismissed as cranks, part of the 'looney left', or ignored. However, Bob Gregory, a distinguished Professor at the Australian National University, who wrote about the impact of mineral exports on the manufacturing and rural sectors was not ignored. His writing caused us some concern. Professor Gregory had analysed the effects of mining on the rural and manufacturing sectors in the period 1964 to 1977. His thesis was based on the premise that export earnings from the sale of minerals contributed to an increase in the value of the Australian dollar. This, in turn, increased the capacity to buy imported goods and services, and affected import-competing industries, most notably in manufactured goods, as well as traditional exports. One negative result would be tougher competition and job losses. Gregory concluded from his work that, 'mineral discoveries have had a much greater effect on these sectors than the recent across the board 25 per cent general reduction of tariffs',[1] implemented by the Whitlam Government in 1973. As the financial press and other economists picked up on his work, Gregory was criticised by both the mining sector and by the left wing of the union movement. CRA Economist, John Macleod, in an article in the *Australian Quarterly*, complained about an off-key 'Gregory Chant', sung by 'self-appointed disciples',[2] who used his work as a basis from which to argue for restricting mining growth. It was an easy step for some trade unionists to reduce the complexities of structural change in the manufacturing industry to a simple slogan such as 'Mining Undermines Manufacturing'.

This debate aside, we all shared a sense of optimism. Even the trade union movement was not immune, and in late 1981 400 000 metalworkers won a 24 per cent wage increase, with a collective bargaining agreement ratified by the full bench of the Arbitration Commission. I also recall that coal miners were awarded large increases in the early 1980s; these rises flowed on to rail workers on the argument that, while they did not mine the coal, they were the ones who had to cart it. This air of prosperity encouraged a general wages explosion further disadvantaging the manufacturing sector, which was already dogged by structural change. In 1982 wages rose across the board by 16 per cent, and they rose by a further 13 per cent in 1983.

As it turned out, the predicted embarrassment of riches from the mining boom was only partially realised, not because of the concerted actions of anti-mining groups, but because of market forces. The international economic downturn of 1982 and its flow on to Australia in 1983 meant the mineral products were not required to the degree anticipated.

It was against this background of optimism bordering on euphoria that the Bank remained discontented about the level of government regulation and continued its campaign for financial market reform. In September 1981, the Campbell Report had amply illustrated the inefficiencies of the financial system, and provided a blueprint for that system which would underpin the prosperity, and some would now argue the demise, of the Australian economy of the 1980s.

The Report was the first major review of the financial system since the Napier Royal Commission Report in 1937. In a nutshell, the Committee took the general view that the most efficient way to organise economic activity was through a competitive market system subject to a minimum of regulation and government intervention. In my view it was long overdue. Any industry which was as highly regulated as the Australian capital market should have been subject to a wide ranging scrutiny at regular intervals. The Committee Chairman, Keith Campbell, to his credit, gave a good public airing to key issues.

In our draft submissions to the Campbell Committee we strongly criticised the Reserve Bank, and I found myself editing down to lessen our disapproval. Even so, in our final submission we were faint in our praise and strong in our criticisms, prompting the Governor of the Reserve Bank to phone me to express his concern. All I could reply was that he should have seen the material I took out!

The reality was that the central bank was overseeing a financial system which was outmoded and out of step with other industrialised countries. I believe these events reflected the pent-up frustration in the minds of middle managers from the Bank over continuing regulatory controls which precluded them from assisting many of their customers with reasonable financial requests. In fairness, it should also be said that I felt a considerable degree of sympathy for the Governor and other senior officers of the Reserve Bank, who were obliged to administer a system which conformed with the official policies of the Treasury and their political masters.

The main thrust of the Bank's submission to the Campbell Committee was to the effect that control over banks should be relaxed so that they could compete on a more equal footing in financial markets. We also suggested, but only as a second best choice, that extension of controls over banks should include other intermediaries. Frankly, it was not a solution. Apart from extending interference with the free flow of money and credit, extension of controls would inevitably have given rise to new forms of intermediation specifically designed to escape those controls, and the type of problem we were facing would reappear.

I was not surprised that the Campbell Committee's recommendations were not acted upon immediately. But I did not think they would more or less lie dead and buried until the 1983 election. However, I was struck by the irony that here we had a free-market oriented Liberal Government which sat on the Report, and a Labor Government – historically associated with nationalisation – which implemented the findings.

Not surprisingly, the newly elected Labor Government set up another inquiry. It was headed by Vic Martin, who was then Executive Chairman of the Mutual Life and Citizens' Assurance Company, but who had earlier been the Managing Director of the

Commercial Banking Company of Sydney, before its merger with the National Bank of Australasia. Vic Martin had resigned from the National Bank, and his appointment to head up the committee to review the Campbell Committee's report could hardly be interpreted as a move by the newly elected Labor Government to reject the concept of deregulation. The Martin Committee recommended deregulation in the following areas: removal of the bank deposit maturity restrictions by August 1984, and the abolition of interest rate ceilings on bank lending under $100 000 in 1985. The ceilings on other lending had been removed earlier. There was one notable exception – the interest rate ceiling on housing loans of 13.5 per cent remained.

That ceiling was well below the market, but housing was, and remained, one of our most sensitive political issues. Since we were unable to raise deposits within the ceiling set for loans, new bank housing loans rapidly disappeared from the market place.

In the aftermath of the Martin Committee's report, changes occurred rapidly and thus it was that, in the space of just a few years, the Australian financial system moved from being highly regulated to virtually unregulated. Most of the changes took place during the eighteen months immediately following the floating of the Australian dollar in December 1983. In this period of rapid change the longer-term effects took some time to work their way through the economy.

Until December 1983 Australians operated with virtually a fixed exchange rate, pegged originally to the pound sterling, and then the US dollar, and finally to a basket of currencies. In capital-hungry Australia the purpose of exchange controls was to protect our overall capital position – hence the surveillance over capital transfers by the Reserve Bank of Australia.

As a result, the trading banks had imposed upon them a complex set of foreign exchange regulations. Westpac and all other trading banks were obliged to settle any net purchases or sales of foreign exchange with the Reserve Bank at the end of each day, and we were not permitted to hold foreign exchange positions. As an agent for the Reserve Bank, Westpac could authorise transfers of Australian dollars within well-defined limits, and we had a statutory obligation to make sure the work was done properly. The

Bank's exchange control section kept pace with the paperwork. Every transaction involving foreign exchange above the discretionary limit set down by the authorities had to be approved by the Reserve Bank. In pre-computer days there were drawers and drawers of forms, some partly completed, for various trade or capital transactions. Whenever a transfer of this kind took place, it was noted on the forms.

We had lived with this intricate set of exchange control regulations since the beginning of the Second World War. They were designed to ensure that funds were not transferred at all for purposes other than to finance legitimate trade transactions, travel, etc. With Australia's need for capital it was necessary to administer exchange control regulations in a way that would not discourage foreigners from investing, transferring or lending to Australians. The Reserve Bank, acting as the government's agent, refused to give guarantees to approve the future repatriation of funds, but it was prepared to give assurances that approvals would never be withheld in all reasonable circumstances or where there were previous agreements providing for repatriation. For example, mining and oil companies would obtain approval from the Reserve Bank to remit capital on a month-by-month basis in a nominated currency. I have no personal experience of legitimate agreements not being honoured. However, there were always hapless entrepreneurs who neglected the exchange control aspect of their business arrangements only to be told by our staff that they could not repatriate their profits to nominated tax havens or other off-shore accounts.

In the lead up to the 1983 elections, large volumes of capital flowed out of the country – something of the order of $3 billion between early February and 7 March 1983. Business and investors had a perception that a Labor Government would permit a higher budget deficit, higher inflation, and a higher current account deficit, and that this in turn would lead to downward pressure on the Australian dollar.

I found it interesting, if not disturbing, that in a controlled regime backed by an intricate set of exchange control regulations, we could have a sharp, substantial and disastrous level of capital outflow in such a short period. However, if the authorities were to encourage a continuing favourable climate for foreign investment, they could not at the same time put up unreasonable barriers to prevent this substantial level of capital outflow. These transactions would have been for early repayment of overseas borrowings, and early payments for imports or for any other transaction which could be brought within the exchange control regulations and could be brought forward or crowded into this short period prior to the election. Those concerned were involved in a one-way bet, in that the more money they took out, the more certain they were to make a profit. There was nothing illegal in this; corporate treasurers were taking what they considered to be a prudent course of action. From the perspective of a practical banker, our resources were stretched alarmingly in servicing the heavy volume of capital transactions in that confined period.

Westpac had a substantial share of overseas business, and most of this business was conducted at 341 George Street, down the hill from the Reserve Bank. We were obliged to make sure there was no delay in investors getting their money transferred. As one of our senior staff in the exchange control section recalled, 'We just had to get stuck into it [the volume of work] . . . Everyone worked overtime and everybody lost weight.' No wonder! When the applications were urgent, the staff walked up the hill, also known as Coronary Hill, to the Reserve Bank to deliver the applications by hand.

When the Labor Party won the election, one of the early priorities for the newly elected Treasurer, Paul Keating, was to face the consequences of the one-way bet on the currency value which had been imposed upon him. To his credit he moved quickly and decisively with a devaluation of 10 per cent. I suppose it was not surprising that the money began to flow back immediately, and the imbalance on the current account was corrected. It would be difficult not to conclude that the capital flows of 1983 were due to speculative movements, but, on the other hand, corporate activity was intense with entrepreneurs making acquisitions and takeover bids.

When the corporate treasurers withdrew Australian dollars to buy their overseas dollars, the Bank's liquidity came under strong and sudden pressure. Because the country was in an election mode, we were unable to adjust our interest rates to inhibit the outflow or transfer some of the cost to the corporate treasurers who were seeking to profit from the situation. And so it was again, for the second time, that we had to suffer the indignity of borrowing from the Reserve Bank to preserve our liquidity ratio at the minimum level of 18 per cent. I was somewhat resentful of the Reserve Bank's attitude at this time, because there was no doubt that we were faced with a situation which was not of our own making and yet we had to pay a penalty rate of interest for the temporary Reserve Bank credit we were obliged to use. We had a large share of international business and had to borrow about $500 million at punitive rates from the Reserve Bank. Before the election we also melted about $1 billion in government bonds and then had to buy them back at a much higher cost. Market interest rates rose accordingly; bank bill rates were of the order of 15 per cent. In simple terms, over $3 billion flowed out before the election at one rate of exchange and most of it flowed back following the election at a lower rate of exchange.

We were not permitted to increase bank interest rates until the first business day following the election and by then, of course, it was too late. As I look back, I am struck by the fact that this was a major crisis in our foreign exchange markets, and yet it took place in a substantially regulated environment. It was in itself an argument against regulation, and it involved a substantial cost, probably running to some hundreds of millions of dollars. There was no doubt that it was an extremely costly exercise for Australian borrowers, Australian banks and Australian taxpayers, yet those involved in the foreign exchange movements finished up with a handsome profit.

When I expressed my concern to the Reserve Bank about the cost of the transactions to Westpac, their reply was unsympathetic. There was a time during the crisis when we were being paid less by our borrowers than we were paying the Reserve Bank for our loans. In a sense, it could be said that we were obliged to pay a penalty to borrow back our own money to observe a liquidity ratio now considered irrelevant. Comparing this episode to the instability in financial markets in 1975, it seems that the major difference was that in 1983 capital flows were more dramatic and rapid.

In spite of the devaluation in March, currency movements remained volatile throughout 1983. The Reserve Bank made a number of adjustments to allow freer floating exchange rate arrangements; it withdrew from the forward market, leaving banks free to quote their own rates to customers and banks were given more flexibility to hold foreign currency balances. By October 1983, Westpac reviewed the situation and concluded that the market signals were stronger than the Reserve Bank's ability to control the exchange rate, and that the dollar would probably be floated – although we had no idea of when that might be. We then had to think about the exchange control section which would no longer be required.

We also considered the future of our foreign exchange operations. Although the Campbell Report had recommended the dismantling of exchange controls and the deregulation of foreign exchange markets, we did not know that the Reserve Bank had studied this scenario and had prepared itself with its now famous 'War Book'. We certainly did not foresee that the floating of the dollar and the abolition of exchange controls would occur in the first nine months after the election.

Westpac already had a modest foreign exchange dealing operation, but not a lot of expertise. How could we when the last bank officers to have experience of a free foreign exchange rate would have been working in the 1930s in a much different market? The Bank recruited many talented people to its principal Australian and overseas branches. Our operations in London, New York, Hong Kong and Singapore assumed a new significance, since they were already located in free foreign exchange markets. And it became even more necessary for us to achieve our ambition to open a branch in Tokyo – that became possible when the government announced its intention to license new foreign banks, including three banks from Japan.

The floating of the dollar and the associated development of our foreign exchange dealing activities provided us with a major challenge as we endeavoured to recruit qualified people and establish suitable systems. It was obvious that our customers and others were not going to wait until we put down maximum controls and systems; so it was necessary to take some risks as we developed the business. We had a few hiccups in setting up our operations, but nothing really major. And when the Bank scored well in the international surveys about the service we provided, we felt justifiably pleased with our efforts.

Much has been written about the politics and economics of the float, about whether the dollar should have been floated and who took what side in the debate leading up to the decision. From my perspective, the Australian monetary authorities may have been able to refrain from their decision for a while longer by imposing tighter exchange controls, using mechanisms such as a Variable Deposit Requirement (VDR) to control destabilising inflows, but ultimately the market signals were too strong. The float was yet another episode in the opening up of our economy. There was no going back because most of our principal trading partners had a floating exchange rate regime and we were out of step. My good friend, Sir Harold Knight, former Governor of the Reserve Bank, used to say that, 'When the tide is going out or coming in there is not much you can do to stop it.'

When the Australian dollar floated in December 1983, the rate was about 92 cents to the US dollar, and over the next few weeks, the rate floated up to about 97-98 cents to the US dollar. However, we were to become victims of the general volatility which attended international foreign exchange markets, largely due to the desire of world leaders to adjust exchange rates in the light of the serious imbalance between the two trading giants, Japan and the United States. In the 1990s, there are many who perceive inadequacies in the floating regime, and we can but wonder what will follow.

Traditionally banks seem to attract the blame from governments when conditions in the economy are not going well. There is no question that they were held partly responsible for the serious events of the great depression, and it was a conservative government which appointed the Royal Commission in the mid-1930s to investigate the financial system. The banks' relationship with the Fraser Coalition Government attracted criticisms from time to time, particularly on the score of interest rates. Mr Fraser had promised an interest rate reduction of 2 per cent in 1978. When that promise looked as if it could not be fulfilled, I was summoned to Canberra in my capacity as Chairman of the Australian Bankers' Association, together with the Governor of the Reserve Bank, Sir Harold Knight, to explain the reasons why it could not to the Economic Policy Subcommittee of the Cabinet. I remember that I remarked to Sir Harold that this was the first time I had had breakfast and lunch on the same airline on the same day between Sydney and Canberra, and his reply was that he, not infrequently, had all three meals on flights between Sydney and Canberra.

I think there was considerable speculation in March 1983 as to what sort of working relationship would develop between the banks and the newly elected Labor Government. I can only say that, subject to the inevitable policy differences, I enjoyed a first-class working relationship both with John Howard, as Treasurer of the Coalition Government, and with Paul Keating, as Treasurer of the Labor Government. The Hawke Government seemed more pragmatic, moderate and less rooted in the socialist ideology of its predecessors. During the eight years the Labor Party was in opposition, I had taken the opportunity to become acquainted with many of its leaders, some of whom have remained friends.

In April 1983, only a few weeks after taking office, Bob Hawke made good an election campaign promise by convening a National Economic Summit. The Summit had no doubt been carefully planned, I suspect in conjunction with the ACTU and some of the government's business friends. The ACTU had a considerable advantage in that it was organised as a co-ordinated delegation, whereas the business representation was fragmented. There were many independent people in attendance who were not associated with any particular organisation. The banks were represented at the Summit by the then Chairman of the Australian Bankers' Association, John Milne of the ANZ Bank.

My impression is that the business community generally came away with a feeling that they had been personally associated with a communique which had been prepared and written before they got there. Perhaps the Summit was chiefly a vehicle for the business community to endorse the ACTU-Government Accord. Although some employers registered their discontent on the floor of the Parliament, the atmosphere was such that none of them rejected the final document with the exception of the Premier of

Queensland (and he was not representing the business community).

Before the government's economic policies were in place, I found it difficult to see how a high interest rate regime and inflationary pressures could be avoided. Yet to its credit, the trade union movement delivered modest wage restraint. In 1984 wages rose by 2.1 per cent and subsequent rises were between 6 per cent and 7 per cent until 1988. But unemployment hovered around 8 per cent and youth unemployment remained at destructive rates. Consumer prices rose by 4 per cent in 1984 and fluctuated between 6.7 per cent and 9 per cent between 1985 and 1988. It seemed to me that Australia would have to continue to rely on monetary policy because the government's capacity to reduce the budget deficits was limited and would in time limit the opportunities for lower interest rates. Inevitably interest rates crept up to record levels.

I suppose one of the main benefits of the Summit was that some of the more naive business and trade union leaders discovered neither side had horns growing out of their heads. But mostly the Economic Summit highlighted how disunited business was in comparison to the well-oiled and highly professional ACTU-Labor Party machine.

The business community was determined it would never again appear so fragmented and disorganised. This fragmentation was not a new phenomenon. The Confederation of Australian Industry (CAI) had been formed some years earlier with much fanfare and ambitious expectations. Centred in Canberra, its membership consisted of the various industry organisations or associations. The principal founding members were the Chambers of Manufactures and their equivalents in the various states, together with the employers' organisations of the various states. Added to the membership were organisations like: the Metal Trades Industry Association, the National Farmers' Federation, the Retail Traders' Association, the Australian Bankers' Association. There were ultimately three boards of three divisions: one for trade and investment, one for industrial matters and the other for international business. Board meetings were attended on a rotational basis by an appropriate business executive, supported by a professional from his association. As the permanent representation rested with the professional employer association executive, the tendency was for the professionals to dominate the agenda rather than the practising company executives with direct exposure to their respective businesses. It was not surprising, therefore, that as the 1980s progressed we saw a series of defections from the CAI, and this was probably reflected in the performance of business at the Economic Summit.

To prepare for the future, the Melbourne-based organisation, the Australian Industry Development Association (AIDA) met with the Business Roundtable, a Sydney-based organisation, to discuss amalgamation to form a new business organisation which would be truly representative of big business.

The two organisations met at the Hilton Hotel in Sydney on the night of Tuesday, 19 April 1983, and following some heated discussion and strong determination on the part of the visiting delegates from Melbourne, a decision was taken to establish the Business Council of Australia and to appoint Geoff Allen as Executive Director. In the confusion at the end of the meeting, and following the somewhat spirited discussion, it was decided to designate a couple of people to prepare a communique. At that stage Milton Bridgland, President of AIDA from Melbourne, offered to be helpful by producing a draft communique from his pocket. There was an immediate outcry from a Sydney representative to the effect, 'Look, they have even written the press release before they got here.'

And so the Business Council was born, but with some very firm rules which confined its membership to the eighty or so largest companies in Australia, and restricted membership of the Council to the chief executive of the participating companies with no right of delegation. This reflected a strong determination to unite business at the chief executive level, and to limit the role of employed professionals. The Business Council was extremely successful because its newly appointed Executive Director strongly supported and practised that policy. I was present at the foundation meeting in my capacity as Vice President of the Business Roundtable, but I did not then foresee that I was to have a prominent role in the Business Council as its second President.

Over the years the Business Council made substantive contributions to diverse issues such as Australia's foreign debt, the importance of equal opportunities for women in the workforce, and the environment. But it was the Tax Summit in 1985 which put the Council in some strife. While I have no intention of retracing the steps of the tax debate itself, as a former President of the Business Council and the leader of its delegation to the Tax Summit, I should like to set the record straight.

The concept of a tax summit was introduced by Prime Minister Hawke during the 1984 election campaign, but tax reform had already been on the agenda of the Economic Planning Advisory Council (EPAC). Two members of EPAC who were also members of, but not representatives of, the Business Council, Alan Coates and Bryan Kelman, had advocated a consumption tax and a capital gains tax as components of an overall tax reform package. But the capital gains tax component had already attracted widespread opposition not only from the Business Council but from business and investors generally.

The basis of the Council's discussion on tax issues by its Tax Committee was established by the government's three options, all designed to improve the efficiency of tax collection and move some of the burden from income tax to indirect taxes. Option A introduced a capital gains tax, a tax on fringe benefits and other measures to improve the efficiency of the system. Option B was a combination of Option A with a modest consumption tax and modification of the existing wholesale sales tax. Option C, the government's preferred alternative, picked up the nasties from Option A and combined them with a broad-based consumption tax. In effect, the Business Council, which strongly advocated the adoption of a broad-based consumption tax, was left with no alternative except to oppose all options, because Option C, the only option with the broad-based consumption tax, contained an expanded capital gains tax and the introduction of the fringe benefits tax. The new interpretation of the capital gains tax was opposed by the Council although two of its members, also members of EPAC, had publicly supported it.

Because of the importance of the Tax Summit, and mindful of the experience at the 1983 Summit, I arranged meetings with the Presidents of the other principal business associations: the Confederation of Australian Industry, the National Farmers' Federation and the Australian Chamber of Commerce. While there were some differences in approach on detail in the application of a broad-based consumption tax, there was no disagreement whatsoever on opposition to the overall package of Option C. From the beginning, and throughout the Tax Summit, the Chairman of the Confederation of Australian Industry and I jointly chaired a daily conference of all business representatives attending, and I am able therefore to refute absolutely the often repeated criticism that the business delegations were divided or inept, or that the Business Council itself was inept.

The simple fact is that Option C did not meet one of the government's own principles of tax reform – community support. It seems that the government had been given the impression that it could do a deal with the Business Council on the basis that the Council would accept the unattractive capital gains tax and fringe benefits tax in exchange for the introduction of a broad-based consumption tax. Of course the Council was not in the business of doing deals, and did not have the authority of the business community to do so. The outcome was that the Summit failed, in that it did not accept any of the government's three options. With the usual skill of those in charge, and some of the media, the Business Council was nominated to carry the blame – even by some of its own members.

In the week leading up to the Summit, I tried several times to speak with Paul Keating, so that there would be no misunderstanding about the Council's approach, but my calls were not returned. No doubt this was due to the tremendous pressures of other constituents who were not on side.

In the public debate about the government's White Paper, it became popular for critics to declare they were on the government's cart or not on the government's cart. The government's approach to the three options was totally inflexible, in that each was presented as a package. In Option C, for example, the consumption tax was not available without a capital gains tax and a fringe benefits tax. Mine was the first speech on the agenda following the Prime Minister's introduction, and when I said that the Business Council was not in any cart, not A or B or C, my strong advocacy of the consumption tax, which was, after all, the major reform proposed, was substantially ignored.

It seemed that a lot of discussion took place outside the

formal framework of the Summit, which was conducted in the House of Representatives, so much so that on the fourth day, the Prime Minister, the Treasurer and the whole of the ACTU delegation were missing from the House. In the lunchtime adjournment on that day, the Chairman of the CAI and I were summoned to the Prime Minister's office to be informed that it was all over, and that it would be announced after lunch that the government would commence work on a revised package. As we were ushered into the Prime Minister's office, we witnessed the end of a conversation between the Prime Minister and the Treasurer which was certainly not a friendly one. I don't have the evidence to describe it as a blazing row, but it seemed like one.

As we emerged, we became aware immediately that a meeting of the business groups had hurriedly assembled, and that it was seething with indignation that the business sector had been excluded from the final decision process. As joint chairmen of that meeting we had considerable difficulty in pursuading the delegates to return to the House to hear the Prime Minister's announcement.

In her book, *Keating – A Biography*, Edna Carew permits herself some fanciful speculation by suggesting that much of the blame for my remarks has been laid at the door of Sir Noel Foley, then Chairman of Westpac and a staunch Liberal Party member.[3] This was of course untrue, and an insult to the integrity of Sir Noel, of the Business Council itself and of my co-leaders of the Summit delegation, Sir Arvi Parbo and Eric Mayer.

The path of the taxation debate in Australia has been long and arduous, and the Taxation Summit was but one detour on which we got bogged down in the quest for consensus. We failed to resolve the issue of tax reform in 1985, and, with some remarkable political agility, we failed again in 1993 to accept the principle. I think we can now say that a broad-based consumption tax is a political 'no-no', but I am convinced that tax reform will remain on the political agenda. Diverse community groups will never agree on the balance of tax between, on the one hand, savings and investment, and on the other hand, spending, and we can only hope that, one day, a dynamic political figure will emerge to resolve the balance for us. I cannot imagine that we will drift to the stage where the IMF will need to come in and direct the necessary solutions.

As I have mentioned, I was privileged to serve as the second President of the Business Council, covering the years 1984 and 1985. It was obvious that the demands of the Presidency would place considerable pressure on my available time, and initially I declined to stand for election. However, the Council made a direct approach to the Board of the Bank. The Board had earlier been strongly in favour of the formation of the Confederation of Australian Industry, and as that organisation had not fulfilled its expectations, the Board was anxious to lend all possible support to the Business Council, and so my earlier decision was reversed.

Of course it would be wrong to say that there were no storms. When I assumed office, my predecessor had drawn attention to the government's substantial budget deficit by saying that his company would not begin to reinvest until the deficit fell to $5 billion. Both the Treasurer and the Prime Minister felt some sensitivity about his warning. And that sensitivity tended to overshadow some of the meetings we had with them around that time.

At the ordinary Business Council meeting which took place on Wednesday, 4 September 1985, at the Hilton Hotel in Sydney, one of the storms erupted. In the run up to that meeting, there had been discussions around the national wage case current at that time, and some of my council colleagues and I had been summoned to Canberra to be warned by the Treasurer and other relevant ministers not to be too soft in these negotiations. Accord Mark III was finalised and I was notified early in the morning of that day to expect a detailed communication from the Prime Minister, so that the Council could respond during the course of its meeting. The details duly arrived, and were remarkable in that they introduced the concept of the 3 per cent compulsory superannuation levy, and seemed in many respects to anticipate the final decision of the Court on the national wage case.

I found myself, as President of the Council, not only faced with a hostile reception to Accord Mark III from my Council colleagues, but saddled with the unpleasant duty of relaying the substance of that hostility to the Prime Minister by telephone. I don't know that the telephone wires actually melted, but I hardly needed the telephone to receive his message. Notwithstanding these periodical differences, the relationship with the Prime Minister and senior government ministers continued to be friendly and constructive, so the problems could at least be discussed if not always agreed. Even so, it became necessary occasionally to allow a day or two for cooling off.

Westpac was satisfied with the outcome of the Campbell and Martin Reports, but there were aspects of the government's economic management it did not like. One of the themes in our public documents was Australia's lack of international competitiveness. We argued that, while the financial sector had been opened up to competitive forces, unless the labour market and other areas of the economy were also deregulated, our competitiveness would continue to be eroded. It was to the government's credit that its partnership with the unions began to deliver industrial peace and restraint in union claims. We felt more could be done in this area, and I continued to press for more deregulation of other sectors of the economy through the Australian Bankers' Association and the Business Council. I was heartened when micro-economic reform was pushed up the political agenda.

The good working relationship between the Bank and the government later paid dividends when the issue of foreign banks was decided. I was impressed when I received a request from Bill Hayden, as Minister for Foreign Affairs, who wanted to meet and talk about deregulation. He said that he would be accompanied by three or four people, and in the end the five who came with him were from the Labor Party's Centre Left faction, which was led by him. The purpose of the discussion was to be sure that, as one of the leading banks in the country, we would be comfortable with the dramatic changes in policy which were likely to take place if foreign banks were admitted. They were concerned to see that the domestic banks would not be seriously disadvantaged.

The entry of foreign banks was one of the most significant events in Australia's financial history. But to say that there was no prior foreign bank presence in Australia is to perpetuate a myth. From time to time, particularly when a credit squeeze limited our loan making capacity and people wrote letters of complaint to newspapers, political notables would threaten to bring in the foreign banks to beef up competition. I recall one Coalition

Government minister saying in early 1983 that, if the local banks didn't smarten up and help the poor farmers, they would get some foreign banks in. I used to smile when I visualised the shocked expressions on the faces of people from Gulargambone or Goondiwindi when an exotic foreign bank opened, with a brand new manager fresh from Wall Street or the Avenue des Champs Elysées. Sometimes when the Wales, and later Westpac, sent a manager out from Sydney, those people would say, 'God, this one's fresh from the tram tracks.'

While it was true that there were only four major banks, the competition in the financial sector was quite healthy. In 1982 nearly one hundred foreign banks had representative offices in Australia. The interests of foreign banks in non-bank financial intermediaries operating in Australia were spread over seventy-four institutions. For them, the spur had been the investment opportunities associated with large resource projects in the late 1960s and early 1970s. As well, foreign banks rapidly became involved in offshore debt financing of Australian industry and government. With the exception of the Banque Nationale de Paris and the Bank of New Zealand, both of whom had been in Australia since the last century when licences were not required, there had been a long standing prohibition on foreign banks obtaining Australian banking licences. It was now effectively over. The lucky ones were no longer confined to representative offices. While lacking an Australian balance sheet, these offices proved sufficient to facilitate offshore loan assessment.

By 1982 foreign banks began to issue offshore letter-of-credit arrangements to Australian companies to facilitate their merchant bank subsidiaries. Through them foreign banks played a major role in the establishment of cash management trusts. I was aware of the benefits which could accrue to Australian development by an injection of additional resources and bank expertise, but I was equally aware that it would not take long for the foreign banks, given their familiarity with the Australian financial scene, to make strong inroads into our banking market.

At Westpac we were concerned that foreign trading banks would tend to confine their market penetration to the wholesale end of the market, leaving the costly collection of household deposits to existing domestic banks. We were also worried that unrestricted foreign bank entry in the early years after deregulation could unnecessarily fragment the institutional structure, or that overly aggressive competition could discourage new domestic entrants and lead to an unacceptable loss of resident ownership and control.

At that time, Westpac held the view that, given the limited ability which Australian banks had to meet existing foreign bank competition, licences should not be granted to non-residents unless or until regulations under which Australian banks operated were lifted. In a deregulated environment, the Bank would not oppose controlled entry of foreign banks in an orderly fashion. It did not mind the door being opened, but saw no need to rip it off its hinges.

There was a considerable amount of apprehension in the minds of Australian bankers whenever the subject of foreign competition came up. This sentiment was aptly expressed by one banker who said that, 'When you have a dog perpetually tied up on a chain and then let it off, you don't let a bunch of new savage dogs into the street at the same time.' Even the gentle riposte from the Bank of Tokyo that, 'It was not a savage dog, only Lassie come home' did not allay our fears. Lassie had been here before the war as the Yokohama Specie Bank, the former name of the Bank of Tokyo, and was now really coming home.

When in 1985 some seventeen banks were offered licences to operate in Australia, most Australian bankers were surprised – the door was indeed ripped off its hinges. But we had been given adequate warning of the need to accept competition as something which was inseparable from deregulation. The two had to go together. The period of grace gave us time to smarten up our own operations, develop new products, evaluate new strategies and invest in our mainstream operations. Our earlier merger with the Commercial Bank of Australia was a strategy now vindicated.

By 1985 we had crossed the great economic and political divide – from a highly regulated to a less regulated financial market environment, from a Coalition Government to a Labor Government and, furthermore, we were integrated more completely into global financial markets. The processes of deregulation, together with the new exchange rate environment, continued to offer new opportunities for domestic and international banking. For Westpac it was all go from then on.

10 IT WAS ALL GO FROM THEN ON

The jury is still out in its assessment of financial market deregulation and its impact on the so-called 'decade of the 1980s'. I suppose, twenty years from now, economic historians and other interested commentators will still be arguing about the pros and cons of the policy decision taken in a decade which ended in the worst economic collapse since the 1930s. One aspect on which the jury will not need to deliberate was the pace of activity. At the time I felt it was frenetic.

In one fell swoop, the number of banks operating in Australia had been doubled. The entry of foreign banks into Australia was one outcome of deregulation which brought lasting and tangible benefits to the financial sector. In our capital-hungry country, short of domestic savings, foreign capital inflow alleviated this shortage – although some would argue it permitted even more frenzied 'entrepreneurial' activity. The agreement by the country in which the foreign bank was domiciled to grant reciprocal rights to Australian banks was a condition of foreign bank entry. Reciprocity arrangements were a golden opportunity for us, and fitted into our corporate plan to become a global bank. We were determined also to establish a presence in the western Pacific consistent with Australia's aspirations in the region.

The Wales had long operated internationally, but one tangible benefit to flow on to Westpac from foreign bank entry to Australia in 1985 was the opportunity for greater international expansion. Over the years, the Wales had built up a wide network of correspondent banks all over the world. The strategy of correspondent banking relationships, rather than expansion abroad, probably arose to some extent from a more stringent regulatory environment; or in earlier years it arose from the colonial mentality. But the relationships we cultivated with correspondent banks were paramount in our international operations. Managers from the International Division responsible for our correspondent banking relationships travelled extensively to discuss with each correspondent bank the business exchanged, helped by a comprehensive set of statistics of all the banks' transactions in and out of the country. As can be imagined, in the pre-computer days, thousands of pieces of paper were sent from one corner of the world to another as reconciliation clerks worked in their respective banks to keep the accounts more or less straight. Our accounts with other banks were known as *nostro* accounts and their accounts with us were known as *vostro* accounts.

A legend of the 1950s told of an impasse in the reconciliation of the *nostro* and *vostro* accounts of Citibank in New York and Lloyds Bank in London which so worried Lloyds Bank that it sent two experienced officers to New York to sort it out. So pleased was Citibank with the result that it enticed the two Lloyds experts to stay with higher pay. The legend is hazy on the reaction of Lloyds Bank.

From the 1950s onwards, when the US investors came here to put up their factories and open up banking relationships, we got a great deal of business through our correspondent banks, because the US bank would notify us when one of their important clients was coming. We used to take the trouble to meet them at the airport, help them through the customs formalities and acquaint them with our banking facilities. During my time as Manager Sydney Office, I used to dread a visit from potential overseas customers when one of our infamous credit squeezes was on. After our International Division staff had extended such a warm welcome, in the pleasant atmosphere of tea and scones, I was the mug who had to tell them we had no money to lend, or that it would be difficult to provide a large amount of finance for a long-term investment.

Of course we needed foreign investment, and we had to encourage investors who wished to set up operations in Australia. The dilemma was that we wanted them to bring money with them, and not borrow our money for the purpose. On the other hand their natural desire was to borrow locally to test the market before they brought their own money in.

Correspondent relationships began to lose their impact in the middle 1970s when the foreign bank representative offices opened for business. But then, in 1980 or thereabouts, correspondent banking revived as we began to think of other reciprocal arrangements. Also, the other banks began to realise that certain banks were expert in their field; our strength was in preparing foreign exchange transactions and dealer transactions. But one difference was that price rather than the relationship became the driving force. The 'old boy' network was by then disappearing.

Although Asia was to become a major focal point for the Wales, our American representation, an initiative of Sir Robert Norman, was important. San Francisco was our original point of entry, but New York with its representation elevated to agency status in 1975 was a priority. The global oil crisis of 1973 focused attention on Australia's abundant energy resources, and on Houston, Texas which became known as the energy capital of the world. The important oil field in Bass Strait was a joint-venture between BHP and the Houston-based operations of Esso, and we considered it essential to have representation in Houston to provide the first port of call for potential investors in our energy resources. The office was opened in 1981. Our research on North America revealed the obvious: although we could hold our own in the North American market against intense competition, and in a market which was becoming increasingly self-contained, our success was likely to be limited.

As Australia's traditional links with London and Europe faded, the US dollar became more important to us as the medium for our international transactions, and so too did New York as a clearing house and as a base for our international treasury operations. The New York representative office opened in 1970 (for the second time in the Bank's history), and when it was upgraded to agency status in 1975 we were able to withdraw US correspondent bank arrangements and settle the growing volume of dollar transactions ourselves. At that time, the Standard Bank of South Africa confessed to us that a major factor in the establishment of their agency in New York at the turn of the century was that they had been appointed New York agent for the Bank of New South Wales. Their publicity and advertising at the time even boasted of that fact.

Our research on Asian markets also made me conscious of the potential interactions between countries in the Asia-Pacific region, including Australia, and the business opportunities flowing from them. The demand for multi-currency loans, sophisticated foreign exchange dealing and options for trade finance would grow as new markets opened up. As the regional economies 'took off', the prospects for Australia as a trading nation to participate more fully in the regional economy were bright. I felt that with careful preparation we should be there, and should get in early. AGC, our finance company subsidiary, already had a presence through a joint-venture established in 1963 in Malaysia. Faced with the expenses of running non-income producing representative offices, we reassessed our earlier approach and began to upgrade our international representation to provide the banking services our customers needed. In addition, I was much influenced by discussions in international forums such as the Pacific Basin Economic Committee (PBEC), and I suppose I was encouraged because of the regional prosperity. In 1985 the Asia-Pacific region generated about 45 per cent of world GNP, and trade expansion had been dynamic. With Japan emerging as regional leader, pulling its neighbours along with it, the region's share of world trade had grown from 33 per cent in 1975 to more than 40 per cent a decade later.

If I have had a mission in life, apart from promoting the Bank, it has been to promote the western Pacific as the growth area of the future. When asked by a European banker how Australia could make its way in Asia with its cultural background I said, 'It just goes to show how little Europeans appreciate what's happening in this part of the world. You just learn to live with those cultural barriers progressively being broken down. And there's a tremendous amount of Asian immigration into Australia now. It would be putting our heads in the sand to say that we couldn't adapt in the cultural sense to living with, trading with, and doing business with, the western Pacific.'

Australians have learnt much in recent times about developing business relationships in Asia, particularly with Japan and China. As I graduated to the senior ranks of the Bank, and in view of the importance of Australia's relationship with Japan, I expended a lot of effort in getting to know more about the country and in developing good relationships with senior businessmen and bankers. Shortly after my return from London in 1974, and only a few days after moving into my last house, I had to leave Molly to attend to the moving problems so that I could undertake my first visit to Japan. That visit extended over three weeks involving calls on banks and customers in Tokyo, Osaka, Nagoya and Hiroshima. It was to be the first of some twenty-five visits, and during that time I formed many friendships, some of which continue to this day.

As a result of my growing familiarity with Japan I became Vice President of the Australia-Japan Business Co-operation Committee, which met annually. I was also appointed by the government to its Consultative Committee on Relations with Japan. I remember the Treasury representative on the committee being quite visibly surprised at the size of the banking facilities we extended to Japanese companies operating in Australia in the early 1980s.

Because of the Bank's active interest in international business, I was automatically a member of the International Monetary Conference (IMC), a Washington-based body under the umbrella of the American Bankers' Association, and was elected to its Board in the middle 1980s for a term of three years. The regular annual meeting, confined to the chief executives of the top one hundred international banks in the world, was invaluable, because the meetings lasted for two-and-a-half to three days and provided excellent opportunities for frank exchanges on a variety of issues of concern to the international banking community.

It is interesting to reflect on the differences in bank reporting requirements between countries, particularly in the area of disclosure. In many instances, Australia included, and in contrast to the strict reporting requirements of the US Securities and Exchange Commission, banks did not then disclose their inner reserves. In one such discussion, the Hongkong Bank representative observed that the American banks undressed in public to an extent which was embarrassing to the rest of us. The short sharp response from his counterpart at Citibank was to say, in effect, the difference was quite simple – if he did not undress in public, he would go to jail.

Gerald Corrigan, Head of the Federal Reserve in New York, now retired, issued a warning to that elite group of bankers to the effect that, 'What you guys have to realise is that at the end of the day you can't hedge the whole bloody world.' That comment was made in the context of the growing volume of off-balance sheet transactions, or, in today's parlance, derivatives. The subsequent explosion in the use of derivatives, and their impact on the balance sheets of banks, speaks a lot for the foresight of Gerald Corrigan, a banker for whom I had a great admiration. Perhaps someone, some day, will be able to write the sequel to this phenomenon of the late twentieth century.

As Asia prospered, the pressure for greater representation in international forums such as the IMC increased, but not all of the would-be participants could be accommodated. In 1980 Masao Fujioka, Executive Director of the Export-Import Bank of Japan, and later President of the Asian Development Bank, invited me to join a small group to form the Asian-Pacific Bankers' Club. Modelled largely on the IMC, the chief executives in the Asian-Pacific Bankers' Club also focused on education and training for bankers, particularly on aspects of international finance. The Club was a useful forum in the Asia-Pacific context, and in 1983-84, as its President, I worked closely with Fujioka in arranging regional meetings to promote greater awareness of financing facilities in the developing countries of the region.

Probably one of the most frustrating experiences in my involvement on international committees was my failure to facilitate the admission of China to the membership of the Paris-based International Chamber of Commerce (ICC). The ICC, as the world business organisation, plays an important role in oiling the wheels of international trade and investment.

In 1987 I had been appointed for a three-year term to the Board of the ICC. As an Australian, with my proximity to and understanding of the Asian region, I think I had a different perspective than that of my more Eurocentric colleagues. Although the ICC is strongly free enterprise, I could see that as China became more integrated into the world economy and became more market-oriented, there should be a mechanism for its participation in international trade forums. How could we encourage China to adopt the normally accepted rules for international trade and investment if we kept them out of our tent? The opposite argument was that the ICC had to be sure that it was not admitting a member which was in effect quasi-government. Drawing on the resources of Westpac's Economic Department, I submitted a paper to the ICC advocating China's case. I felt that I was making some progress, because the ICC had invited representatives from the China International Trust and Investment Corporation (CITIC) to Stockholm to its next meeting. The fates were against me on this one. Four or five days before the meeting we had Tian'anmen Square and China's case was set back once again.

Balancing the demands of my international commitments with those in Australia often required careful juggling and reliance on the Bank's senior officers. Occasionally one of the juggling pins spun out of control, but on the whole the structure of the Bank – three senior executives responsible for services, retail, and corporate and international, plus a Deputy Managing Director – meant that I could go away for a few days. As Bill Reddin so colourfully put it: as Managing Director, I didn't need a desk – only a few chairs.

Aside from the rewards of visiting new places for the first time and the pleasure of being accompanied by Molly on some occasions, travel did not rank high in my enjoyment, as I did not particularly like flying on the busy international routes. Molly and I travelled together to the annual meetings of the World Bank/IMF, the International Monetary Conference and the Australia-Japan Business Co-operation Committee because they were traditionally mixed meetings. Molly's participation in the women's agenda helped to nurture the personal relationships I developed in my ten years at the helm. Of course there were countless visits on a solo basis.

Developing international business relations required a great deal of dedication and patience, but the results were worth the effort. When I was awarded the prize of *Asian Finance* magazine's Banker of the Year in 1984, jointly with the chief executive of the Korea Exchange Bank, In Yong Chung, I felt another step had been taken to integrate Westpac into the region. From my perspective, Westpac's involvement in the international community was one of our most significant strategies. We made many valuable contacts and friendships during those years. The value of these contacts would be difficult to quantify in this age of bottom-line-driven banking, but the benefits were still tangible.

When we were thinking about setting up in Japan, I received some excellent advice from a longstanding friend, a Japanese banker, about gaining access to the right people. I had become disillusioned with the lack of response to written submissions. He said there was only one way, and that was to keep calling, because they would be so polite they would always receive me. If they received me, they would make a note of it, and if I called often enough, I would become so well known that I would be the first one they would think of.

Acting on that advice, I established a regular visiting program to the Ministry of Finance in Tokyo to stake a claim for a banking licence as soon as the Australian authorities granted licences to our counterparts in Japan. I was always received with great courtesy at the Ministry, and I recall that they and the Bank of Japan, 'the central bank', were impressed by the fact that we had already taken an expensive lease of space some time earlier in anticipation of approval to open a branch. We did this because of demands on available space in Tokyo, and because we did not wish to suffer any delay once the approval was granted.

One of my vivid recollections of the time was my surprise to find such spartan conditions in the Ministry of Finance in Tokyo. The parquetry floors were showing signs of wear, the building was modest, and conditions were crowded and lacked privacy. The conditions provided for bureaucrats in this extraordinarily wealthy economy were in marked contrast to those one might have seen in Canberra.

With all the formalities completed, we opened our office in Tokyo on Friday, 4 October 1985. The opening took place only a few days after the so-called Plaza meeting of the group of seven international leaders, when the decision was taken to readjust global exchange rates. At the time of our opening in Tokyo the exchange rate was 210 Japanese yen to one Australian dollar. Less than a decade later, the Australian dollar is now worth under a third. It is incredible that despite this massive adjustment, Japan's external account remains in surplus while ours remains in deficit. However, having recruited specialist staff in Japan to manage our foreign exchange operations, we were able to cover the substantial set-up costs of the branch within a relatively short period of time. The most serious hiccup was a fairly major earth tremor on the night of our opening party, so severe that I was obliged to walk up several flights of stairs to my hotel room when the lifts ceased operating. In the wake of the opening cocktail reception and a subsequent get-together for the new staff, it was in all respects an exciting night. My ability to conquer the stairs illustrated either my restraint in celebrating the occasion or my staying power, because I always found it a demanding exercise to receive and farewell a couple of hundred guests in a foreign city.

Over the years the Bank's investments grew markedly, and continued to generate a good income. We had established our name in the region; we had built up a solid core of expertise, and understood the risks and dynamics of 'doing business in Asia'.

Another player in the complicated story of the 1980s was the 'market analyst'. During the first seven to eight years of my term as Managing Director, I hardly ever heard the term market analyst. This species began to become more and more aggressive in the middle 1980s, and it was with increasing frequency I heard the expression that 'we had to worry about the analysts'. I had some concern with their growing influence on our decision-making processes and I was concerned because the customary time horizon of the analyst was the next quarter or the next half year.

In this, Australia was not unusual. I can remember the chief executive of the Canadian Imperial Bank of Commerce, when addressing the Institute of Directors in Sydney, talking about the same development in Canada. He had had a meeting with a group of analysts who asked him about the next quarter. He suggested that they leave if their time horizon was limited to the next quarter, because his focus was on the next five to ten years, as was ours. It is my view that in some instances corporations have traded off underlying, long-term corporate strengths for short-term gains in order to satisfy the market analysts. Focus on the 'short-term' partly arose because of the fear of hostile takeovers.

I think it is unfortunate for business generally that higher percentages of shareholdings are now in the hands of professional fund managers, from whom the analysts earn their keep. The fund managers live in a highly competitive world, particularly with the expanding market of compulsory superannuation. Naturally they see their quarterly performance comparisons as their best marketing tool. In this environment the short-term profit potential in the share price of a company tends to outweigh the long-term prospects of the same company. Not surprisingly, the bigger, listed companies now feel obliged to employ professional investor relations experts capable of talking a common language with the analysts.

Of course there are competent and highly respected analysts, and of course I am not arguing against the need for efficiency or productivity reforms, but those reforms need to pass the test of customer-impact. In the reform process of the 1980s, I required a customer impact statement with submissions coming before the Bank's executive committee. The business of banking is about service, and it is about long-term customer relationships. Because banks enjoy some privileges recognised by a licence to conduct banking business, an element of public responsibility is also involved. It is difficult for an analyst to offset the abstracts of service, maintenance of long-term relationships and public responsibility against a range of profit or productivity ratios calculated from a range of companies listed on the stock exchange. However, those managing banks can be sure that higher profit and productivity ratios cannot be achieved forever without some adverse impact on the three abstracts mentioned: service, customer relationships and public responsibility. By the same token, they can be sure they will be marked down if they are perceived to be inefficient.

The takeover battles of the 1980s naturally involved Australian banks. No doubt there have been instances where banks were asked to participate in negotiations on behalf of one customer not always to the advantage of another customer. Usually, potential conflicts of interest were resolved with a minimum amount of discord. The period saw a major shift in the relationship between the corporate customer and the banks; in some cases the status quo in banking relationships was fundamentally, if not irreversibly, disturbed. The Bank's 1985 *Annual Report* attracted a lot of criticism because it featured three photographs. The first was of a Westpac Group Account Executive talking with two senior executives of

Molly and I with Sir Julius Chan, Prime Minister of Papua New Guinea, 15 December, 1980.

'The gentlemen of the Wales' succeeded.
The late Bill Mitchell, Weekend Australian, May 16-17, 1981.

I launch Australia's first EFTPOS terminal at Woolworths, Neutral Bay, 9 April, 1984.
Photo: Trevor Dallen, Fairfax Photo Library

I addressed the Petro - Pacific Conference at the Hilton Hotel, Melbourne, 1984.

The honour of Banker of the Year was bestowed upon me in 1985 and 1987. The covor of *Australian Business*, August 21, 1985.

The branch where it all started in 1940, in the Murray River port of Echuca.

55 years on...progress at the expense of character.

Capturing me for posterity – the tradition at the Wales for all Chief Executives.
Painting by Judy Cassab.

Back home at the Conargo pub in 1994.

It's still safe at midday on Conargo's CBD intersection in 1994!

Where it all finished...Westpac Head Office, 60 Martin Place, Sydney.

The authors: Bob White and Cecelia Clarke.

Adelaide Steamship Company – described as a long-standing banking relationship, and it was because it dated back to the last century. The second photograph was of Robert Holmes à Court, Chairman of Bell Resources, shown with Peter Alexander, Manager Project Finance. The third picture was of the home of Bell Resources in Perth, for which Westpac was the lead bank, managing a $US220 million Syndicated Revolving Euronote Issuance facility.

Such was the attitude of the day that BHP's Chairman expressed his concern to Westpac's Chairman about the publicity afforded to certain other customers of the Bank. The incident was distressing, because the Bank had never intended to give the public an impression that it favoured one customer over another. The two relevant customers had had an aggregate relationship with the Bank for more than a hundred years. All we were trying to do was to emphasise the value we placed on our long-term banking relationships, and our desire to build on them. But this episode was only a sign of things to come.

From a small start in Western Australia, Robert Holmes à Court developed and continued his association with the Bank. His early takeover of the Western Australian Woollen Mill was followed by Bell, a civil engineering and transport group in Western Australia. We followed Robert Holmes à Court through many of his activities, and subsequently he became, arguably, one of the Bank's most important corporate customers. Nevertheless, we declined to become a leader in his various earlier attempts at a BHP takeover until he had achieved a degree of success not previously thought possible. In building up a shareholding in BHP, and in the light of his substantial relationship with the Bank, particularly measured against the dominant Melbourne bank participation in the business of BHP, we felt obliged to accept a lead role in his final takeover bid. The amount was substantial, and we were aware the principle was of huge significance.

The subject was discussed at length in the Bank, and was considered at a special Board meeting. Ultimately it was decided that we had an obligation to our shareholders to go ahead. In May 1986 the Bank decided to lead a multi-currency line of $500 million for Bell Resources to support an amended offer by Bell for ordinary shares in BHP. It was decided that I should inform the Managing

Director of BHP, immediately before the takeover bid was announced, and explain our reasons. It was not a task I anticipated with a great deal of pleasure. All hell broke loose, and the hostility with which my information was received confirmed my worst fears. We did not enjoy a large relationship with BHP, but from that day we enjoyed no relationship until subsequent events had cooled the atmosphere.

Westpac became more focused on the future. The basic planning document, the 'medium-term' plan, looked three years ahead, concentrating on expanding our global network based on our core strengths. It was never our intention to buy a gold bullion dealer in London or a securities dealer in the USA. In 1986, however, when these two 'out of plan' opportunities arose, we carefully assessed them (or so we thought) in order to take advantage of the prospective good business. The result of these unplanned acquisitions was mixed. Both organisations developed problems. One was a success despite some initial cross-border management problems and the other a dismal failure when the operating environment of the US government securities market was changed.

Both episodes provide illustrations of managing from a distance. I am not saying that an organisation should never stray from its core business, although the two out-of-plan acquisitions demonstrated the risks of not sticking to one's knitting. The Bank had, with reasonable success, long concentrated on diversifying into non-regulated activities to escape from the burden of regulation. In the deregulated environment perhaps we failed to appreciate that non-core activities required much more careful analysis than was otherwise the case, particularly when they were based overseas. It is crucial that management fully appreciates the local operating environment. I think there is also an argument that strategists/ planners who bring forward plans for acquisitions, should not then also be involved with implementation if a regime of checks and balances is to be maintained.

The gold market has traditionally been an important market in the Australian economy. In 1986 this market was strong, and mines which had hitherto been abandoned came alive again. Westpac was already in the business of dealing in gold bullion, having acquired in 1983-84 a 75 per cent interest in a bullion dealer, Mase. Warren Magi, the Managing Director, was a founder of Mase.

The London Gold Ring, of which Johnson Matthey Bank (JMB) was one of five members, handled a substantial slice of the South African gold production. In an almost coffee shop arrangement, where the players talked each morning and fixed the price, gold was sold through a 'fixing mechanism'. The business was split between the five members, with JMB's share at about 20 per cent. It was a privileged market position. London, it was believed, controlled as much as 50 per cent of the bullion trade, with the bulk of the residue being handled in Switzerland. London's pre-eminence was being threatened by New York, Hong Kong and the Swiss.

In 1984 JMB nearly collapsed, and the Bank of England took it over. In 1986, having completed the rescue operation, the Bank of England sought to dispose of JMB and invited interest from Westpac. What better neutral solution than an Australian bank? It seemed like a good fit. The purchase, which took Westpac to the heart of the gold business in London, gave us membership of the London Gold Ring, and an opportunity to develop important relationships with central banks around the world. I thought the invitation was an accolade.

Unlike its Australian counterpart, the Bank of England takes a more active role in financial market governance. For example, it was well known around the City that, as a bank, if you 'were sent for', you were in trouble. Not long after my arrival in England in 1972, the Wales's Deputy Chief Manager, Bob Norman,* and I went to the Bank of England to see the Supervisor about a special purpose subsidiary which we were contemplating. While we were sitting in the waiting room someone we knew from one of the foreign banks arrived. In greeting our colleague, Bob Norman almost instinctively said, 'We have not been sent for.'

The Bank of England had (and probably still has) an old boys' network, which was regarded as the leading employment agency in the London financial markets. Foreign banks always had some bloke who understood how it all operated. When, for

* Not to be confused with Sir Robert Norman.

example, a foreign bank opened shop, the Bank of England was keen to ensure the new bank had the required local expertise. It was often remarked that the Bank would say something like, 'Your number two or three will be so and so; he is retiring in the next few months.'

Having mounted its rescue operation of JMB, the Bank of England reverted to its normal supervisory role – a policy known as 'four eyes'. This colourful phrase refers to the Bank of England's policy that in a licensed bank at least two people – four eyes – should be in charge of decision making, particularly credit decisions.

Westpac became the owner of JMB, and appointed the manager of Mase-Westpac Australia, Warren Magi, to be Managing Director of the new Mase-Westpac Ltd., now a London licensed bank with a business scope considerably broader than his Australian operation. The Chairman was to be David Murison, then about to retire from his role as Westpac's chief executive in the UK and Europe.

The sudden illness of David Murison in June of 1986, more or less at the outset of the new ownership, was most unfortunate, and L.T.G. (George) Preston was appointed Acting Chairman. George Preston was an 'elder statesman' of the London banking community, with extensive experience in the Bank of England. He had been working on the JMB operation on behalf of the Bank of England, and we retained his services as a member of the Board of the newly named Mase-Westpac Ltd. His acting appointment seemed to be the best solution to a sudden problem in this new venture a long way from home, particularly with a chief executive who was strange to London, and from a non-banking background. The contrast between George Preston and Warren Magi was marked. Preston was twice Magi's age, and probably three times more conservative than the energetic and imaginative bullion dealer. The newly arrived Australian, a non-banker, suddenly found himself responsible to an experienced London banker as Chairman.

The responsible executives in Sydney also did not fully appreciate that Mase-Westpac, as a London licensed bank, was quite a different animal from Mase-Westpac Australia, where the reporting line was short and direct. This difference led to a failure to appreciate the role of the London Board Chairman and the relationship with the Bank of England. On the other hand, the newly designated London Chairman, with his long experience in London and in the Bank of England, and having nurtured this bullion bank through its intensive care period, was in no doubt whatsoever about his responsibilities and what the reporting lines should be.

Had I had an inkling of what was going on, I would have expected a telephone call from George Preston to warn me that he would probably be obliged to surrender his role as Chairman. When it came, it was a nasty shock. I did not hesitate to make a hastily organised trip to London in July 1986. Since JMB had already been in intensive care at the Bank of England, and since the Bank of England had trusted one of its favourite sons (Westpac) to take it over, the prospect of a problem sent shivers down my spine.

After I arrived in London, I began to appreciate the situation more fully. When Mase-Westpac had been set up, insufficient attention had been paid to the organisational structure. The new Managing Director was given a direct reporting line to Sydney, rather than reporting through his Chairman. He also had a 'dotted line' responsibility to the Westpac General Manager, European Division. As expected, Warren Magi's view, based on his brief from Sydney, was that the real power rested with him and his seniors in Sydney. Apart from a monthly Board meeting, his impression was that he needed to have little other contact with the Chairman of Mase-Westpac unless the Chairman had to be briefed on a particular matter.

In briefing him, the senior executives in Westpac Sydney also had apparently formed an incomplete view of what the responsibilities of the Chairman of Mase-Westpac should be, further compounding the problem of woolly reporting lines. Their brief to the Managing Director of Mase-Westpac sums it up well: 'No doubt it could be expected that the Chairman would be in a position to be able to give guidance to the Chief Executive Officer and to his fellow directors.' In other words, the Chairman's role would be largely ceremonial, and therefore in conflict with the Bank of

England's policy of 'four eyes'. The Chairman should have been given a more active role and the reporting line should have been from Magi through the Chairman to Sydney.

One problem always seems to lead to others. The Bank of England, well aware of the differences, expressed its concerns at a meeting in July 1986 particularly on the requirement that at least two individuals effectively direct the business (the four eyes policy). Mase-Westpac, as it was then operating, did not meet that requirement and the Bank of England was also worried about the credit committee. It is unusual for the chief executive officer of a bank to chair credit committees, and it was contrary to the customary arm's length independence. The checks and balances provided by an independent credit committee had been undermined.

There was an enormous benefit in my being on the spot and speaking individually to all the parties concerned. The episode convinced me that when serious disputes arise between senior executives, it is the responsibility of the 'top person' to become involved, to get his or her hands dirty. However, not everyone agreed with that approach, as I learnt later. The important sequel is that Mase-Westpac went on to be a successful business and I got the impression that the Bank of England appreciated the concern acknowledged in the form of my personal visit.

The problems involved in the management of multinational businesses have loomed large in recent times as conglomerates grapple with the conflict between management by business units and management by geographic units. The smooth-sounding solution is matrix management. Whether that will be adequate to meet the competing requirements of national and corporate sovereignty may well be the subject of another book.

In 1985-86 investment banking was the flavour of the month (although the definition of investment banking was imprecise). The Bank's executive committee was of the view that the future growth in international banking would be in institutions which could put together business arrangements on a broader scale than just of lending. It was a view that I shared. Anxious to explore possibilities in this area, we engaged a consultant to investigate possible investment banking activities. Our investigations revealed that Westpac could not hope to compete globally as an investment bank. However, we took a modest and low risk approach and appointed another lateral recruit to be General Manager, Investment Banking in London. His job was to explore the possibilities of growing our investment banking business.

In 1986 when the opportunity arose to purchase the US-based William E. Pollock Government Securities, Inc., the level of support in the Bank was quite strong. The Australian government securities market, unlike that in the United States, was straightforward. In fact, it was compulsory for Australian savings banks to invest in government securities under licensing requirements. Dealing in US government securities was a different story.

Pollock was one of a select group of about forty bond dealers recognised by the US Federal Reserve authorities in New York as primary dealers. This arrangement with the US Fed to 'recognise' them and to limit their numbers conferred considerable advantage on those organisations. Because of the special privileges they enjoyed as members of this group, they attracted a high premium. A further underlying advantage for Pollock was an abundant supply of government securities. The US government had a huge deficit, and it seemed likely that its deficit funding policy would not change in the near future, particularly as large buyers of government securities could hardly avoid US government stock.

In conjunction with our American adviser, the executive in charge of Research and Planning in Sydney began our investigations. The terms of the sale were that it would be a 100 per cent buy-out, not a joint-venture. The owners set the price: it was a goodwill component of 100 per cent; that is, two times the book value. Although the management of Pollock would be contracted to stay on, they would not retain any equity. We concluded that here was an opportunity to buy another key component of an investment banking operation. During our investigations we discovered that a major British bank was also in the market to acquire Pollock. The proprietors of Pollock had established a price, and price therefore was not a factor in the competitive bids.

At the conclusion of our negotiations, Westpac was selected as the favoured purchaser. Immediately following the announcement of that decision, I had a telephone call from the Chairman and Chief Executive Officer of the other bank, expressing regret and suggesting we might consider a joint-venture. They were very keen; perhaps our second mistake in this episode was in not going with them.

Even with some of the best brain power in banking and finance, errors occur. Our fundamental approach to acquisitions was that we would never 'bet the Bank', and although the acquisition of Pollock was a disaster, it was by no means a major disaster. We made two fundamental errors. First, none of our strategists had examined the risk of what would happen if the operating environment changed – that is, if our market position was no longer privileged. We had paid so much for an operation based on that market advantage, yet we did not factor the risk of the ground rules changing into our purchase price, and into our future income stream, and as a result the purchase price was too high.

A change in the ground rules is precisely what happened. About a year after we became the owners of Pollock, the US government changed the operating framework of the bond market. With the admission of a number of other dealers to the market, Pollock's major market advantage was destroyed. The proposition to acquire Pollock had been strongly supported by those on the spot who apparently did not recognise the imminent change in the rules and the impact that would have on the operations in the market.

In the aftermath of my retirement, I believed that the second error was that those concerned with the management of Pollock appeared not to accept the consequences of the new operating environment. At the end of 1986 it was an acquisition that attracted the value of twice the net tangible assets. In 1990 it could not attract a buyer and was closed down. By acquiring Pollock, Westpac joined the club of other solid and reliable organisations which made expensive mistakes in the so-called investment banking arena.

Throughout a good part of my career, my overwhelming preoccupation was the emphasis on the safety of lending. I had vivid recollections of the manner in which lending authorities were delegated so as to avoid the concentration of too much power in one individual but especially to set up a dividing line between the customer seeking to borrow and the officer with the authority to approve. This was an example of the elementary 'checks and balances' concept or, if you like, a manifestation of the Bank of England's 'four eyes' dictum, developed from long experience which teaches that there are inherent risks in the business of banking or lending money.

Amid cries of protest about the implications of the word 'control', a new division, Credit Policy and Control, was established in 1984, under the late Frank Ward, within the Corporate and International Banking Group. Its charter was to establish a credit policy and the mechanisms for controlling a whole range of exposures through maximum limits for any one individual group; for countries graded in a range of A to F; for international banks; and for industry groupings, etc. Frank was also to review delegated authority levels and other approval processes through the executive committee for ultimate approval by the Board.

To facilitate the global operations of the Bank's treasury, a global limits system had been established with on-line access to all of the treasury and dealing operations of the Bank now spread throughout the world. To ensure the independence of the credit process, neither the chief executive officer nor the executive committee had any lending authority. It was unfortunate that the AGC group, only partly owned, remained outside the jurisdiction of the Credit Policy and Control Division.

As we pursued policies to stay abreast of the developing sophisticated lending techniques and to ensure that we managed our big account relationships professionally, the data prepared by Frank Ward's new division showed that our risks and our exposures were increasing. I came to the conclusion that it was therefore necessary to enhance the independence and standing of the Credit Policy and Control Division by lifting it out of the Corporate and International Business Group and giving it bank-wide jurisdiction reporting directly to me. I had concluded that an independent and professional credit policy and control unit was essential to balance the pressures on account managers, to perform by increasing their loans or meeting their targets, against, prudential requirements established by the Bank's overall culture. Those pressures on the account manager could also be driven by the persuasive power of a high revenue producing customer or the bonus incentive which would be determined by his boss. Of course, there would be tensions in resolving these conflicts but these would be better managed if the approval process were independent and seen to be so.

There were strong protests about the proposal to elevate the Credit Policy and Control Division to a direct reporting line to the Managing Director, and the change was not achieved until late 1986.

The Economic Department, which was responsible for economic input to the credit policy function, particularly in respect of country and industry exposures, was briefed to be objective in its assessments and not to be influenced by the Bank's marketing goals. My co-author, as a Westpac country risk economist, recalls in the late 1980s an overture to regrade a 'country risk' to facilitate a proposal essential to the achievement of the lending officer's target. If the concept of a professional and independent credit approval process is not underwritten by the Board and the chief executive officer, the pressures on the credit officer will ensure that he or she quickly becomes less effective. It is my judgment that the commitment of the Board and the chief executive officer to the independence of the process was overtaken by the commitment to growth following my retirement at the end of 1987.

Looking back to the environment of the early 1980s, deregulation was a global phenomenon which imposed tremendous pressures on banks as they strived to compete. As I headed towards the end of my career, I witnessed developments which were threatening the existence of many of the big banks of the world like the Continental Illinois Bank, the Bank of America, the First National Bank of Chicago and the Midland Bank. While I was not free of worries, I had no inkling that Westpac could face the risk of joining that group. The thrust into Asia and the USA had been relatively smooth, the long established London business was struggling to find a future but the Mase-Westpac acquisition promised potential. The Pollock acquisition was to be a costly mistake. Steps were in hand to apply the concept of checks and balances to the future 'all go' environment of the rest of the 1980s and the independence of the Credit Policy and Control Division was an important, although not lasting, component of that concept.

THE LEADING EDGE OF TECHNOLOGY IS A MOVING TARGET

11

In reviewing published material for this book, I was puzzled to find that the Bank's computer technology project, CS90 (Core Systems for the 1990s), was perceived to have been fanned by the financial euphoria of the 1980s. This was not the case. The driving force for the large investment lay at the heart of the Bank's determination to enhance its competitiveness and profitability.

Every basic payment transaction is really a communication function. A cheque is a form of communication with a bank to pay somebody. Having had first hand experience with the problems of too much paper I have always been able to see the advantages of the computer. It seemed sensible to substitute electronic transactions for paper and having taken this view, to continue with our program of investment in technology. Technological applications have limited the growth of paper-based transactions and because of this we have been able to communicate more efficiently with our customers. Being on the leading edge of technology was part and parcel of staying on top.

The ledger system is the life blood of a bank. When I first joined the Bank fully bound ledgers were posted by hand, as they had been since the Bank opened for business. For reasons of checking accuracy and preventing fraud, the work was checked by two officers other than the ledgerkeeper. The process known as the 'call-over' was an early morning daily ritual in every branch of the Bank in pre-machine days. I can picture in my mind the familiar sight of the manager standing at the ledger, and the second officer beside him with the cheques calling the details of each cheque and each deposit. The only major difference as we moved into the 1940s was that the bound ledger book had been replaced by a loose leaf book which was locked and new sheets, which were numbered, had to be signed for. But the processing system had not really changed.

As the volume of paper grew in the post-war period, the Bank moved into machine posted ledgers.

As Assistant Manager Sydney Office in 1964, I saw we were encountering more and more serious problems in coping with paper. In addition to a large savings bank, the 25 000 customer accounts made that branch larger than the Bank of Adelaide. Accounts were processed by twenty ledger sets on the ground floor of the building. Twenty ledger sets meant twenty ledger machines, twenty statement machines and a ledger examiner for each set. Some 100 people worked just to process this ever increasing volume of paper. Because of the building design, ventilation and light were poor to say nothing of the noise. With ever increasing volumes of cheques that had to be processed on the day of presentation, bottlenecks occurred and when this happened ledgerkeepers often received much of the criticism. The sharp escalation in the number of cheques at the month's end when most people paid their bills had to be seen to be believed. Ultimately the number of people needed to handle the ever growing volume of paper would outgrow the capacity of our buildings.

In the late 1950s and early 1960s, a technological innovation changed the face of banking across the world. Specially designed numerals printed in ink containing iron particles, could be read at high speed from small documents. Magnetic Ink Character Recognition (MICR) special font numerals, when printed on the bottom of cheques, allowed nearly all the information on the voucher to be read by a computer. High speed MICR Reader/Sorters were developed to read and sort cheques and other vouchers at speeds of up to 700 a minute. These highly sophisticated machines were the Boeing 707s of the banking industry and they propelled the banks into computer technology more deeply than most other industries.

When the Bank's first computer, FABACUS (First Australian Banks' Accounting Computer Used in Sydney) was introduced in 1964, I could see the immediate benefit to the ledger system, to customers and to the people who worked in the Bank. Even this primitive system provided better and faster information. It was the first great leap forward in the Bank's technological progress. Because computer programing was in its infancy, the FABACUS programs were written by a group of keen, young bank officers who had been seconded from the business side of the Bank to its fledgling technology section. Their major strength was that they combined hands-on banking experience with technological competency. It was a credit to them that the ledger system they built held together for so many years. It was also amazing that until the addition of some new computers in 1970-71, we ran the Bank on 64K of memory, and although the comparison is not strictly valid, that is less capacity than some personal computers have in the 1990s. Within a decade of installing FABACUS most cheque sorting, account updating, interest calculation, fees collection, statistics gathering and customer statement preparation were done by computer.

The first plastic card to be issued by the Bank was 'Bankcard' which was initiated in October 1974 by a co-operative of all banks. It was the first and last credit card issued on an unsolicited basis to customers of all banks. Its wide distribution and acceptance guaranteed its success which resulted in a dramatic impact on peoples' lives and their shopping habits.

In May 1980 the Bank crossed a major divide into electronic banking when it introduced automatic teller machines (ATMs) marketed under the name 'Handybank' at twenty-five selected locations. 'Handycard' was issued to access the machines. The computer-linked facility enabled customers to perform many banking transactions, notably deposits and withdrawals, on a 16-hours-a-day and 7-days-a-week basis. So readily did our customers accept this innovation that by late 1984, 274 ATMs were handling more than two million money transfers per month. About the same time we continued to make great strides with the extension of front office customer service terminals allowing customers to make paperless transactions at all branch counters.

Throughout 1983 our corporate image advertising told the Australian public, 'We're rolling our sleeves up' – and then we announced what we had up our sleeves. It was exciting to work in a Bank that was excelling in the application of technology.

The point of sale terminal was to follow. The problem of transporting cash was huge, the costs to the customer and the Bank of delivering cash economically and safely were rising. We envisaged that point of sale terminals (EFTPOS) would reduce the volume of cash transactions while at the same time satisfying the basic transactional needs of our customers simply, conveniently and reliably. They could be used Australia-wide in major retail outlets such as Woolworths, Dick Smith, Food Plus, BP and Amoco service stations.

We hit the mark with EFTPOS. It was an outstanding example of a new service widely accepted by customers and by 1988 35 per cent of the Bank's total transactions were electronic – up from 16.9 per cent in 1984. I launched Australia's first EFTPOS terminal at 11.00 a.m. on 9 April 1984 at the Woolworths supermarket, Neutral Bay, by wheeling a trolley of goods up to the check-out. I remember the occasion very well because Ron Friend, who taught me mathematics in Year 10 at Deniliquin, came forward to introduce himself. I had not seen him in forty-seven years. I could picture myself in 1937 in the classroom at the Deniliquin Intermediate High School sitting at the old fashioned desk, not a calculator in sight, blackboard out front, without even a dream that I would initiate Australia's first EFTPOS transaction.

Coincidental with the expansion in the ATM network, extension of front office terminals in the branch network and the introduction of EFTPOS terminals in retail stores, the Bank made further strides in 1984 in establishing Westpac's proprietary cards: the Westpac MasterCard, a combined credit and debit card for international and domestic use, and the WestpacCard, a debit card, with each card providing access to the full national Electronic Banking System. At that stage there were 1.6 million Westpac cards on issue. The slogan was 'The card is the bank and the bank is Westpac.'

With deregulation well under way, the customer of yesteryear with his or her cheque account was transformed into a customer with a range of diverse interests serviced by the bank, for example a current or cheque account, a savings account, a fixed interest loan, a bill acceptance line, a superannuation account, a cash management account, etc. But we did not have a common data base to give us the total customer profile. In any event, we knew that the product range would keep on changing. There was no other answer but a total revamp if we were to cope with management information needs for the new products which were emerging in the new financial market environment.

The major revamp was approved in 1985 and called 'Domestic Core System'. The Domestic Core System was a complex and radical step forward in technology applications for the finance industry. With a huge network of branches connected to a central computer, we envisaged a sophisticated communication system which could be used to transmit many kinds of information and instructions and which was related to more than just banking. I was all for it.

By August 1987 the core systems project had evolved in complexity and the Bank announced a major program of technology investment aimed at replacing and consolidating the Bank's independent computer software systems into a single integrated system. The project, known as Core Systems 90 (CS90), had the potential to revolutionise the delivery of financial products thereby increasing the Bank's overall capacity to do business while holding down operating costs. The system was to be jointly developed by Westpac and the Federal Systems Division of IBM. Based on the concept of 'reusable modules', CS90 would allow much greater flexibility in the development of new products than was possible with the existing systems. We forecast that the Bank's customers would see the first benefits of the project in the second half of 1988.

In proceeding with CS90, Westpac was breaking new ground in two important areas. We were trying to build an engine for all future business applications and secondly we were trying to build an integrated system where all parts could interact. Because of the amount of new technology and early difficulties with project management, we encountered problems in the early stages with timing and quality, much to the disappointment of many in the Bank's business area. In addition to technical problems, there was a certain level of dissociation by the business side of the Bank from the project. This was in part, a legacy of a cultural rift in the Bank which began in the 1960s when computers were first introduced. One group believed in computers and worked hard to make sure their introduction was successful. The other group did not believe in computers. With CS90 the lack of support by this latter group was partly due to nervousness and a rising sense of frustration with technical problems and a lagging schedule.

Yet input from the business side of the Bank was a critical element in the project. In the earlier stages of the Bank's technological systems development, the front line bankers developed the computer programs and understood their complexities, such as they were. In contrast, with the Bank's later computer technology there was a separation of tasks. The technical side was left to the computer technologists specially recruited for their expertise; although these might have been regarded as the elite, they were nevertheless in need of much help not only from the business side in designing the new systems but from their predecessors. This arrangement was less successful than using technologists with hands-on banking experience. Although many of the elements of CS90 were successfully introduced, in some instances it proved too difficult for the business side to describe what they wanted from the system and for the systems people to deliver the goods.

More importantly, if there is a plan for something new, innovative or partly experimental, it is more attractive to a conservative banker to sit back and wait rather than move out in the front with support. What I learnt from this experience is that systems development projects are as important as the business side of a bank and must be both understood and championed by the Top Team. At times I was unnerved by the glazed expressions of some of my colleagues and in the boardroom, when presentations on systems development were made. I could sense that their lack of understanding of the project and interest would not work in favour of CS90. By the time I had retired as chief executive officer, we had a sophisticated distribution system with on-line front office terminals in every branch, 1000 teller machines and a growing bank of EFTPOS terminals successfully serviced by a central computer in Sydney but we had not completed the core systems project. With my retirement and the retirement a few months later of Peter Douglas, Chief General Manager Management Services, the project lost its two senior level champions.

I sensed a growing disenchantment with CS90. I was left in no doubt about its future directions when, at the Board meeting on 15 June 1990, the Chairman foreshadowed the appointment of consultants to look at various operations. In an implied criticism of CS90, he strongly endorsed an observation from another director that 'The leading edge of technology is a moving target'. I found the comment mind boggling because it was somewhat akin to saying 'The sun rises every day.' The policy implication of this statement was that the Bank should no longer be a leader; it should be a follower – hopefully a fast one. Without a champion, and particularly at the Board level, it was not surprising that as the level of investment and commitment dropped off, the total development of CS90 eventually met its demise.

It is of course difficult to make a judgement in hindsight on CS90. It delivered a number of successful releases such as account opening, term deposits, interest bearing deposits, personal loans and the customer information system which emerged as the ongoing substitute. Perhaps I can sum it up by saying: If you are with it, you will make some mistakes; if you are not, you will fall behind.

One can but wonder what sort of world we would be living in today if the leading edge of technology was *not* a moving target!

SKIRMISHES ON THE LABOUR FRONT

12

One of the lessons that I learnt during my fifty years in banking is that you can become overpowered by the formality, and even by the legality, of the industrial relations structure to the point where you forget the concerns of the people for whose benefit the structure was designed. Relations between employers and the people who are the backbone of organisations have often been fraught with complexities and contradictions.

In banking, union activity and membership did not begin seriously until the 1920s, and, probably because of the relative conservatism of bank employees and the generally favourable employment terms and conditions provided by banks, employer/employee relationships were traditionally stable.

In the 1970s and 1980s employers and employees in the banking sector have grappled with technological change, financial market restructuring and the changes in tax laws arising from the government's efforts to raise taxation revenues without introducing a consumption tax. Naturally, the Bank did not always see eye to eye with its employees or with their representatives, the union. But from time to time industrial issues and the manner in which they were managed prompted me to ask: whose interests are being served? Is it the people or is it the so called 'industrial relations club'? Being a people-oriented person, I sometimes found myself concluding that the people got the short stick.

As a fledgling bank officer in the early 1940s from a background which was certainly not privileged, I was neutral towards the union movement. I was of course ambitious to make something of my life, but I saw that as something which I alone could achieve. However, I joined the Australian Bank Officials' Association (ABOA) in 1941, and remained a passive member throughout the war and until the Association decided not to fight the government's attempt to nationalise the banks. It has never been easy to resign from a union in Australia, so I had to wait until my transfer to London in 1955 before I could resign. In the post-war period I was not attracted to the union movement because of continuing industrial disruption, the influence of communists in key positions in some unions, and because of the general satisfaction I had with my employer. In that period the Bank, of its own volition, had introduced a medical benefits scheme for its staff and a third superannuation scheme for its wages staff – it already had long established such a scheme for men and women on the salaried staff.

As a result of my service in the army, I had developed a strong sensitivity to the importance of people relationships in any form of activity. The memories of war-time life in the Northern Territory had provided me with ample opportunity to observe patterns of behaviour and the degree to which those patterns could be influenced by leadership. In that environment, particularly, I had time to assess the leadership styles of the officers to determine what made some of them more effective than others.

On our arrival in the Northern Territory our unit acquired a new, humourless commanding officer (CO) whose main concerns were with the 'trappings' of the job – the staff car, the uniform. His ability to interface with the troops from behind his dark glasses was about zero. We had a little dog which we had adopted as our mascot. Private Sox, so named because he chewed socks, was given an identity disc to hang around his neck similar to that provided to the rest of us. The disc was engraved with his rank, name and blood group, and for obscure reasons the same regimental number as our commanding officer. On an inspection one day, the CO noticed the disc and his curiosity drove him to examine the engraving – all hell broke loose. Had that man, the leader, been able to share the joke with his troops, his standing with them would have risen immeasurably.

The more effective leaders were able to lead their peers and subordinates into believing that working together in an environment of mutual satisfaction was more productive than working in an atmosphere of friction. Whether such leaders were conscious of their management styles I do not know, but I do know they achieved good results. The less effective officers, in contrast, sought to impose their will and to extend their authority in an autocratic style.

In the days leading to the peace with Japan, the army called for volunteers to undertake a crash course in the Japanese language, and then to join the British Commonwealth Occupation Force in Japan. What a wonderful opportunity, I thought. I had had three years service with my unit, most of it in Darwin. I had reached the exalted rank of Lance Sergeant. With the war drawing to a close, the unit would undoubtedly wind down, leaving me undecided about the future, particularly as I felt I had exhausted my prospects. Without hesitation, I volunteered for the Japanese assignment. I then was called before the commanding officer, given a lecture about 'deserting the ship', and informed that my application would not go forward. Leadership is about building individuals and certainly not about tearing them down. That CO's style was in stark contrast to that of his predecessor. Clem Usher, our unit's original leader, set about training, building teams, injecting pride and discipline by encouraging the troops to think that their unit was among the best, if not the best. Fifty years later the shrinking residue of that small army unit marches down St Kilda Road in Melbourne on Anzac Day behind a banner which says 'Usher's Mob'. The name of Clem Usher's successor never gets a mention. Such are the measures of success and failure in the management of people.

I was able to test some of my theories in the time I occupied the position of personnel officer in the Victorian division of the Bank prior to my London transfer, but my memories of that period are dominated by the harmony of people relations in the Bank and the comfortable and satisfying personal relationships which I enjoyed.

On arriving in London, I discovered that the 'people' scene was in stark contrast. London in 1955 was still recovering from the impact of the war, and the Bank people felt they were not as well treated in comparison with others. Their pay and conditions were influenced by the 'Sydney' approach, and were thus not necessarily equal to or ahead of their counterparts in other London banks. As they saw it, their conditions should have taken into account the impact of the war, the different cost of living, and the more limited career prospects which were part of working for such a small bank away from the home base. I sympathised with them, and my conclusion was that the situation was exacerbated by expatriate managers who dominated the personnel function in London, and by personnel managers based in Sydney. I was disturbed by what I perceived to be the adoption of the worst features of British 'people management' practices, and ironically I also sympathised with the staff because they lacked a representative body to speak for them. Only a few of the staff were members of the National Union of Bank Employees, and that union was heavily pre-occupied with the relatively gigantic local banks.

On my return to Australia in 1958, I discovered that the local scene was also changing. There was a growing desire both on the part of the Bank and of many concerned members of its staff for a separate Bank of New South Wales Union. Shortly after my return, the first step in that direction occurred with the formation of the Wales Staff Council. In view of my then recent experience, I was asked to be a quasi-representative of the London staff at the inaugural meeting, and as a result the London staff later formed their own staff association.

The principal difficulty in the development of a separate Wales union lay in the formal structure of the Australian industrial relations system, with awards carrying the imprimatur of the Arbitration Court determining a whole range of minimum conditions of employment in areas such as rates of pay, hours of work, overtime rates and holidays. We perceived that the establishment of a separate Bank of New South Wales award through the Court would be a difficult, if not impossible, process and so the Wales Staff Council was an informal body, not recognised by the Court. It was restricted in its consultations with the Bank to matters outside the award, such as mobility involving change of house, education of children of officers moved to remote country areas, superannuation, and other fringe benefits.

The ABOA was also changing, or becoming more 'hairy chested'. The old system of separate associations in the states was discontinued when the Melbourne-based ABOA, the only one registered in the federal jurisdiction, acquired the others and later changed its name to the Australian Bank Employees Union (ABEU).

A union of employees rather than an association of officials seemed to be more appropriate terminology for the future. In the eyes of the conservative bankers, the unthinkable occurred when it affiliated with the Australian Council of Trade Unions (ACTU). The banks were then also part of a complementary formal structure through the Banks' Industrial Relations Committee (BIRC), loosely affiliated with the Australian Bankers' Association.

It is not surprising that industrial confrontation has become a feature in the skirmishing from which awards have evolved. Economic expansion increased the pressure from unions for a bigger share of the cake, or for better terms and conditions, and those pressures provided opportunities for employees of the communist persuasion to advance to key positions in the unions. The politicians were divided in their approach, and in some cases even the unions fought to protect themselves from communist influence. Victoria, probably because of its wider industrial base, was the principal centre for industrial disputes and the home of political divisions.

Such is the adversarial system based on confrontation. Over the years the system has become more sophisticated; both parties developed expertise in the so-called practice of industrial relations, becoming capable of speaking and negotiating with their counterparts 'in the same jargon'. Practices like the 'ambit claim' grabbed attention and created a dispute, a necessary pre-requisite for the Court. The system grew even more absurd as legal counsel were employed to present and argue cases before the Court. Much of the posturing that occurred on both sides was so foreign to my idea of personnel relations; moreover, it was above the plane of ordinary human relationships. In this environment, it is no wonder that there was a sharp division between award conditions and non-award conditions. As a result, employers, including me, developed a strong conviction that non-award conditions were outside the jurisdiction of the union.

As the chief executive officer, I faced the dilemma of disenchantment with the formal system which seemed to be built on confrontation plus a measure of distrust because I had a strong desire to promote an atmosphere of good staff relations in the Bank built on open consultation. In the prevailing 'them and us' atmosphere, there seemed to be no avenue for an open consultative process which I so valued. How would I breach this gap in the communications line? My dilemma was not helped by the requirement that each new employee of the Bank was required to become a member of the union.

It was a relief to discover that John Sanders, the General Secretary of the ABOA (soon to become the ABEU), was of a like mind. He too thought they and the Bank should set up a joint consultative process to fill the gap created by the formal industrial relations machine. As we proceeded to negotiate the details, I could sense nervous vibrations from the Bank's industrial relations experts that this new inexperienced CEO should be embarking on such a silly if not dangerous path. They also had the industry perspective to worry about through their membership of the BIRC, but nevertheless the arrangement was implemented with meetings to be hosted alternatively by the ABEU and the Bank.

Prior to the establishment of elected staff consultative committees, I broke new ground with the ABEU. In late November 1978, as I arrived at the ABEU headquarters to attend my first meeting on their turf, I felt a sense of history in the making, and I could not help but wonder if some of my illustrious predecessors were turning in their graves with this 'senseless' new development. I felt the consultations with the union were worth the time and effort we devoted to them; we achieved an exchange of views at the top level, a fact reported to every member of the staff over our joint signatures.

The next step in an endeavour to move outside the formal industrial relations club was taken in 1981-82 when we set up staff consultative committees in each state, independently elected by the staff. The system was to provide for consultation at state level on state issues, with unresolved issues and national issues coming before a national consultative committee at head office. The system was too detailed for my personal involvement, but with the most senior executives delegated to attend and resolve issues raised we all had high hopes of success. However, in the early stages the process seemed to be overwhelmed by bureaucratic procedural issues, while numerous unresolved matters were flagged forward. As time progressed the process became more successful, but I was never really satisfied with the range of issues or level of discussion. People seemed to be more focused on 'tea, towels and toilets', the small issues which should have been resolved at the local level, while the more important matters continued to creep through the bureaucratic process. The mere fact that the mechanism was available was seen by the staff to be a good thing. There was an avenue of communication right to the top, and there were some notable achievements, such as pay for the job as against a scale built on age and service.

In the 1970s, as the number of armed hold-ups increased, security in the bank branches was a growing problem. The old-fashioned idea was that every officer on the counter was armed with a loaded revolver, and officers were taught how to use revolvers at the shooting range on the rooftop of 341 George Street. But as staff turnover increased, with more young people, particularly women, employed on the counters and with changing social attitudes towards the use of firearms, the practice faded. Armed hold-ups continued to increase, and other solutions had to be found. The use of bullet resistant glass screens was discussed with the ABEU. While the safety of our staff was of paramount importance, the wholesale installation of screens presented other problems. They created difficulties of communication for both staff and customers and they had the potential to increase the risk of hostage taking from the customer's side of the counter. Notwithstanding these perceived problems, the installations proceeded in those branches considered to be at greatest risk.

Typical of the Bank in those days, reaction time in the bureaucracy was often slower than one might have wished. One incident which remains fixed in my mind occurred at the end of the day on Friday, 13 June 1980, when a special delivery letter came to my office after 5.00 p.m. It was a petition signed by every member of the staff, including the manager, at Homebush, a Sydney suburban branch with a staff of nine. It transpired that the branch had that morning been held up by an armed gang which had menaced the staff, and particularly a teller who was about five months pregnant. More seriously, it was the fourth such hold-up in twelve months, and the same teller had been involved in all four.

The communication from the staff was an appeal for help,

because in failing to respond urgently to the distressing series of hold-ups, the Bank, they felt, had not demonstrated any concern for their safety. I was furious that such a state of affairs had been allowed to develop. Early on the Monday morning I instructed that an armed guard be posted at the branch immediately and I telephoned the manager to inform him that I would visit the branch that afternoon following the conclusion of business.

When I arrived, I discovered that the manager had provided refreshments, so I was able to mingle with the staff in an informal atmosphere and give them strong assurances of the Bank's absolute concern for their safety. It seems incredible that the installation of a bullet resistant glass screen in this instance had not been treated with the urgency it deserved, but these are the problems which arise with too many layers of management or long lines of communications. In fairness to those concerned in this instance, there had been some difficulties between the Bank and the local Council in obtaining formal approval for the installation to be put in train, but with the right sense of urgency, those difficulties evaporated. In mid-July 1980 I fulfilled a promise to return to the branch to host a small staff party to launch the newly fitted-out branch, where the staff themselves had been permitted to decide the decor. The pride and team spirit generated by that small concession was remarkable.

In a subsequent discussion with Barry Amos, the Federal President of the ABEU, I expressed surprise that the union had not taken us to the cleaners over that incident, and his reply was to the effect, 'We knew you had become involved.'

I have often reflected on this incident, which had the potential to become something of a public and staff relations disaster. I have concluded that failure to act quickly when the signs were so strong, both before and after the earlier hold-ups, and particularly when a safety issue was involved, was symptomatic of the 'slumbering giant' which was so difficult to wake up. What was also surprising about the incident were the muted criticisms of the manager for having subscribed to the petition, and of me for my spontaneous intrusion.

As technological change developed as a more significant issue, the ABEU's anxiety grew. The union sought prior discussions well before changes were introduced, and it emphasised its concerns on continuity of employment. It foreshadowed a major publicity campaign seeking wider round table discussions including the government.

The introduction of ATMs was a major watershed in the banking industry. Their intensive use exemplifies the changing interface between customers and banks. When we were in the planning stages, we forecast that widespread acceptance of the ATMs by the customers would take business away from the front counter, but with new savings bank and other retail products, we envisaged that our peak load times would also change. We had peak times at lunch and on Thursdays and Fridays. We thought that the employment of part-time tellers in conjunction with the introduction of the ATMs was a better way to service our customers.

The ABEU was nervous about the ATMs because it thought employment opportunities would be reduced. It was also concerned that the introduction of part-time work, the new work practice to cover peak loads, would undermine career progression in an environment where full-time work and years of service were still the norm, and the telling function an important step in the career ladder. Lastly, the union was concerned that the extensive use of ATMs and part-time workers would reduce the capacity to increase union membership. Hours of work, based on full-time employment, were part of the award conditions of employment and therefore in the union's province. But I felt that the union's right to have a say in the introduction of new technology should not be incorporated into the award, although I was happy to discuss it as part of the informal consultative process we had established with the union.

The Commonwealth Bank Officers' Association, as an in-house union, was able to negotiate over the whole spectrum. We were nevertheless surprised that the Commonwealth Bank agreed to the principle of a rostered day off (RDO) in exchange for an agreement on the introduction of ATMs. This agreement cut the ground from under all the private banks. We were forced to abandon our consultative process with the ABEU when they demanded an up-front guarantee of improvement in conditions or a right of veto as a pre-requisite to consultation on technological change.

In the continuing technological debate, the union's ambit claim was the introduction of a rostered day off in return for the introduction of ATMs and an extension of part-time work. The Bank's problem was that it could not agree to RDOs, where the cost, if not the disruption, could be measured, before the financial benefits of ATMs could be calculated. We had now regressed to the confrontationist mode, since the hours of work and RDOs were matters covered by the award.

One of the more colourful aspects of the campaign was its introduction to the public arena. A noisy demonstration was held in Martin Place outside the Bank, with a band and songs which had been composed about technological change:

> . . . But there's no one to talk to. No one at all.
> And it won't join the union – this hole in the wall.
>
> . . . So come all you bankees, and listen to me.
> Beware of the price of new technology.
> Take heed of your union and answer their call
> Or banking will be nothing but a hole in the wall.
>
> And there'll be no one to talk to. There'll be no one at all.
> For what can you say to a hole in the wall?[1]

The union campaign against technological change was unsuccessful. ATMs were introduced and their use widely accepted by the community. Sadly, the topic of technological change brought a premature end to the consultative process about which I had such great expectations.

The Bank became involved in the Mudginberri abattoir dispute in the mid-1980s; Westpac was the banker to Mudginberri, and we were financing the operation which was producing buffalo meat for export from a remote work place in the Northern Territory. The maintenance of our customer's business and the protection of our finance were important considerations and inevitably our continuing support was a major issue in the dispute. More importantly, that dispute confirmed the weaknesses of the structure which governed work place behaviour, and which attempted to prescribe rules for all the complex issues which arise between people simply because they are in the relationship of employer and employee.

The proprietor of Mudginberri, Jay Pendarvis, had entered into an agreement with his employees, the terms of which fell outside those usually sought by the relevant union in other places. As one might expect, the conditions agreed upon reflected the remoteness of this part of Australia, and the appropriateness of different work practices. So far as the Bank was aware the Mudginberri employees were not coerced by their employer, and wished to continue to work under this agreement. After all, they had travelled great distances to take on this employment. The unions' response was to place a picket line to cover the entrance and exit to the works.

Because the meat produced was for export, it had to be cleared by inspectors. However, the inspectors declined to cross the picket line, and the works had to close down. The Bank, as the financier, had a problem. For Australia, the abattoir was lost, as was the valuable export market it serviced. Lengthy court proceedings ensued; Jay Pendarvis won damages but lost his business, and the workers lost their jobs. On New Year's Day, 1985, Jay Pendarvis was named the *Australian* newspaper's Australian of the Year. I often asked myself why did it all happen and who benefited?

All of the collective wisdom accumulated over the years by the Bank was insufficient to save us from what was probably the worst industrial dispute in the Bank's history. It began at the end of 1986 and centred on Victoria, but the issues were nevertheless relevant to the whole Bank. It was perceived to be about the impact of the fringe benefits tax, against which I had argued so vehemently and so unsuccessfully at the Tax Summit a year earlier. Because of long-standing management practices, some extending into the last century, and some in the nature of our business, the Bank was a big provider of fringe benefits to staff. Almost from the very beginning, bank managers had been provided with a residence, on which the managers properly paid a tax equivalent.

For as long as I can remember, the Bank had granted low interest rate loans for motor cars to managers who used their cars extensively for business purposes, particularly in rural areas. With the growth of staff numbers after the war, the trend towards home ownership and the introduction of credit cards, the volume of loans involving a concession grew likewise.

Following the 1985 Tax Summit the government decided to impose a tax on these concessions, to be paid by the employer and not the employee. For the Bank this was a major concern, not only because of the cost involved, but also because of the compliance problems. Just think of the complexity and cost of calculating the benefit to a young bank officer using his or her credit card in the range of a few hundred dollars at an interest rate below the public rate. The uncertainty created among the staff about the future, particularly in the housing loan area, combined with some implementation difficulties, gave rise to general dissatisfaction with the Bank's handling of the change, and ultimately to strike action.

By the end of 1986, the ABEU had developed a general campaign under the slogan 'Income Protection' to raise fear in the minds of their members that many benefits were under challenge. In one pamphlet the amount at risk was estimated at $4,823 per annum, made up of cuts in award benefits, cuts in fringe benefits, downgrading of superannuation improvements, and cuts in real wages.

This was a wildly extravagant, if not fictitious, version of what was likely to happen, but the uncertainty had been created by the government imposing the fringe benefits tax on the employer and Bank employees were fearful that pay and other benefits would be downgraded.

Private banks and the ABEU had discussions under the umbrella of the Arbitration Commission in November 1986. Although decisions had been made to reverse some earlier changes, including plans to increase credit card rates, the banks were adamant that they would not become involved in negotiating on fringe benefits, since they were non-award benefits. In retropsect, I was wrong to think that the union would remain aloof from this discussion. In the meantime, on 11 November 1986 the Prime Minister said in the Parliament that protests by the Commonwealth Bank officers were against the action taken by the bank, and not by the government. How convenient.

With the general announcement to the staff of the profit results on 13 November 1986, I announced that, although the profit result fell just under the level required to trigger the profit sharing scheme, the Board had nevertheless decided to pay a profit share. I added that we had decided to reverse the increase on credit card rates, and that I was concerned that some of our staff had been alarmed by talk of further cuts in benefits. As an employer with shareholder responsibilities I believed the Bank was being fair and generous to its staff. In the same announcement I gave an assurance that no further cuts were planned by Westpac.

Regrettably, these assurances were of limited help, because on 21 November the Victorian Branch of the ABEU issued another pamphlet, headed 'Income Protection', to coincide with further stop work meetings in NSW and Victoria. We had 121 branches closed for that meeting in Victoria, compared with 15 for the other two banks, indicating that we were in greater trouble. The problems of rationalisation and integration posed by the merger with the Commercial Bank of Australia were greatest in Victoria, because in that state the two banks were approximately of equal size. I felt that despite our assurances at the time of the merger there remained a residue of uncertainty about the future prospects of our managers and other classified officers. One manager was displaced each time two branches were converted into one.

I visited Melbourne on 26 November 1986 for a discussion with a large gathering of managers in an endeavour to gain a better understanding of the underlying problems. The emerging picture was a complex one. It seemed to me that the ABEU campaign and the fringe benefits question were a cover for other issues. These were related to the pressures created by new work practices which had been introduced in the Retail Banking Division, and which were aimed at greater productivity. Inadequate communication rendered the atmosphere explosive. In my darker moments I felt that those senior executives who were responsible for implementing changes in work practices were dunderheads sitting on a volcano.

I circulated a report of my impressions of the state of affairs to the responsible executives at head office, but I was forced to conclude that they were reluctant to become too involved even though they were directing some of the changes which gave rise to the pressures on the staff. Rightly or wrongly, I suspected a strong undercurrent of thinking – there he is, intruding again, but he will be retiring soon.

In early December a progress report on the ABEU campaign indicated that industrial action was continuing with little or no response in states other than Victoria, where 67 branches were applying bans and 147 were operating within restricted hours. On 17 December the ABEU distributed newsletters indicating that the ANZ had agreed to negotiate, and that they had achieved some progress with the Commonwealth Bank, and with the state banks in Victoria and NSW. In other words the employers had broken ranks. Westpac, it was claimed, had made the most vicious attack on staff benefits of all the banks; it was added that the bans had forced Westpac to make some changes, but that these were still not good enough. Action continued against us despite the payment of the profit share, and I ruefully thought: so much for the concept of profit sharing.

A few days later, the General Manager for Victoria placed an advertisement in the Melbourne press in the form of a message to Westpac staff telling them of the misinformation being circulated, and pointing out that the claim that the ANZ had caved in under union pressure was just not true. However, our Bank continued to be singled out. At a further stop work meeting at the Melbourne Town Hall on 13 January, federal officials of the ABEU recommended that all industrial action be suspended to allow further discussion with the Bank on award restructure and superannuation, and to monitor the Bank's attitude to fringe benefits. The focus of the dispute seemed to be changing, with fringe benefits now slipping down the totem pole of importance, and the meeting reacted angrily to the Federal Executive of the ABEU.

The Bank's next step was to run full page advertisements in the Melbourne press on 15 January 1987, in the form of a message from me to customers and staff in Victoria. The message endeavoured to cover all the facts of the situation, and appealed to the staff to examine their own situation before continuing with further industrial action. The Victorian Branch of the ABEU responded with its own advertisement aimed at promoting the dispute as a state matter. There was some lessening of the impact on customers and staff, but it was only a lull, because we were soon to face a series of wildcat actions inflicted at key points. At Box Hill District Operations Centre some thirty members of the staff walked out at midday on 28 January.

When a further stop work meeting was called for 30 January it ran for about three and a half hours, with about 1000 people present, and endorsed further strike action. In contrast, a similar meeting in Hobart was attended by only thirty-five people, and in Launceston by none.

The campaign began to take on a nasty overtone. On 3 February, at around 1.30 p.m., the City South District Operations Centre was put under picket by about thirty people who proceeded to chant and voice their disapproval of the staff on duty. Many of them later entered the premises and began to bang and push on the glass doors, threatening the staff. Two of the pickets were identified by staff members: one as an ABEU organiser and the other as a former member of the staff. Staff were harassed and abused, and on one occasion the union organiser attempted to impede staff members who were leaving their cars. The police were called and rendered assistance in extreme cases. The District Operations Controller suspected that non-members of Westpac staff had been involved, because several of the staff members' cars were adorned with BLF (Builders' Labourers' Federation) Resistance Fighter stickers, on one of which Westpac was spelt incorrectly. Some of the picketers left about 3.15 p.m. to harass staff and customers at the neighbouring 409 St Kilda Road branch, returning some fifteen minutes later. A Channel 10 News Team arrived around 3.40 p.m. to cover the story. Several more demonstrations of this kind took place, including one at the Westpac Gallery in the Melbourne Arts Centre. The theme for that demonstration was 'Spending money on art not staff'.

While these latter events were taking place, a letter from Len Hingley, Federal Secretary of the ABEU, was in transit. It informed me that the stop work meeting on 30 January had instructed him to advise me of its strong criticism of the Victorian administration and of its demand that I immediately intervene to restore some semblance of sanity in the staffing levels of the Victorian Division. The information was conveyed in strong terms, and talked about 'insane pressures' on staff members endeavouring to maintain service, causing immense distress not only to the staff members but also to their families and loved ones. Fringe benefits had dropped off.

In fairness to the Victorian Division, the staffing and work measurement policies were part of the overall approach of the Retail Banking Division, and it was unfortunate that the architects of that approach remained aloof from its impact at the branch level, even to the extent of voicing some concerns about my 'intrusion'. It is perhaps also unfortunate that I had grown so far apart from the ABEU that my only remaining contact was Len Hingley. To add to that misfortune, he was away in another state for most of the dispute, following a family bereavement, and his letter was our first communication on the subject.

For a long time the Bank had held the strong view that the Managing Director should not become involved in industrial disputes, particularly in face-to-face negotiations with the union representatives. The practice of industrial relations and the tactics used had become highly developed and complex, suggesting that managing directors lacked experience for face-to-face negotiations. And, in any event, the unions would no longer respect the managers responsible for industrial relations if they knew they could get access to the managing directors. But I had already broken with that tradition. I believe that it is the duty of a managing director to become directly involved when a problem is not responding to the actions of subordinates, and when it is damaging to the company.

This dispute had been with us for over three months, with over a hundred branches at times providing limited or no service. It was becoming a national disgrace, and the moment had arrived when I had no option but to intervene. The other catalyst was a direct phone call from the manager of a small suburban branch who wanted to speak to me about his concerns, which were shared by many of his colleagues. I asked him to come to Sydney to see me. His story followed the theme of Len Hingley's letter, and I decided to visit Melbourne immediately to see for myself.

I made a call to the computer centre, a critical area to the Bank. It had kept functioning during the dispute, and naturally we wanted to ensure that it did not close down. I had to cross a picket line to enter the building, an unpleasant experience. Who enjoys being booed? By the time I left the building the picket line was three times as large. While they didn't jostle me, they made sure that I had a very narrow passage to walk through.

As I was leaving, I heard a voice from the crowd asking if he could talk to me. I said only on one condition – that he was an employee of the Bank. He was, and our impromptu discussion was held under a tree nearby. What I learnt made my hair stand on end. The dispute which had escalated so dramatically, and which prompted that employee to join the picket line, was based on totally unfounded fears of all the sorts that I had tried so hard to put paid to. After I finished my conversation, I was actually cheered by the picket line as I got into my car to drive away. Isn't it remarkable that my willingness to speak with a member of that group so dramatically changed the mood of that picket line? I left this venue in an air of unreality; I was dumbstruck, greatly disappointed that the Reddin principles were not being applied, and angry that we had been so outclassed by the union in communication. I was determined to change that deficiency from then on.

Having made the diagnosis that a process to rectify this unhealthy situation had to be put in place immediately, I used the Reddin approach and called one hundred people from all over the state, at all levels in the Bank, to a meeting. I wanted them to tell me directly what was wrong. My approach was that I could not fix the problem for them. The solutions lay with them, and I believed they had the capacity to deal with it. My job was to ensure that the problems, once identified, were fixed, and to ensure that the staff knew the Bank did care and that they were not out there on their own.

Small groups working from a short set of prepared questions discussed the issues and reported back to a plenary session. Through a series of subsequent discussions and reports back, we were able finally to identify the ten most significant issues facing the Division. Spokespersons appointed by each group were given the floor in the plenary sessions, with no holds barred other than a limit on time. This was seen as open participation at its best, particularly as the key responsible executives from both Sydney and Melbourne were present.

With the problems now identified, we instructed that several task forces be formed and set various report back dates. A disciplined program of follow-up communiques to all staff was also set in train. The impact was remarkable.

Surprisingly, there was still an overhang of criticism of me – too much 'hands on', and too prone to intrude into the territory of his subordinates. However, I was surprised when I was forced to defend my decision to hold the problem-solving meeting at the Hyatt on Collins, one of the most prestigious Melbourne venues. I was accused of extravagance. My response was: why shouldn't we hold this conference at one of Melbourne's leading hotels? What more important conference could we be having, and why not this venue? If you want people to extend themselves and contribute, it is sensible to make them feel good.

When we produced a video with highlights of the conference and the subsequent reports back, there was a debate about its distribution. This was a high profile dispute, as was the problem-solving conference, and I felt there was value to the Bank, especially in the attitude of the staff towards the Bank, if the video were circulated to all branches. I thought curiosity and uncertainty would be aroused if circulation were withheld. Notwithstanding all the difficulties of the previous three months, there were still executives who felt that the video should be suppressed because it might taint others with the problems of Victoria. The video was circulated, and the results were positive.

Service, quality and a highly motivated workforce depend on the culture of the organisation, and when one of the business units fails to get the balance right – it might be profit ahead of service, or it might be productivity ahead of human resources – the image of the organisation will deteriorate. The check, at that point, is the intervention of the CEO.

The dispute in this instance may or may not have arisen from the Victorian Division alone, but its impact had national and international consequences. Analysts were publishing negative opinions because of suspected deep-seated problems in managing industrial relations within the Bank. Regular publicity concerning the number of branches not offering full service was immensely damaging well beyond the retail business unit, and beyond the state of Victoria.

Notwithstanding the changes which have taken place in the formal practice of industrial relations, the foundation of any business in the service sector is its people. Even with the advance of technology, the business of banking will continue to rely on people who are motivated, who identify with the organisation and who enjoy coming to work each day. Those worthy goals cannot be achieved by a Human Resources Division or by an Electronic Banking Division. They can only be achieved by the leadership of the CEO through his or her line managers.

I THROW IN THE TOWEL

13

As 1987 approached, I knew that further changes were in the wind because the age requirement of the Deed of Settlement would oblige both the Chairman and Deputy Chairman to retire at the Annual General Meeting at the end of January 1987. That reminded me my time as Managing Director must also be drawing to a close and I began to think about my own retirement, which the Board had already agreed should be extended to my 65th birthday in October 1988.

I had a feeling of some uncertainty arising from the pending departure of the Chairman, Noel Foley, who had been my mentor and with whom I had worked harmoniously for the previous nine years. There had been an open and mutually supportive relationship between the Board and the management. Power was not my driving force and, as a result, there had been a devolution of power down the line; I sensed that forces were at work within the Board that would certainly seek to change their role and perhaps even the balance of power following Foley's departure. My assessment of the outcome left me with an uneasy feeling.

In a large public company the Board of Directors is the guiding force, but individual personalities leave an imprint which sometimes influences the organisation long after they have departed from the scene. There had been few changes in the structure and management style of the Board characterised by an adherence to practices and to stability of membership, but now that was about to change.

My first contact with the Board was on my appointment as General Manager's Accountant in late 1961. At that time there were only seven directors who met every Tuesday and Friday. The Board was 'hands on' with little delegated authority vested in the management. In Victoria in the 1950s the head man for that state had a discretionary lending authority of only £10 000; everything above that had to be sent to Sydney for approval. The Deed of Settlement also required that the Board approve the appointment of every manager including all of the branch managers, and by the time the number of branches had increased to 1000 or more, the routine work load had grown substantially.

Because of their small number, there was a high degree of fellowship. The Chairman of the Board, called the President as required by the Deed in those days, was elected by the members following each Annual General Meeting of the proprietors. As a member of the General Manager's immediate staff I was well aware of the formalities and traditions of the Board and its operations and over the years I developed a special feeling for them and for the boardroom on the first floor of the head office.

The directors were all businessmen with major responsibilities in addition to those to the Bank and, unlike the practice in later years, the President did not have his own office nor did he come to the Bank every day.

The Board usually finished meeting before lunch and in those more spartan days, there was no tradition to lunch at the Bank. A bowl of fruit and a tray of drinks were on the sideboard. When the meeting adjourned some had a piece of fruit, some had a drink. In the corporate folklore there is a tale of one newly appointed director who, after finishing his drink, set his glass down and said that he would have, in the Australian vernacular, 'the other half'. Whereupon he was taken aside and told quietly – one drink or one piece of fruit but no more. After they had all departed, I must confess that there were times when the personal staff sampled the leftovers.

The name Cadwallader first appeared in the list of directors in 1945, when he was only aged forty-three. He became the President in 1959 and remained in that position until his retirement at the Annual General Meeting in 1978 because he had reached the age of seventy-five. Cadwallader was my mentor when I became the chief executive officer in 1977. He had then been on the Board for about thirty-two years and was deeply immersed in the traditional values of the Bank.

When the Board was discussing the distribution of the

annual profits, perhaps as a result of his experience in the depression of the 1930s, his first concern was to ensure that an adequate amount had been set aside in the provisions for contingencies. Even as late as the 1960s the Bank did not disclose the total amount held as a provision for contingencies (the general provision) nor did it disclose the annual charge against the profits to increase the general provision. Because the industry had not adopted the modern practice of full disclosure, the Bank had greater discretion over how it would publicise the profit level. It could, if it had a good year put a bit more in the kitty or if it were having a lean year, it could put less in the kitty. Of course, the purists thought the practice was wrong and open to abuse. But it operated well because of the high degree of integrity of the directors.

John Cadwallader was never tempted to produce a good public result at the expense of the cautious policy of carrying adequate provisions for unexpected contingencies. I have always admired his determined attitude towards that question. In keeping with the cautious approach of the Board, Cadwallader told me that when he first joined the Board in 1945, some six months elapsed before he was spoken to in the boardroom and more than twelve months elapsed before he dared to initiate a comment at a meeting.

In the late 1960s my predecessor, Sir Robert Norman, succeeded in persuading the Board to reduce the frequency of its meetings to weekly. He also broke another tradition in that he was the first Bank executive appointed to the Board. The caution with which they approached that decision is reflected in the amendment to Clause 37 of the Deed which merely conferred on the Board the power to appoint to the office of director a person holding the office of Chief General Manager. In effect, they were not about to make it mandatory for the chief executive officer to be a member of the Board. This explained the continued use by the Bank of the term Chief General Manager rather than Managing Director.

It is difficult to imagine in the 1990s that the chief executive of any large company would not be a member of the Board. I remember being forewarned not to expect that I would be appointed to the Board as a matter of course. Such was the caution which governed change in those days.

By the time I became chief executive officer the Board had

increased from seven to ten members. It still met weekly and it was my ambition to have this changed to fortnightly in order to reduce the demand on executive time. However, one complication was that share transfers could only be approved by a committee of the Board. As well, it was necessary for it to approve loans and advances in excess of the authority it delegated to the executive. A compromise was reached: there would be a full agenda meeting every two weeks, while on the alternate week a short meeting would approve share transfers, loans and advances and other matters of an urgent nature. That procedure continued for ten years.

The acquisition of the Commercial Bank of Australia was another milestone. That bank had three executives on its Board: their Managing Director, David Dobbie; his deputy, Harold Byrnes; and an Executive Director, Tim Marcus Clark, in charge of Subsidiaries and Related Services. To harmonise with the Commercial Bank's practice, the chief executive officer of the Bank of New South Wales was renamed Managing Director of Westpac with two other executive directors to be known as Deputy Managing Directors.

Following the merger, the number of directors on the Board jumped from ten to seventeen. The intimacy disappeared and with the growing complexity of the business, orientation towards strategic planning, performance against objectives, the time occupied by meetings expanded considerably. Sir Noel Foley, now Chairman of the Board, had succeeded Sir John Cadwallader and he was supported for the first time by a Deputy Chairman, Stephen Kimpton, the former Chairman of the Commercial Bank of Australia. Because the Melbourne directors had such a broad range of experience, they brought additional fire-power. They also brought the influence of 'the other city'. The Board would now also meet frequently in Melbourne.

The provisions of the Deed had once again been amended by 1987 to require directors to retire at the AGM following their 72nd birthday instead of their 75th birthday. This was the reason Sir Noel Foley and Stephen Kimpton both retired in January 1987. I think the Board must have been experiencing some succession problems, because for the first time in its history it appointed a non-resident of Sydney, Sir James Foots, of Queensland, to succeed

Sir Noel as Chairman of the Board. Sir James was seventy when he took up office and destined to serve only two years because he would be required to retire in 1989. We had reverted to the tradition of not having a Deputy Chairman.

After Sir Noel's retirement, I proposed that the frequency of meetings be reduced to once a month, a practice almost universally followed by other public companies. I also recommended a series of committees to handle more detailed work requiring the attention of the Board. I had in mind a credit committee to overview large loans and credit generally; a human resources committee to oversee human resource policy, and an audit committee to meet with the external auditors and review audits and compliance. The process of reaching consensus on these changes was difficult. Finally, we agreed to adjourn to a meeting at the Bank's staff college, Mahratta, on the weekend following the meeting of 15 May 1987. After a long and laboured discussion, during which I heard several cautionary comments such as, 'wary of Board committees' or 'edgy about audit committees', the Board finally agreed to a schedule of monthly meetings and to establish the three committees already mentioned. At last, we had a structure common to popular usage.

In my ten years of office, the composition of the Board had changed markedly. I was conscious that these changes had led to a break in the relationships I had enjoyed at the time of my appointment. With the retirement of Sir Noel and Stephen Kimpton the numbers on the Board fell again to the pre-merger total of ten of whom only three had been in office at the time of my appointment. Of the remaining seven, three had joined from the Commercial Bank of Australia and four had less than three years service. Again there was no Deputy Chairman and again I was the only executive on the Board. Before the year was out, there would be three newcomers.

It would be wrong to say that my relationship with the Board had deteriorated, but it certainly had changed. With the retirement of so many longer serving members, it became less enjoyable and more formal. Although my term would end on 31 October 1988 the selection of my successor had not been settled. I was conscious, and so too was the Board, that we had to agree on my successor before much of 1987 had passed.

The results for 1985 and 1986 had been satisfactory with profit growing from $306 million in 1984 to $380 million in 1986, with the dividend per share increasing from 25 cents to 28 cents. Notwithstanding the results, the pressures of new competition largely associated with deregulation were becoming more severe. The regular review of lending policy in April 1987, now in the deregulated environment, disclosed that the outstanding Australian dollar financing facilities of all trading banks had increased by a whopping 28 per cent in the year to March 1987 whereas in Westpac the comparable increase was 13.7 per cent; these increases compared with growth of the broad money supply of only 8 per cent. Our rate of growth was considered prudent despite that achieved by other banks and consequent loss in market share; we were comfortable with the lower rate of increase in our figures but we were becoming less comfortable with the trend in bad debt performance. The charge against our profits to maintain our general provision, the kitty for the rainy day, and to cover the increasing write-offs or planned write-offs, had grown from $85 million in 1984 to $125 million in 1985 and to $237 million in 1986.

I was pleased that I had finally succeeded in 1986 in elevating the Group Credit Policy and Control function to a separate division reporting directly to me, although the move was not favoured by the head of the Retail Bank. Notwithstanding the increase in the charge against profits, the actual net write-off for 1986 as a percentage of net year-end loans at 0.31 per cent for the Group was low and considered satisfactory.

Change always affects a corporation's digestive ability. Part of the $237 million kitty was a provision against the delayed time bomb planted at the time of the merger. In acquiring the Commercial Bank we also acquired General Credits, its wholly owned subsidiary finance company and sometimes known in the market as 'generous credits'. Both General Credits, 100 per cent owned following the merger, and AGC already 76 per cent owned, were substantial public borrowers and so it was essential to amalgamate them. To overcome AGC's reluctance, the Bank was obliged to enter into a warranty agreement with AGC to protect it from future losses arising in General Credits.

The merger also brought under the Westpac umbrella the Commercial Bank's 51 per cent owned NZ subsidiary, CBA Finance, of which Marcus Clark was Chairman with Alan Hawkins as Chief Executive Officer. At the end of 1983, Hawkins walked out to form Equiticorp; Marcus Clark resigned to become Managing Director of the State Bank of South Australia and joined Hawkins on the Board of Equiticorp. The aftermath involved the Bank in a take-out of the minority shareholders in CBA Finance which became Westpac Merchant Finance.

Although the Bank was performing well in the market place, the analysts and the media criticised our bottom line performance. The size of our workforce and the related ratio of our expenses compared unfavourably with the National Bank. Although we had recorded some improvement in the level of our assets per salaried employee, R.A. Holdaway, arguably one of Australia's leading bank analysts, said in his survey of 19 March 1987 that we showed up poorly in the comparison of operating profit after tax per salaried employee against the National and only marginally ahead of the other two big banks.

The need to improve productivity had been receiving a lot of attention but as this translated into added pressure throughout the network, staff turnover began to increase. Some younger staff found it difficult to cope with the pressures to develop product knowledge and to sell the growing variety of new products available since deregulation.

I had always insisted that we be a service driven bank but our driving force was defined as 'profitable servicing of customer needs'. However there were differences of view, with some executives suggesting that too much emphasis was being placed on profitability and that in the process people were being switched off. More aggressive executives expressed the contrary view that there was not enough emphasis on improving profitability. I was concerned about what I perceived to be a decline in staff morale.

In early 1987, we introduced a series of programs specifically for selected potential executives of the Bank to be conducted at the Australian Graduate School of Management at the University of New South Wales. These one-week, intensive programs concluded with a feedback session with the Managing Director.

When I attended two of these sessions I was unpleasantly surprised by the aggressive nature of the feedback, even though the intent of the program was no doubt to encourage an aggressive and thrusting approach.

There seemed to be opposing views. One group concentrated on the urgent need to become more profit driven by recovering costs on unprofitable products, by contracting out certain services such as legal, share register, transport or by pruning staff numbers. In contrast, the other group referred to the need for excellence in the provision of customer service in response to the powerful new wave emerging which required higher quality service.

In a service organisation such as the Bank the dominant costs are: people, computers and buildings. If the organisation continues to improve its expense ratio and bring about greater productivity, a point will come where the expense line crosses the service line. There is a limit to the extent to which expense ratios can be improved, and if that limit is exceeded, the resulting inferior service will have a negative impact on the customer. This would appear to be the problem confronting the banks in the 1990s. If we do indeed reach the day when the customer will not qualify to speak face-to-face with a human being unless he or she has some thousands of dollars on deposit, other financial intermediaries will emerge or we shall see further dramatic changes in the way we do our banking business. There may well be another story emerging about the provision of financial services in the last half of the 1990s.

All of the debate was good stuff and an encouraging sign that executives of the future would be quick to remedy the defects they had identified. However, a worrying overtone throughout these feedback sessions was the implied criticism levelled at my style as Managing Director. Were they worried about the change in style which would inevitably follow my retirement? They were greatly concerned by the uncertain succession and went so far as to say that it was destabilising and the subject of wide comment outside the Bank. I was worried too, but because I could not share my thoughts on the subject other than with my wife who had often played the role of trusted confidante, I reacted rather angrily when the topic was raised openly, on the grounds that surely it was not reasonable to expect me to respond in public. I was surprised that they did not appreciate that I was in no position to discuss the succession of the top man. The decision, I explained, was not mine. I began to wonder if that was why they pursued other criticisms.

I was further criticised for my reluctance to pass down decision-making and for my intrusion into many administrative processes. When I sought examples, the one most quoted was my 'intrusion' into the industrial dispute in Victoria. I was puzzled, greatly puzzled, by the thought processes behind that observation given the seriousness of the dispute, its impact on service and image, and the apparent inability of the responsible line executives to solve it after three long months.

At the time I found it difficult to make the link between operational difficulties which could be corrected and the succession of the Managing Director. In reflecting on these sometimes heated discussions, I dismissed the idea that these up and coming executives thought the Bank was not being managed properly. Rather, I concluded that they wanted to hitch their star to the right wagon and were worried about making the wrong choice.

Westpac made the outside cover of the May 1987 issue of *Euromoney* with the caption 'Struggles at White's Westpac' as a lead in to a profile by S. Karene Witcher. In her article Karene Witcher discussed some of the strategic decisions and aspects of the Bank's cost structure and she offered some comments on my management style. She also noted that there were two contenders for the top post and the question was which was the more likely to make a name for the Bank in the global capital markets. A further comment highlighted an observation from one of her inside observers that everybody was spending time talking in the corridor about who was going to run the Bank instead of running the Bank. The general thrust of her investigation accurately reflected many of my private thoughts at that time.

It is not unusual that uncertainty in the lead up to this major change should have produced a variety of reactions and comments. I have learnt during my fifty years in the workforce that it is important that people in positions of leadership read the signals and know when to let go of the reins of power. Of course I found these comments unsettling. They reinforced my determination to try again to resolve this question of succession with the Board so that we could make an announcement to remove the uncertainty. Unfortunately the problems of succession were further compounded by the effects of deregulation and other growth-generated issues.

I needed little convincing that the brave new world of deregulation would not be an easy one to traverse. All of those appendages or subsidiaries the Bank had collected in the regulated era had now substantially lost the advantage which had led to their creation. The two principal subsidiary interests developed to give the Bank access to the less regulated segment of the market of earlier years were Australian Guarantee Corporation Limited (AGC) and Partnership Pacific Limited (PPL).

Both AGC and PPL quickly realised that they faced the risk of decline as financial intermediators. The finance companies had 24.5 per cent of financial intermediation in 1980 but by 1986 that share had declined by about half, and of course, their returns had likewise declined. It mattered little to their managers that the parent bank had been the major beneficiary of their misfortunes, and not unnaturally the same managers quickly decided that they had to sharpen their act or broaden their vision if they were to survive. They still nurtured the view that the conservative banking owners had failed to maximise the benefits of deregulation, and that view reinforced their determination to pursue opportunities to stay in business.

PPL, now a wholly owned so-called merchant bank, sought to develop expertise in project finance and other innovative activities. One of PPL's initial successes was financing the Sydney Harbour Tunnel. AGC, in contrast, sought to broaden its traditional consumer finance and leasing business and move into merchant banking, project finance and other offshore activities. Inevitably, some of AGC's ambitions would clash with those of the parent bank. It was illogical, for example, to expand AGC's so-called merchant bank subsidiary, Bill Acceptance Corporation Limited (BAC) since the Bank already owned PPL. It was also illogical to the Bank that AGC should expand offshore where its activities would be perceived by the offshore central banking authority as part and parcel of the parent bank.

In the struggle of will which ensued, the Bank was

impeded by its partial ownership. I often heard the noble advice that the Bank must at all costs avoid any inference that it was suppressing the interests of the minority shareholders. That particular argument conveniently ignored the fact that the child would unquestionably look to the parent for help in the event of trouble, and that the parent would be forced to help in that unlikely event to safeguard its standing as a bank.

AGC was, and had been since the 1920s, an independent, listed company with its own Board. The Bank first took a 40 per cent interest in 1957 and at that time, publicly affirmed its intention not to interfere with AGC's management and traditional independence. Similar assurances were given whenever the Bank increased its investment. Although the Bank had some representatives on the Board of AGC, the independent hierarchy operated without much difficulty until AGC began more aggressive moves in response to the threats posed by deregulation.

In March 1987 Westpac's Board reviewed the impact of deregulation on AGC and its subsidiaries. This review led it to conclude that it had to address the growth issue in BAC's assets and that perhaps we needed to seek additional representation on AGC's Board with the object of removing current or potential overlaps in the respective businesses. The particular legal constraints associated with partial ownership and which were of concern to the Bank were that Westpac executives could not direct AGC to take a particular action; that AGC directors had full control over company assets; that AGC directors could not bind themselves to vote in a particular way for a particular purpose and that the Bank could only outline its views on business matters but not give direction to AGC directors.

The Bank was unable to change these legal constraints but as a result of this review we endeavoured to improve the linkages between the AGC and the Bank's Board of directors. For example, we appointed one of the independent directors of AGC to the Bank's Board. Westpac's Board was conscious of the legal position of minority shareholders but it believed that the Bank's objectives were consistent with the needs and expectations of other AGC shareholders.

To maintain its asset share, the AGC group took on more

assets, and my experience told me that asset growth to improve market share inevitably raises the risk profile because the new loans must be those which were less attractive to the competition. AGC was not prepared to forego its independence because of its perception that the Bank was too slow or lacked the flexibility to manage and promote the kind of business at which it was so successful. That arrangement had been fine in the past but the 1980s heralded the ending of the convenient dividing line between what was AGC business and what was Bank business.

The growing concept of deregulation was changing all that and it was also changing the approach of the Reserve Bank to its responsibilities. A more prescriptive definition of central bank prudential requirements was emerging from discussions led by the Bank for International Settlements in Basle.

Although AGC and its subsidiaries were outside the direct control of the Reserve Bank, the Reserve's prudential requirements imposed on the Bank were growing. They embraced AGC and its subsidiaries within the figures of the Group. All banks under the Reserve's control were constrained in their asset growth because of the Reserve's requirement that a certain ratio of capital be maintained to support assets of the whole Group – whether in the parent bank or a subsidiary.

The crisis created in 1979 by the failure of Finance Corporation of Australia, a subsidiary of the Bank of Adelaide, was a sharp reminder of the impact on a licensed bank of the misdemeanours of one of its subsidiaries. It was one thing for the Reserve Bank to demand that banks specifically deny responsibility for deposits raised through their finance companies' prospectuses, but it was another thing to enforce such a denial in the event that the finance company required support. The problem was solved in the case of the Bank of Adelaide when the Reserve Bank virtually insisted that it arrange to have itself taken over.

One of the principal backdrops to the Bank's growing concern was with the high profile South Yarra development known as the Como project. This ambitious project in a prominent position in South Yarra was initiated by the Jack Chia group with strong support from the Victorian Government because of its potential contribution to the state's economy. The Bank had been approached some time earlier to participate in the financing but had declined because the project was more suited to the role of a property developer. The proposal was subsequently approved by a committee of the AGC Board with BAC to lead a syndicate to finance the project. Unfortunately some deficiencies in the management of the syndicate obliged BAC to release the other syndicate members leaving the AGC group responsible for the whole project.

Tensions between a parent company and a subsidiary are nothing new in the annals of corporate history. It was interesting to contrast my AGC experience with my experience as a director of a local, listed company, majority owned by a large offshore group. In one case the discussion was often dominated by the interests of the minority shareholders and in the other case, it was often dominated by the interests of the major shareholder, but directors in such cases, have to determine, in the final analysis, what is in the best interests of the shareholders as a whole. Certainly the Board of Westpac did think about the limits of its authority and from time to time I was called upon to impose the will of the Bank on AGC but on all occasions the Bank was motivated by the interests of all the shareholders who would have to share the pain in the event of a problem.

On 4 March 1987 AGC and interests associated with Jack Chia (Australia) Ltd. announced that AGC would purchase the Jack Chia group's interest in the total Como project and continue the development work. The press release said that the project had suffered, in common with other construction projects, from a number of external influences: cost escalation arising from excessive demand in the construction industry, devaluation of the Australian dollar, industrial disruption and the extremely wet 1986 winter. The greatly increased funding requirements caused the partners to review their financial involvement and their separate responsibilities. The statement went on to say that it would be a further five years before the project would be completed. Subsequently, the financing of this project and the further decline in the supply-demand situation in Victoria resulted in continuing and substantial losses for AGC and for the Bank group and of course to the detriment of all shareholders.

At the end of 1986, the *Australian Financial Review*'s

magazine ranked CEOs in Australia. The winner was Sir Eric Neal of Boral and by then a director of the Bank. Following him were: John Gough, Pacific Dunlop; John Elliott, Elders; Brian Quinn, Coles Myer; John Spalvins, Adelaide Steamship; Robert Holmes à Court, Bell Group; Ron Brierley, IEL; Stan Wallace, AMCOR; followed by me in position number eight. When I reread this form guide, my earlier quibble in being ranked behind some of the other seven evaporated as I asked myself: where are they now?

One of the few bright spots of 1987 came when I was named Banker of the Year by *Australian Business Magazine*. This was particularly pleasing because I had also been named Banker of the Year by the same magazine in 1985. Included in one of the supporting articles by banking writer, Tim Blue, was the comment, 'Reinforcing the vote – as if it were needed – were some spontaneous comments added to ballot papers in praise of lesser ranked executives within Westpac, particularly within its corporate finance, foreign exchange and leasing departments.'[1]

On 20 October, just as I had finished sashing the prize-winning ram at the Dubbo sheep show, I was informed by my worried secretary that the stock market was taking a nose dive and the Bank's share price had plunged.

The *Sydney Morning Herald* of Thursday, 5 November quotes me as saying that, 'The sudden and sharp adjustment to share markets has concentrated the minds of international policy makers on fundamental distortions in the world economy. Similarly, it has provided a timely reminder to Australian policy makers of the vulnerability of the Australian economy to a downturn in world trade.' The values of most of the leading stocks in Australia quickly recovered but what was interesting was that the leading banks were to be major beneficiaries as investors turned to safety and security following the October crash. We must have been doing something right.

Amid these many diversions, I had initiated a serious dialogue with the Chairman concerning my successor. As the Bank was structured in 1987, three Chief General Managers were on one level below me: Peter Douglas, Chief General Manager Management Services, was shortly due to retire and therefore was not a contender for the job. The other two were Stuart Fowler in charge of the Retail Banking Group, and Warwick Kent in charge of the Corporate and International Group. Two years earlier, the Bank had reversed the roles of Fowler and Kent so they could broaden their experience in the two principal business areas of the Bank. I had known both of these officers for about thirty years and I was totally familiar with the performance of each in a variety of areas of the Bank. I had developed a particularly close friendship with Stuart Fowler since we had served together in London on two separate occasions and also in New Zealand.

One of the primary responsibilities of the Board is to appoint the chief executive. Other people would say that one of the primary responsibilities of the CEO is to identify his or her successor. My task was to prepare a variety of choices and to confer regularly with the Board on the matter. To add to my personal difficulty, I had long favoured Warwick Kent as the more appropriate successor against my long standing friend, Stuart Fowler, but I was having difficulty in persuading the Board to follow my advice. It was a lonely decision but for me totally clear cut. Because of my difficulties, I sought the views of a close colleague who was also in a position to make a judgment. He unreservedly supported my view and it was arranged that he would inform the Chairman.

The Board convened for a special dinner meeting on the night of 15 October with the objective of making a decision. I argued strongly against the appointment of Stuart Fowler, but on returning from a short absence to retrieve some material to support my argument, I felt I had already lost the battle. When I affirmed my conviction that there would be a strong reaction against his appointment from our colleagues, one director retorted that it mattered little who was appointed, they would come running. As I left at my own suggestion to enable them to make the final decision, I thought the last retort probably reflected something of the style that was to come. After a lonely twenty minutes or so in my office below, the Chairman came to tell me that Stuart Fowler had been appointed.

When the Board reconvened on the following morning, I asked that it be placed on record that I was extremely disappointed with the decision and that I would be seeking to retire earlier than previously agreed. I long ago concluded that once one's successor has been named, the sooner one gets the hell out of it, the better. My comments were received in silence but later the Chairman attempted to persuade me not to retire on the last day of December but to remain for a few months and to see out the AGM scheduled for 29 January 1988. I declined but it was agreed that there would be no public announcement until the mid-November Board meeting when the Bank's annual profits would be announced.

I had been invited to rejoin the Board following my retirement as a non-executive director and I accepted the offer. To preserve absolute confidentiality, it was left to me to prepare an action plan to cover the various announcements and to prepare drafts for the Chairman's approval. This was a miserable task because I found it so hard to find the right words to describe the events and particularly my appointment as a continuing member of the Board. I also found it irksome to discover that the words I had used on my draft had been altered to downplay the 'fiction' of the Bank's good fortune in retaining my services as a non-executive director.

The 1987 profit result was announced on 19 November. The Group Operating Profit after tax was $409 million, up by only 0.6 per cent. However, it was clouded by a number of non-recurrent items, such as a provision of $75 million for third-world loans written some years earlier and a much higher tax charge of $398 million, some of which was recovered a couple of years later. The underlying performance of the Bank was best illustrated by the operating profit before tax of $848 million, up 26 per cent. (The minority interests of $41 million account for the difference in the calculations.)

The impact of tax aside, I was pleased with my last profit results. However, the press responded without much excitement. The *Australian* reported: 'Third World Debt Trims Westpac Profit', while the Melbourne *Age* headline said: 'Westpac profit pegged back by debt provision.' The headline in the *Australian* on 20 November said that Westpac had ended the uncertainty by naming Stuart Fowler as chief of Westpac.

The Chairman had earlier indicated that the Board felt it should reinstitute the role of a Deputy Chairman so that there would not be a repetition of uncertainty when the Chairman retired the following year. The successful appointee was Sir Eric Neal who had been on the Board since 1985. His appointment was announced simultaneously with that of Stuart Fowler.

And so it was that I threw in the towel on 31 December 1987 after ten years and eight months as the chief executive officer of the Bank.

I was left in no doubt that it was all over when I went to my office the day following my retirement to clear the accumulation of papers from the past ten years. It was New Year's Day and I could hardly get in because a group of workmen were already at work to redecorate the office, remove and replace the furniture, paintings on the wall and the curtains. It was to re-open on the first business day in 1988 with a clear message that the office was under new management.

LIKE CATS IN A FISH SHOP

14

The Bank was under new management. The *Times on Sunday* heralded the change with the headline, 'New boss, new fees at Westpac', and said that Stuart Fowler had already signalled a new era for the Bank once labelled 'the slumbering giant'.

I attended my first Board meeting as a non-executive director on 15 January 1988 and I feel sure that I said nothing of import at that meeting because I could feel the eyes around the table staring at me silently questioning, 'How will he handle this?'

An earlier step to take over the shares in AGC held by the minority shareholders had been completed and the initial reaction, not surprisingly, was that the Bank's offer was too thin.

At the next Board meeting, the Deputy Chairman asked the Managing Director to bring AGC takeover matters directly to the Board and not to consult the executive committee on the grounds that, 'They might be good bankers but they know nothing about takeovers.' I had a feeling that the balance of power would shift under the new hierarchy, and I decided to plot the course of that change as best I could as a case study for the future.

An executive committee comprising the top team of executives to review major proposals was an essential ingredient of my philosophy of checks and balances but always within the constraint that all power vests in the Board. There was no question that the executive committee was usurping power from the Board because the committee decided only those matters which had been delegated to it by the Board. The exclusion of the executive committee from the review process may be seen as appropriate by some professional directors but it does change, if not weaken the system of checks and balances.

The takeover of AGC minority shares raised the difficult question of further investment in a business, the prospects of which had been prejudiced by deregulation and the price of which was inflated by the Bank's major shareholding. However, notwithstanding those difficulties, the course proposed was the correct one, if not the only one, particularly in the absence of another bidder. Later in the year it proceeded, coming to a successful conclusion.

After the share price crash in October 1987, a short period of uncertainty gave way to renewed confidence. The fear generated by the crash and the resulting pressure on the Australian dollar persuaded the authorities to support the dollar and to ensure that there was adequate liquidity in the system. The new management of the Bank was thus able to commence with complete freedom from restraint and bolstered by a healthy inflow of deposits as investors returned to the banks.

Preliminary results for the first quarter, that is the last quarter of the calendar year 1987, were well ahead of plan. At the Board presentation the Financial Controller's forward estimate for the half year included some additional provisioning that he believed might be prudent but, notwithstanding the good result anticipated, he was told that it was not his role to foreshadow provisions ahead of the event, because a good result was needed and the shareholders were entitled to expect it. Without suggesting that there was any desire to produce a particular net result, I could not help but feel that this rejoinder signalled a change in emphasis from the traditional approach to the general provision which was the 'kitty for the rainy day'.

In the run up to the March half-year, the Bank's senior managers adjourned to a retreat in the Southern Highlands to plot the way ahead. The output presented to the Board on 12 May 1988 was positive with lots of talk about values, vision and the need to convince the investing public that Westpac's shares warranted a major re-rating. This provided the backdrop to the March half-year profit results and the announcement of a substantial issue of new capital.

The group's operating profit was up 76 per cent on the same period a year ago, and one new share was to be issued for every four held, to be supplemented by a bonus issue of one new share for every five held after the issue just mentioned. As a result, the number of shares would increase by 50 per cent and the rights issue, scheduled to raise $740 million of new money, was not to be underwritten. Such was the standing of the Bank at that time. What a bonanza!

With the announcement, the directors foreshadowed their intention to revalue the Bank's own properties and to include the new values in the balance sheet at the end of the accounting year. The amount involved would be in the region of $1 billion and would represent something of another bonanza.

This move shattered the comfort I had long derived from the inner reserve in the unrealised value of the Bank's own real estate. Once it was taken into the balance sheet, it was no longer available to cushion unexpected losses. From then on, the profit and loss account would need to reflect any downturn in values because property assets would be in the balance sheet at estimated market values. Unfortunately, the senior managers' plan document was on a different wavelength from what was to be the market trend, in that it assumed the trend would continue upwards. The plan prescribed an annual increase of 7 per cent in the market value of the property portfolio. Additionally it set an objective to be amongst the top fifty banks in the world by 1992 – that would have represented an increase in size almost threefold.

The mid-June Board meeting devoted some time to general questions concerning the property portfolio. This meeting dealt with the Managing Director's recommendations that priority be accorded to investment in the high-growth central business district, against the medium-growth urban areas and the low-growth country areas. In supporting the Managing Director's general approach, the Deputy Chairman again sought to shift the agenda from the executive committee on the grounds that the committee members might be good bankers but not property experts. Therefore the alternative of a property committee comprised of Board members was canvassed.

One of the agenda items dealt with at this meeting was the $4 million proposal to refurbish the top floors of the head office building embracing the Boardroom, Chairman's office and executive offices. It was criticised selectively because of its sketchiness of detail and because of its cost but it was approved. The work on mahogany row proceeded without modification to the plan.

The press, ever vigilant in its reporting of the corporate vanities of the late 1980s, referred to the mahogany row refurbishment as the 'Golden Dunny'. The Bank's attempt at a serious riposte was published under the header, 'Flush freedom for all'.

Other items on the June agenda were the integration of AGC, now that it was wholly owned, and the need for strategic investments in minor banks and building societies. It was the AGC integration plan that forced me to forsake the somewhat passive role I had adopted since my retirement.

As a partly owned subsidiary, separately listed on the stock exchange and with its own independent Board of directors, the question of a delegated authority had not arisen until then. But with 100 per cent ownership, the Bank was in a much stronger position to ensure that AGC and its subsidiaries pursued policies that were not only consistent with those of the Bank but not likely to generate undue risks for the group results. After all, the investment community, the customers, the rating agencies and the Reserve Bank were more attuned to the Bank's consolidated results rather than just the results of the Bank itself.

I was decidedly uneasy about the revised structure in so far as the loans committee was to be chaired by the Managing Director of AGC with a delegated limit of $100 million for individual loans. I was able to recall past loans from AGC's merchant bank subsidiary which had caused concerns. When I questioned the plan, the Chairman responded that the limit had been agreed following full discussion in the interests of a harmonious integration.

In recalling these events, I am not criticising the Managing Director, but rather, I am criticising the departure from an important banking principle which is to remove the large loan decisions from the coal face. My protest about the delegated authority was in vain. One favourable aspect of the integration plan was the decision to sell AGC's merchant bank subsidiary but in the end, perhaps not surprisingly, there were no buyers.

The 1988 full-year results announced on 17 November were greeted by the *Australian* on the following day with the headline that Westpac held the lead after profit soared by 70 per cent. The *Sydney Morning Herald* chose to exclude abnormal items from the profit and reported that Westpac was out of the doldrums with a 45 per cent lift.

The issue of share options to senior executives was another innovation for 1988. The largesse was spread with a hefty increase in the dividend, generous bonuses and increases to the executives; and as another symbol of the progress achieved, a new Mercedes 560 appeared in the car park for the Managing Director along with an array of Jaguars and other Mercedes to replace the humble Ford LTDs provided under the old made-in-Australia policy. The *Annual Report* issued at the end of the year promoted the Bank with the new title: 'Australia's World Bank'.

Prior to the announcement of the 1988 results, the directors met in the absence of the Deputy Chairman and Managing Director to consider the appointment of a new Chairman. There was some controversy and a decision was deferred for another week. The outgoing Chairman, Sir James Foots, asked me not to attend the second meeting because I was thought to be too close to the management.

The Managing Director, Stuart Fowler, and I were together at a social function on the evening of 16 November 1988 when a message came through that Sir Eric Neal had been 'unanimously' elected as Chairman. The *Sydney Morning Herald* two days later said that Sir Eric had ruled out becoming an Executive Chairman, but said he would be a 'busy chairman' and that his new job would be his principal role. Sir David Zeidler, just short of 71 years of age and formerly on the Boards of BHP, Metal Manufactures and Coca-Cola Amatil, was elected Deputy Chairman.

A few months after becoming Chairman, Sir Eric called the nine most senior of the Bank's executives together to address them on a variety of issues including the Board, its expectations and the need for changes in direction and emphasis. Some negative perceptions of the Board centring on its age structure had been mentioned in the market place and these were discussed at some length. Those present were urged to speak positively about the directors both inside and outside the bank, as if positive perceptions could be ordained.

The senior executives were also reminded that all power rests with the Board which delegates such powers as it feels appropriate. This did not imply that the executives were being reprimanded for acting outside the limits of their authority. The

Chairman was merely stating the obvious. Past poor performance was illustrated and a number of danger signals in corporate behaviour were displayed on a screen and these included items such as the CEO who boasts that he appoints directors, and that the Board does 'as we tell them'. What was remarkable about this incident was not so much what was said but that it happened to a group of executives with collective business experience of a couple of hundred years.

In mid-1988 plans had been set in train for an active program of visits to Australia by overseas directors and for directors to visit offshore centres. The visit to London by six directors produced strong criticism of the London Advisory Board, the institution of which had served the Bank since the opening of the London Office in 1853. I accept that I may have had a biased view of the value of the London Board having relied heavily on its members for advice and guidance in the midst of a union crisis and a government-imposed pay freeze in 1972. Not one of the Australian directors participating in the visit was a member of the Board in 1972, but that aside, they exercised their prerogative and sacked their London colleagues because, in their view, two of them were in serious conflict of interest.

My grouch was with the manner in which the decision was executed. Although the London directors had all been associated with institutions of considerable standing in London, they were not consulted. Their 'notice', given by letter, awaited them on their arrival at the next scheduled Board meeting. As well, they were 'uninvited' to the Sydney conference scheduled for September. Their names and any reference to a London Board vanished from the 1989 *Annual Report*.

As this drama unfolded I argued to have some gesture of appreciation recorded in the Board minutes. In a moment of reverie, I murmured to myself, 'This is the way things are done around here now.' It reminded me of the term applied to victims in a South American regime, 'the disappeared'. In the report of that 1989 visit to London in which I did not participate, it was noted that London would remain the financial centre of the EEC for the foreseeable future but the activity in Brussels suggested that this city might be considered for such a role. My cynicism must have been growing because I had pencilled alongside, 'About as much chance as Canberra or Washington!'

The results for 1989, announced on 16 November, showed an increase of 34 per cent in the group operating profit after tax to $791 million. However, due to changes in accounting policy, and therefore in the definition of operating profit, it would be difficult to rely solely on the announced result and its comparison with that of a year ago as a guide to the underlying performance of the Bank, without taking into consideration some of the factors which contributed to the result. The charge against the profits for tax had been reduced and, if it were not for this substantial reduction , the 1989 profit would have been lower than in 1988. The principal reason lay in the increased burden of bad and doubtful debts which in 1989 had more than doubled from $232 million to $563 million. Was this to be the price of growth?

In the frenetic market of the late 1980s the opportunity for asset growth was high and the Group's assets had grown by $24 billion or 28 per cent in 1988-89. But the increase in bad and doubtful debts reflected the dramatic increase in higher-risk asset growth.

In the aftermath of the 1989 results, and with a substantial profit in the bag, albeit with the benefit of some windfalls, the Chairman and Managing Director were active to assure the market that the Bank was on the right path.

The Managing Director told the *Sunday Age* on 17 December 1989, that only BHP was making more profit than Westpac. In a wide-ranging interview, he reminded readers that when he took over from me in January 1988, he quickly set about increasing charges to avert the ridiculous practice of businesses using free savings bank accounts to avoid paying fees. He went to some lengths to emphasise that he was bullish about the performance of Australian companies.

It is a verity of banking practice that there are risks for a bank in pursuing a policy of aggressive expansion of its loan portfolio: one is the availability of resources to assess and maintain the quality of the loans being acquired; the other is the pitfall of being saddled with the leftovers of other lenders. The loans market, whether it be manufacturing, property, or retailing is not a bottomless pit. Borrowers should likewise be constrained by the level of the demand they seek to serve. When the provider of loans or services, or the manufacturer of goods, or the miner of resources breaks through the barrier of demand, trouble will follow as surely as night follows day.

Westpac's mood in 1989 was focused not only on organic expansion but also on expansion by acquisition. That too placed an added demand on management resources. As 1990 dawned, the bank was negotiating the acquisition of the French Polynesian business of Banque Indosuez and that had to be demanding because it involved a non-English speaking culture and the opening of a branch in Paris. Other acquisitions were also under active consideration.

Apart from the pressure on resources, I had a nagging worry that neither the Board nor the management of the Bank sufficiently appreciated the increased risks posed by a decline in the quality of the loan portfolio. Both the wholly-owned merchant banks, Westpac Merchant Finance and PPL, had already produced losses in 1989 and, I dwelt on the delegated authority of $100 million to the AGC Loans Committee – a high enough limit to inflict considerable damage to the group if not used cautiously. The 1989 *Annual Report* boasted that the excellent asset growth achieved by AGC should provide a solid platform for medium-term profitability.

A few months after the acquisition of the AGC minorities, all directors of the Bank were appointed directors of AGC under the common chairmanship of the Bank's Chairman. Having served on the AGC Board since 1977, through its ups and downs and with fortnightly Board meetings dedicated to its own affairs, I was unhappy when the new regime dealt with AGC matters as just another item on the agenda of the Bank's Board meeting.

Early in January 1990, the Board had before it loan committee minutes from AGC recording the approval of a real estate development loan of $88 million. The unusual feature about the Board minutes was a note recording disagreement by the Bank's representative on the loans committee, but this notation was of no consequence because the loan had been approved.

I anticipated that my earlier concerns about the level of AGC's lending authority might be mollified, but I was to be disappointed because the Westpac Managing Director described the contretemps as a clash between the classic approach of a conservative banker with the entrepreneurial approach of the AGC property executives. He added that, in any event, the Chairman of the AGC loans committee had the final say, which was a surprise to me having regard to my earlier reservations expressed at the Board.

However, more was to follow, because the Chairman had intervened to say that he had already discussed the circumstances with the Chairman of the AGC loans committee (who also wore the hat of the AGC Managing Director). He concluded that the Westpac officer overseeing the loan proposal had not understood that AGC's lending policy permitted loans against leasehold security. I was confused. As it happened, I had handled the initial recruitment of the Westpac officer in the 1950s, and I knew beyond doubt that he was one of the most experienced credit officers in the group, including, with due respect, the Chairman and the Managing Directors of both the Bank and AGC.

In addition to voicing his disapproval at the AGC meeting, the Westpac officer had written a submission to his superior in the Bank detailing his reasons for refusing to endorse the approval and that was also presented at the Board meeting. On the basis of my own not inconsiderable experience, his reasons were of copy book standard. In brief, he said that the security property was non-income producing; development plans had not been finalised with no source of clearance; there was no assurance that the development would proceed in the then current environment; and that the rating agencies were already concerned with the level of the Bank's exposure to property development. He went on to summarise the difficulties he was experiencing as an unofficial member of the AGC loans committee and to express his discomfort with the level of delegation. In short, this highly experienced officer forewarned of a dud loan in the making.

His submission only succeeded in earning him something of a rebuke from the Chairman for having exceeded his authority: it was the Managing Director's role, and not his, to determine the appropriate level of the Bank's exposure to property development. This was a classic example of what can happen when the checks and balances are overridden because within a matter of a few months, that particular loan was in the doubtful debt list. Five years on, the project was still a hole in the ground.

Less than four months later the Bank's credit rating was downgraded. The *Sydney Morning Herald*, 4 May 1990, reported that the international ratings agency, Standard and Poor's, had delivered a blow to Australia's largest bank cutting its credit rating over shaky loans. The Agency cited declining asset quality, which reflected problems in loans to many highly geared companies and to the domestic commercial property sector. Another downgrade by the New York Credit Agency, Moody's Investors Services, made Westpac the lowest major bank in Australia.

The anxieties I had about a particular AGC lending proposal were compounded by my concerns about the decision-making processes generally. In my view, major decisions coming before the Board should first have had a clear management view developed through the executive committee. But the executive committee was held in such low esteem by one director that he even suggested that the term 'executive committee' be banned from Board papers.

One major decision which appeared not to carry the imprimatur of the executive committee was the acquisition of 7.5 per cent of the shares of the ANZ Bank at a cost in excess of $400 million. After receiving a detailed presentation from the strategic planning area, this investment was approved on the voices – but not mine. I had many concerns: the funding cost at 1990 interest rates would have been substantial and may not have been tax deductible; the market outlook for ANZ shares was not good; with the problems then facing the Bank, the value of the investment as a strategic holding was indeed questionable. In addition to the ANZ investment, Westpac acquired four other strategic holdings in relatively minor and second tier banks and other opportunities were reviewed. Such was the concentration on growth.

Despite these problems, the big picture was well to the fore when the Board departed for its planned week-long visit to the USA. The pre-departure Board meeting on 19 April was a little clouded by news that a report in the following day's issue of *Business Review Weekly (BRW)* would be adverse to the Bank. The content of the article was not known but those present were comforted by a statement that it would be easy to present such an article based on problems which had been generated in the past, and which were now surfacing and adding to present difficulties. Thus comforted, the thirteen directors began their visit program with a dinner in San Francisco on 22 April 1990. Frank Conroy, by then Deputy Managing Director, and I remained in Sydney, but not to mind the shop, because the Chairman had issued a directive that no meetings were to be held during the absence of the other directors.

The visit program was indeed comprehensive, covering staff presentations, lunches, receptions and dinners in San Francisco, Chicago, Columbus, Houston, and Los Angeles, as the directors divided into small groups for the first couple of days. The whole group came together again on 26 April for a Board meeting at the New York Stock Exchange; a customer dinner hosted by the Chairman at the New York Public Library, and further presentations from the America's Division. The up market visit program, designed to reflect the standing of Australia's first bank, was reputed to have cost around $1 million.

It was unfortunate that the events back home were casting a deepening shadow. Some of the directors had travelled on to London and following their favourable report to the full Board on their return, the directors agreed with the Chairman that the full Board should also meet in London a year ahead. Perhaps this was one way to ameliorate the evolving pressures on the home front.

The cover story in the *BRW* on 20 April 1990, 'Westpac's Woes' was indeed unfavourable. There were references to the low level of the Bank's credibility with the investment community, its main union and even its own staff. While many of the comments were neither supported nor attributed to specific individuals, it was of some concern in the Bank that discussions with a 'Westpac director' had been reported. Following the May meeting of the Board, the Chairman convened a meeting of all non-executive directors the purpose of which was to identify any directors who had spoken with the author of the article.

The format of the meeting was unusual, if not undignified; each director individually was formally asked if he had spoken with the author of the article. Only one person had spoken with her but not in the terms quoted, and as far as I understood, no real conclusions were drawn and no action was taken.

I thought that the developing situation was serious but that the Board's attention was misplaced. Instead of concentrating on who said what, we should have been concentrating on what was said in the article as a whole and the impression created by it in the public arena. When I suggested that non-executive directors should meet again away from the pressures of the day and preferably off-site to discuss the situation facing the Bank, there were spontaneous, brief expressions of support from some directors. However, the meeting was terminated without further discussion and no subsequent meeting eventuated. I was not surprised.

The first half-yearly profit for 1990 after tax of $354 million was down 8 per cent but again there were complications in assessing the underlying performance of the Bank. The profit results, were for example, boosted by a transfer from the staff superannuation funds of $325 million, which would attract tax of $127 million, leaving $198 million to be added to the net profit. Without that windfall, the real net profit for the half year was only $156 million and that was down by 59 per cent year-on-year.

The principal reason for the sharp decline was associated with write-offs and provisions for bad and doubtful debts, the charge for which totalled $585 million, much more than double the amount of $226 million charged for the same half in the previous year. It was becoming clear that the Bank had a problem.

It should be noted that the superannuation funds had been examined by an independent actuary at the end of 1989 providing confirmation of a surplus of the order of $1 billion. Since both the Bank and the members had been contributors over the period during which the surplus had been accumulated, the Board and the trustees determined to distribute $650 million of the surplus with half to enhance the members' benefits and the other half to return to the Bank. The Australian Bank Employees Union challenged the distribution through the courts, but it was not successful.

The equivalent result for the National Bank (NAB) was a profit of $440 million, an increase of 6 per cent. Their charge for bad and doubtful debts was also up by $103 million to $247 million, much less than half of the comparable Westpac figure. The NAB's result was not assisted by any windfall distribution from their superannuation fund, prompting Simon Lloyd in the *Financial Review* of 18 May to wonder whether the two organisations were operating in the same industry. Mark Beyer in the same magazine picked up the double bonus of the large surplus in the super scheme because Westpac had also ceased making contributions to the fund the previous year resulting in annual savings of about $50 million. Fortunately, the one bright spot in the week was reported by the *BRW*: Westpac had blitzed the forex field. The heading said, 'Never before has a single bank so dominated the *BRW* foreign exchange poll.'

In the aftermath of the half-yearly announcement, the Bank's management was preoccupied with putting out fires rather than running the Bank. Philip Deer, the Chief General Manager, Corporate and International, had resigned to head up the National Westminster Bank's operation in Australia and his departure had been preceded by Warwick Kent who had also resigned to become Managing Director of the Rural and Industries Bank of Western Australia, now BankWest.

A profit improvement program was set in train. Predictably, the program included an objective to curb asset growth and a critical review of salary levels with no increments intended.

In early June the Board received the long-awaited report of the Board committee appointed in November 1989 to review policies and exposures of AGC in relation to commercial property with particular emphasis on joint-ventures. The report noted that commercial property loans and joint-ventures in property had increased substantially since 1987 with some exposures overdue because of delays in completions and sales, and with a recent blow-out in bad debts.

Our traditional approach at AGC to joint ventures in real estate was to insist on restraint enforced through an overall limit of $500 million based on commitments, not outstandings, with a minimum of 20 per cent equity. A limit based on commitments meant that new projects were not taken on above that limit so delays in completions and sales would never increase the exposure beyond the limit. It appeared that in the transition to full ownership this earlier system had been overridden.

Non-executive directors, particularly more recent

appointees, may not have been familiar with past policy restraints and the background to their adoption and how could they have been? The Board committee did not have the assistance of an experienced and independent executive and, perhaps not surprisingly, had taken over six months to produce their report.

I was becoming more anxious not only about the growing incidence of difficult accounts and the evidence of concentration of doubtful debts, but also about the Bank's capacity to manage these problems.

Early in August one particularly large and difficult exposure was reviewed to the Board credit committee and illustrated, to me at least, how a confused management approached the problem loan. Six levels were directly involved: two junior executives at the account management level; General Manager of the division; Chief General Manager, Credit Policy and Control; Chief Operating Officer; Managing Director and the Chairman.

A letter already sent to the borrower by the account manager in conjunction with two other lending banks and lawyers was subjected to a post-mortem around the Board table. The tone of the meeting seemed to convey such a lack of confidence, if not trust, in the management's approach to the problem that the Board felt obliged to look over the management's shoulder at every step. I felt helpless and frustrated, because in instances such as this, even if I had views, another intervention would only have added to the confusion.

Some months later there was an illustration of the kind of image the Bank was then projecting. It came in two press articles concerning the *Northern Star* and Channel 10 by Mark Westfield in the *Sydney Morning Herald* on 13 September 1990 and by Tom Burton of the same paper two days later. Mark Westfield said that factions in the Bank appeared to have been pushing in different directions in their efforts to find a solution to a problem account. Tom Burton's article had a headline to the effect that the Ten affair showed the power struggle at Westpac.

Substantial losses were looming from a relatively small number of large exposures. It should have been obvious to management that the Bank's asset growth strategy had been so aggressive that neither the availability of skilled resources to manage the expansion nor the credit implications had been fully considered. That situation emphasised the absolute need for the right people who are often in short supply in a climate of excessive growth. At my suggestion, the Board called for a review of the circumstances surrounding a number of the larger losses in search of lessons for the future. The circumstances of two of these cases are examples of what was happening.

Case 1: We had a longstanding customer, who was listed on the Stock Exchange, but taken over and controlled by an entrepreneur from 1986 when the Bank's exposure was $82 million. In 1986, following the takeover, requests for additional accommodation were declined. By March of 1989, when a provisional liquidator was appointed, the overall Bank group exposure had risen to $288 million. In the period of only three years, this account had been overseen by no less than four different account managers.

Case 2: A longstanding customer, listed on the Stock Exchange, was acquired by another company in 1984. In 1988 a high profile entrepreneur gained control. Prior to that, recorded exposure was $52 million in 1985, but the entrepreneur had a relationship with PPL dating back to the early 1970s. Covering the period of the borrowing group's subsequent acquisitions and expansion, there were multiple account managers – three semi-permanents and five relievers from 1988 to 1990. The frequent changes reflect the pressures imposed by the inadequacy of resources. By 1990 when receivers and liquidators were appointed, the total group exposure was assessed at $175 million.

Lack of continuity in account management is hazardous at any time but even more so when the account is deteriorating. I remembered a message from my old boss at the Sydney Office who presided over me and six other subordinate managers. He said 'No problem to lend it son, the problem is to get it back. My problem as the Chief is that sometimes they get promoted too early and leave the problem of getting it back to me or somebody else.'

As 1990 progressed, I became increasingly unhappy with the course of events at the Bank and that unhappiness was compounded by a sense of isolation. It was no longer a joy to attend Board meetings or Board committees because each meeting seemed to produce another problem and so far as I was concerned, the problems were never confronted in open and free discussion. Only the rhetoric flowed freely in the assignment of responsibility. In a way, I was probably too sensitive for high office. Perhaps to my discredit I resented the exercise of power and judgment by a group of 'Johnnies-come-lately' in what I saw as a developing crisis in the Bank which had literally been my life.

Other actions which had been initiated in relation to my professional activities gave me the impression that I was being shouldered aside. The least trivial of these was the Chairman's request in May 1990 that I discontinue my association with the Business Council's Debt Summit Project. The three past Presidents of the Business Council, of which I was one, and the current President had convened a summit in Melbourne on 2 March 1990 to discuss and publicise the alarming growth in Australia's foreign debt, the level of which has almost doubled in the ensuing five years. In the view of the Chairman, this initiative was damaging to Australia, and as a result of my association with it, damaging to the Bank. I had been appointed to the Debt Summit Project in my own right and not as a representative of Westpac. I could not even begin to understand the logic of what he was saying.

With much loss of sleep, and with my wife's deteriorating health, I decided that I could no longer continue as a director of the Bank. I carefully prepared my letter of resignation and submitted it simultaneously to the Chairman and every other director as they assembled for the scheduled Board meeting on 16 August 1990. I wrote:

> Dear Sir Eric,
>
> With deep regret and after a great deal of consideration I have come to the conclusion that I must submit my resignation as a Director of the Bank.
>
> For some time now I have felt increasingly at odds with the general approach of the Board under your leadership and this raises in my mind a growing anxiety that my continuing membership of the Board might well be perceived by the proprietors, customers and staff as an endorsement of the current approach. By itself, that is a worry but because I retire by rotation at the end of this year, it would seem to be

inappropriate, if not a neglect of my responsibility to the proprietors to allow my name to go forward for re-election without some qualification. I think it is preferable that I face the issue now.

It is not my wish, nor is it my intention, to present a litany of the events leading to my decision but one such example was the reconvened meeting of non-executive directors on May 18, 1990, to conduct an inquisition into the identity of the director quoted in the B.R.W. Article (19.4.90). For one of the country's leading Boards, this was an undignified affair which concentrated only on who said what and substantially ignored the more important content of the article. I took the opportunity to suggest that the directors present on that occasion should meet again, informally, away from the pressures of the day and preferably offsite, to discuss the situation facing the Bank. Disappointingly such a meeting was not arranged notwithstanding apparent general support from the directors present.

Another area of my concern arises from my perception that there is now a gulf between the Board and the Executive of the Bank. This is for me a new development not hitherto apparent since I first entered the boardroom on a full time basis over 16 years ago. In a service industry, and particularly in one of our size, it is a prime responsibility of the Chairman and the Board to develop and maintain a working relationship of mutual trust and confidence between the Board and the Executive.

The absence of such a relationship inevitably promotes a demotivating influence at senior levels which is likely to cascade down through the organisation. It is of course difficult to make a judgement on the overall impact of that, and even more difficult to measure its significance on the quality of service to the customers. However, you will recall that I raised, at the last Board meeting, my concerns about the impact on our customers of our current approach and I continue to be greatly worried by what I perceive to be a rising level of customer dissatisfaction.

I hope you will appreciate that the combination of

> these and other circumstances within a structure which severely limits my ability to contribute, leaves me with little option but to submit my resignation.
>
> Yours sincerely,

On the following evening at home, I received from the Chairman a bland 'Dear Bob' advice to the effect that the directors had considered my resignation and accepted it with regret. It included the almost obligatory comment that the Stock Exchange had been formally advised and it conveyed the writer's regret that he had been unable to contact me to convey the information personally.

On reflection I thought had he been able to contact me, and having regard to the contents of his letter, the conversation would indeed have been short. Left unsaid in the letter was the instruction to the Public Relations Department – no press release.

And so ended the career which began fifty years earlier in the Murray River port of Echuca. Sad though I was, I knew that, come what may, this icon of Australian business would survive without me.

EPILOGUE

In stark contrast to the earlier years, major steps were taken in the 1980s to relieve the banks of the regulatory controls which had been a feature of the industry since I joined. Consequences of deregulation and its impact on the banks and their customers have been far reaching and remain the subject of community debate. There are some who question the benefits of deregulation, and there are others who argue that regulation suppresses the regulated sector which then re-emerges in some other unregulated form. Whatever the views, the new freedom brought big changes to the range of services offered to customers and encouraged the banks to seek new opportunities elsewhere as foreign banks were licensed to enter Australia.

The four major banks in Australia, with the privileges bestowed by a banking licence, are probably unique as an industry group in that they play a role in just about every phase of economic activity, and as a result, they touch the hearts and minds of a huge slice of the population, probably as much as 75 per cent. The size of the customer base imposes on banks an almost frightening burden of responsibility as they struggle to balance that burden with the demands of their other stakeholders: the shareholders and staff. Business analysts and governments, consumers, investors, media and public relations experts will have a field day until the community feels that the right balance has been achieved. In the process of deregulation, banks were able to offer loans in offshore currencies, but because there are many unresolved disputes involving those loans, I have felt unable to canvass the topic in this book.

Technological change has revolutionised the way we do our banking business in the 1990s. Those of us who enjoyed the simplicity of a handwritten passbook to show us how much we saved may regret the complexity of present-day banking particularly as the old account cost us nothing and paid us a little bit of interest. But without the computer, we would not be able to use the plastic card at the supermarket check-out, nor would we be able to draw some ready cash from the 'hole in the wall'. Of course it is convenient and of course it is expensive, and so the current debate is about who pays for this convenience. As always, the governments are on the look out for ways to raise taxes – they take a little bit when we put money in and a little bit more when we take it out – not only is it like a tax on breathing, but it adds to the costs of every transaction both for the banks and the customers.

Following my agonising decision to resign from the Board on 16 August 1990 some significant events followed: the return to the Bank of $325 million from the surplus in the staff superannuation fund boosted the 1990 results; a strategic alliance with the AMP Society in 1991 involving the sale to it of the Westpac Life company for a profit of $130 million; and a rights issue in 1992 to raise approximately $1.2 billion of new capital which thankfully was underwritten by CS First Boston Australia because it was heavily undersubscribed.

In the 1992 *Annual Report,* the after-tax profit, which included the two abnormal gains mentioned above, had become a loss of $1.5 billion. On 1 October 1992 five directors, including the Chairman and Deputy Chairman resigned.

For observers of these events, questions arise concerning issues of corporate governance particularly on the question of what should happen when one member of a board feels obliged to resign out of concern for the company. There will be many instances where a dissident director will resign because he or she is at odds with the rest of the board, and it is of course the prerogative of the board in such cases to accept the resignation and get on with the business. One question which arises is whether that course is appropriate in all cases. In my case, I ask myself repeatedly didn't my resignation merit more than just a perfunctory acceptance? Subsequent events seem to suggest that it did. What safeguards, if any, should be adopted to deal with such cases? One course of action may be to require a notification to the Australian Securities Commission of the reasons for a director's resignation. Otherwise how does one meet the requirements for an informed market?

It is easy to make judgments in the blinding clarity of hindsight and perhaps easier still to draw on the mountain of material produced on corporate governance, the duties, and responsibilities of directors. I can do no better than quote the words of that most experienced director and my good friend, the late Sir John Dunlop, one of the co-founders of the Institute of Directors in Australia. In the Institute's publication, *Dunlop on Directors*, in 1987, Sir John said:

> I submit that the partnership between management and board works best when management does everything; when the board is used as a wise uncle, as guide, counsellor and outspoken friend, whose advice is taken seriously, discussed, and acted upon, unless withdrawn after discussion.

This principle – this check and balance – is surely a foundation stone for corporate governance.

ENDNOTES

Chapter 2

1 Royal Commission into the Monetary and Banking System, 1937, *Report*, Commonwealth Government.

2 L.F. Giblin, *The Growth of a Central Bank*, Melbourne University Press, Melbourne, 1951, p. 227.

3 *Notes from General Manager, Bank of New South Wales, on Meeting with the Governor and Deputy Governor of Commonwealth Bank*, 28 February 1947, Westpac Archives.

4 T.B. Heffer to A.H.B. Jones, correspondence dated 10 April 1947, General Manager's Letters, Westpac Archives.

5 T.B. Heffer to A.H.B. Jones, 15 April 1947, General Manager's Letters, Westpac Archives.

6 T.B. Heffer to L.J. McConnan, correspondence dated 2 June 1947, Westpac Archives.

7 S.J. Butlin, 'Australian Central Banking, 1945-59', *Australian Economic History Review*, Vol. 23, No. 2, 1983.

8 *Preliminary Plan for Borderline Electorates and Recommendations*, (hereafter called the Plan), 22 September 1947, Westpac Archives GMA2057, p.5 of Recommendations.

9 T.B. Heffer, Circular Letter to Branch Managers, BNSW, 25 September 1947, Westpac Archives A2057/68.

10 The *Plan*, covering letter, p. 2.

11 G. Blainey and G. Hutton, *Gold and Paper, A History of the National Bank of Australasia, 1858–1982*, The Macmillan Company of Australia, Melbourne, 1983, pp. 232-3.

12 H.C. Coombs, *Trial Balance*, The Macmillan Company of Australia, Melbourne, 1981, p. 117.

13 *Australian Banker*, 9, No. 1, January 1934, p. 3.

14 *Special Report on Proposed Government Legislation*, 28 November 1944, p. 2, ABOA Archives. Also quoted in J. Hill, *From Subservience*

to Strike, University of Queensland Press, St. Lucia, 1982, p. 117.
15 A.H.B. Jones to R.R. McKellar, correspondence dated 29 August 1947, Westpac Archives GMA2057/3.
16 F. Daly, *From Curtin to Kerr,* Sun Books, Melbourne, 1977, p. 60.
17 The *Plan,* p. 9.
18 Notebook containing prepared answers. Property of R.J. White.
19 L.F. Crisp, *Ben Chifley, A Biography,* Longmans, UK, 1960, p. 332.
20 General Manager's Circular Letter, 29 August 1947, Westpac Archives, A20567/68.
21 T.B. Heffer, General Manager's Staff Circular, 20 September 1949, Westpac Archives.
22 Interview with Murray Stewart, 6 September 1993.
23 T.B. Heffer to Staff, 20 September 1949, Westpac Archives.

Chapter 6

1 Commonwealth of Australia, *Report of the Committee of Economic Enquiry (Vernon Report),* Commonwealth of Australia, 1965, pp. 64-5.
2 C.B. Schedvin, *In Reserve, Central Banking in Australia, 1945-75,* Allen & Unwin Pty Ltd, Australia, 1992, p. 168.
3 *Vernon Report,* p. 253.
4 ibid.
5 ibid.
6 Australian Securities Markets, and Their Regulation, Part 1 of the *Report of the Senate Select Committee on Securities and Exchange (The Rae Report),* VI, Australian Government Publishing Service, Canberra, 1974, para 3.7.

Chapter 7

1 'Summer Stupor', The *Economist,* 20 July 1974.
2 'No relief for borrowers' *The National Times,* 21 August 1974.
3 Correspondence, R.A. Norman to R.J. White, 29 August 1974.
4 Bank of New South Wales, *Australian Commentary,* 20 September 1974, No. 38, p. 1.
5 P. Kelly, *The Unmaking of Gough,* Angus and Robertson, Australia, 1976, p. 155.
6 Telex from Bill Hayden to Chief General Manager, Bank of New South Wales, 4 November 1975.
7 Notes of meeting between bank representatives and government

officials held at the Treasury on 6 November 1975.
8 Telex from Bill Hayden to Chief General Manager, Bank of New South Wales, 7 November 1975.
9 Telex from R.J. White to Bill Hayden, 10 November 1975.
10 Memorandum from R.J. White to all Chief Managers, 11 November 1975.
11 R.J. White, personal papers, 11 November 1975.
12 Australian Bankers' Association, Press Release, 11 November 1975.
13 Telex from T. Bell to R.J. White, 12 November 1975.

Chapter 8

1 *The Making of Westpac (A), (B) and (C)* – three part case study, written by Janet Hunter under the direction of Visiting Professor David Zenoff, entitled *The Making of Westpac (A), (B) and (C).* Copyright 1986 by IMEDE, Lausanne, Switzerland. The International Institute for Management Development (IMD), resulting from the merger between IMEDE, Lausanne and IMI, Geneva acquired and retains all rights.

Chapter 9

1 R.G. Gregory, 'Some implications of the Growth of the Mineral Sector', *The Australian Journal of Agricultural Economics*, Vol. 20, August 1976.
2 J.D.S. Macleod, 'The Gregory Chant', *The Australian Quarterly*, June 1977.
3 E. Carew, *Keating – A Biography*, Allen and Unwin Pty Ltd, Sydney, 1988, p. 124.

Chapter 12

1 *The Hole in the Wall*, words and vocal by Graeme Bechaz, arrangement and instrumental by Jan Wositzky and Louis McManus. Extract from a recording produced by the Australian Bank Employees Union, August 1980.

Chapter 13

1 T. Blue, *Australian Business Magazine*, 2 September, 1987, p. 70.

INDEX

n denotes endnote. Compiled by Cecelia Clarke.